Texas: A Modern History

TEXAS:
A MODERN HISTORY

David G. McComb

University of Texas Press   Austin

Second paperback printing, 1994

Requests for permission to reproduce material from this work should be
sent to Permissions, University of Texas Press, Box 7819, Austin, TX
78713-7819.

⊗ The paper used in this publication meets the minimum requirements
of American National Standard for Information Sciences—Permanence of
Paper for Printed Library Materials, ANSI Z39.48-1984.

LIBRARY OF CONGRESS CATALOGING-IN-PUBLICATION DATA

McComb, David G.
    Texas, a modern history / by David G. McComb—1st ed.
       p.   cm.
    Bibliography: p.
    Includes index.
    ISBN 0-292-73048-9 (alk. paper)—ISBN 0-292-74665-2 (pbk. :
  alk. paper)
    1. Texas—History.   I. Title.
F386.M337   1989
976.4—dc20   89-31666

The poem "I Am a Cancer Cell" is reproduced by permission of the M. D.
Anderson Cancer Center.
A brief quotation from *The Best Little Whorehouse in Texas* is reproduced
by permission of Larry L. King.

Contents

Maps

Preface

This is a brief, narrative history of Texas written for the adult reader who wishes to probe into the ethos of a people, taste the unique flavor of the culture, and experience the rhythm of development. In the story you will find triumph and tragedy, sadness and humor, cruelty and compassion, exuberance and depression. It wasn't always easy to be a Texan; it still isn't.

Texas: A Modern History

1. Land and Nature

The land possesses a powerful and haunting beauty, and Texas, the name for this country, is a word of myth and reality. The five letters are so emotionally encrusted that the name defies definition. It means too many things to people. For example, Thomas Jefferson wrote to James Madison in 1820, "The province of Techas will be the richest state of our Union without any exception." Frederick Law Olmsted, a traveler and landscape architect, recorded in 1857, "'G.T.T.,' (gone to Texas,) was the slang appendage, within the reader's recollection, to every man's name who had disappeared before the discovery of some rascality. Did a man emigrate thither, everyone was on the watch for the discreditable reason to turn up."

"Other states were carved or born, Texas grew from hide to horn," stated Texas poet Berta Hart Nance around 1930. And in 1962, after traveling with his dog Charley, John Steinbeck wrote, "Writers facing the problem of Texas find themselves floundering in generalities, and I am no exception. Texas is a state of mind, Texas is an obsession. Above all, Texas is a nation in every sense of the word."

To say the least, it is huge—267,000 square miles stretching 770 miles from east to west and 800 miles north to south. This second largest state takes in 7 percent of the area of the United States, and if you rode a bicycle around the entire border you would cover 3,800 miles. To the Travel and Information Division of the Texas Department of Highways and Public Transportation, the state is a "Land of Contrasts," as indeed it is to almost everyone who has pondered its nature and character. There are reasons for this, and a major one is geographical.

Texas, like a beautiful damsel, has many charms and attractions, but it is not entirely faultless. Indeed, there is no such place as a perfect elysium on earth. . . . But its many beauties will hide a multitude of faults; or render them light and easily borne.

AMOS ANDREW PARKER,
A TRAVELER IN TEXAS, 1834

Portions of four of the eight major physiographic regions that make up the terrain of North America divide the state. The Rocky Mountain system decorates far West Texas with islands of low, clustered mountains set in beige desert basins. The highest point, Guadalupe Peak, reaches 8,751 feet; there are only six others over the 8,000-foot level. With the exception of this intermontane segment in West Texas, the state consists of three gently sloping plains separated by escarpments. They formed about 100,000 years ago. If you could accelerate the erosion process to smooth the land to an even surface, you could place a bowling ball at the 4,600-foot elevation of the Panhandle, and it would roll southeastward into the Gulf of Mexico. The momentum and the continued tilt might even carry the ball underwater until it dropped off the edge of the continental shelf six miles from the shore.

This is the reason why all the major rivers—Rio Grande, Nueces, San Antonio, Guadalupe, Colorado, Brazos, San Jacinto, Trinity, Sabine, Red, and Canadian—flow in the same general southeastern direction. They are not the businesslike, rushing streams of the Northeast with the power to turn waterwheels and inspire industry. Their descent is gentle and meandering. Their brown waters take the time to build sandbars and explore new channels before reaching the shallow waters of the Gulf. In the early years the streams barely tolerated small steamboats, and they have never been good for hydroelectric dams or even waterwheels to any extent.

Beneath the land and extending beyond state borders, in addition, are six major freshwater aquifers. They collected their precious water over thousands of years and held it in sands and porous rock. Along with mineral deposits—salt, sulphur, petroleum, natural gas, gypsum, helium, limestone, lignite, quicksilver—which became part of the subsurface some 180,000,000 years ago, the water resources had to await the advance of technology before they could be extensively utilized.

The Great Plains with its subdivisions of the Llano Estacado and the Edwards Plateau splits the Panhandle, thrusts through West Texas, and crosses into Mexico midway up the Rio Grande. The Balcones Escarpment with its dramatic limestone cliffs and choppy hills marks the southeastern boundary of the plains in Texas. In West Texas near Post and in the Panhandle near Clarendon the rising Cap Rock, an exposed hard-pan layer, announces the eastern line of the Great Plains.

Although occasional badlands and colorful gorges such

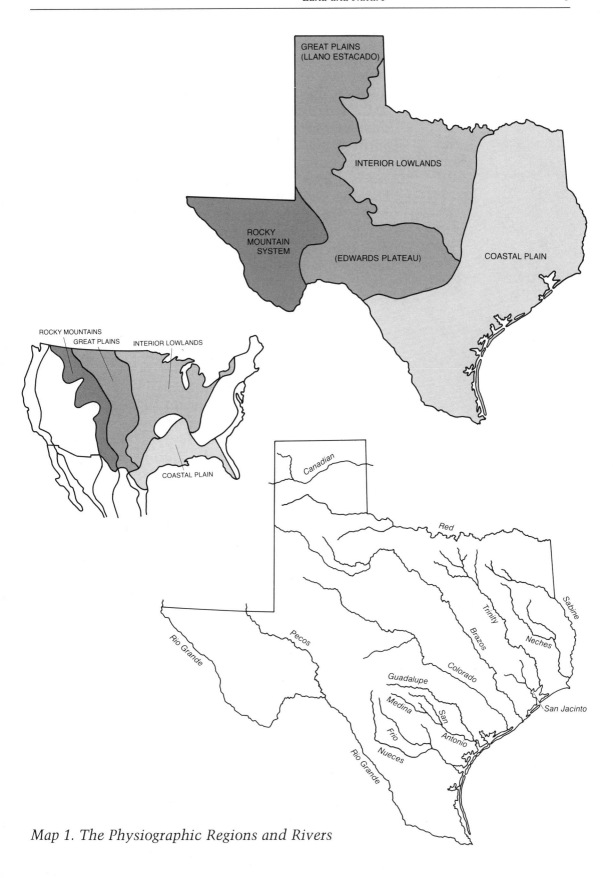

Map 1. The Physiographic Regions and Rivers

as Palo Duro near Canyon challenge the monotony of this landform, it is an area that early wayfarers faced with dread. "The traveler, in passing over it, sees nothing but one vast, dreary, and monotonous waste of barren solitude," wrote Randolph Barnes Marcy, a trailblazer of the mid-nineteenth century. "It is an ocean of desert prairie, where the voice of man is seldom heard, and where no living being permanently resides. The almost total absence of water causes all animals to shun it; even the Indians do not venture to cross it except at two or three points, where they find a few small ponds of water."

And yet there can be an addictive attraction to this near-desert expanse. As artist Georgia O'Keeffe commented about the Panhandle, "I lived on the plains of North Texas for four years. It is the only place I ever felt that I really belonged—that I really felt at home. That was my country—terrible winds and wonderful emptiness." To her friend Anita Pollitzer she wrote in 1916, "I am loving the plains more than ever it seems—and the SKY—Anita, you have never seen SKY—it is wonderful."

More comfortable for most people are the gently rolling plains of the southwestern tip of the interior lowlands, a physiographic landform that stretches through the midwestern United States from the Great Lakes to north-central Texas. It joins the Great Plains on the west and the even lower coastal plain on the east. The coastal configuration, for its part, extends from New York, follows the Atlantic seaboard, and swings around the Gulf into Mexico. It is less than 1,000 feet above sea level in Texas and was once under water. This gently sloping plain mildly slips into the Gulf waters and continues descending to form the shallow continental shelf.

The shoreline, characterized by easy surf, depthless bays, and salt marshes, nurtures shrimp, oysters, and aquatic birds of all sorts. Offshore sand barrier islands such as Galveston and Padre guard the mainland from the fury of West Indian storms, and serve, as they have since the early days of settlement, as a place of retreat for overheated Texans. Inland on the coastal plain the first Anglo-American settlers found the climate and black clay soils compatible with their cotton, slaves, and manner of life. The maelstrom of the Civil War caught them there, and thus the coastal plain of Texas became the geographic and historic terminus of the Old South. Its border with the interior lowlands even today denotes the point at which the South meets the West.

This east-west separation, traced roughly along the

ninety-eighth meridian by Interstate 35, is not the only division. Average rainfall drops with a steady beat from fifty-eight inches per year in the extreme east to eight inches in the extreme west. Generally, people of the coastal plain expect forty inches or so; along the Balcones line they anticipate thirty inches; and beyond the Cap Rock ranchers predict twenty inches. People have gathered in greatest numbers in central and eastern Texas, but the extra dry west has a reputation for the healthiest climate. "If people there want to die," so the folk saying goes, "they have to go somewhere else."

Heavy snowfalls are uncommon, but there are blizzards on the high plains, one of which set a record of thirty-three inches in 1956. In other places, such as Houston, snow is so unusual that when it comes the schools adjourn for the fun of the occasion. On rare occasions Galveston Bay has partially frozen and people have been able to scoop up the stunned fish with nets. Droughts have occurred, commonly during the odd-numbered decades—1850s, 1890s, 1910s, 1930s, 1950s, and 1970s.

A German traveler, Benno Matthes, noted in 1856–1857 that the Brazos and Colorado rivers were so low that

Tornado funnel over Austin, 1925. Photo presented to Frontier Times Museum by Mrs. William Braune, Bandera. Western History Collections, University of Oklahoma Library.

they could be crossed on horseback. Huge cracks in the earth, fifty feet long, three feet wide, and twelve feet deep, creased the prairies. The same conditions prevailed one hundred years later, threatening urban water supplies in north Texas and creating dust storms so thick that the automatic streetlights in Dallas turned on at midday.

South-central Texas, moreover, is the southern end of "tornado alley," a 200-mile-wide zone which points like a gun barrel northward to Iowa. This is the most tornado-prone region in the world—131 in Texas in 1986, 232 in 1967—and the springtime months are the most dangerous. Warm air from the south, cool air from the north, and a fast-moving jet stream aloft cause these deadly, tight-whirling storms. They customarily form and strike during the afternoon when warm moist air rises in advance of a cold front.

This happened in Waco in 1953 when a "twister" slashed through the downtown section, destroyed 185 buildings, and killed 114 people. The one that struck Wichita Falls in 1979 killed 42 people and caused $400 million in damages. In 1987 the small Hispanic town of Saragosa in West Texas suffered a tornado at sundown which obliterated the settlement and killed 30 people, many of whom had gathered at the community center to celebrate the Head Start program.

Greater devastation, however, has come from hurricanes striking the Texas coastline. Warm humid air rising in the mid-Atlantic from June through November creates the condition for these broad storms, which roar out of the Caribbean to ravage the shoreline with heavy rains, tornadoes, and winds of over seventy-five miles per hour. In 1900 Galveston experienced the worst natural disaster in terms of mortality in the history of the United States when a major hurricane flooded the island and killed six thousand people. Hurricane Celia, which struck Corpus Christi in 1970 with gusts of wind measuring 161 miles per hour, caused eleven deaths and $454 million in damages. Allen, a hurricane that hit the same general area in 1980, resulted in three deaths and $650 million in damages. Alicia, which assaulted the Galveston area in 1983, killed eighteen people and caused property losses of $3 billion.

Much more common for the discomfort of citizens than these unusual storms, however, are the northers of winter and the stifling temperatures of summer. The "blue norther" approaches as a fast-moving, heavy bank of dark purple clouds on the northwestern horizon. It arrives with a howl and proceeds to break tree limbs, slam shutters, and lower the temperature by as much as twenty-four degrees in one hour. It can be either wet or dry, but it is always cold. As an editor in Galveston commented in 1876, "The norther has many ways of demonstrating its affection for animal objects. It can come about as near getting over, and under, and around, and inside of a thinly clad specimen of the human species as almost anything else."

In its own way the "blue norther" can be inspiring. Pecos Bill, a Texas cowboy tall-tale character invented by journalist Tex O'Reilly, supposedly rescued a dog running ahead of a norther with a 600-pound block of ice on his tail. Bill broke off the block and took the dog inside to warm up, but the cold of the storm had frozen the barks of the grateful animal, who joyfully opened his mouth without sound. Bill picked up some of the frozen barks and warmed them in the skillet, and the cabin was soon filled with noise, much to the bewilderment of the dog, who searched the room for his canine rival.

Even without such exaggeration, wide temperature ranges during the year are common. Amarillo, for example, has recorded from −16 to 108 degrees Fahrenheit; Dallas from −8 to 113; and Houston from 5 to 108. Texans have learned that April with its refreshing spring rains and bluebonnets and October with its bright periwinkle blue skies are the best months for the comfort and temper of human beings.

In spite of prevailing southerly breezes, the summer months sizzle, and during the heat wave of 1980 temperatures of 105 to 110 were common throughout the state. Recordings in the 90-degree range are to be expected during July and August. This explains why Texans were the first to experiment with air-conditioned sports arenas, why Houston is the most air-conditioned city in the world, and why the comment of Philip H. Sheridan—while a junior officer at Fort Clark in 1855—is the most widely known Texas joke. "If I owned Texas and Hell," he said, "I would rent out Texas and live in Hell."

As might be expected, temperatures remain warmer longer in South Texas and permit an extensive growing season. In the southern tip the season lasts 330 days; in the extreme northwest it is 180 days. This means that the lower valley of the Rio Grande is a prime citrus region, an industry that began in the 1920s. Still, there can be trouble. The "big chill" of December 1983, which held Texas in a frigid hammerlock for seventeen days, killed

The Bluebonnet

A type of lupine, the bluebonnet grows fifteen to twenty-four inches high with the flowers blossoming for two to six inches at the top of the stem. Each flower has five blue petals that form a tiny bowl large enough to hold a drop of rainwater; the upper petal has a white spot that turns red with age. The wildflowers grow extensively over the state but are most prominent on the hillsides of Central Texas from March to early May.

The bluebonnet was first called buffalo clover, wolf flower, or *el conejo* ("the rabbit," because the bit of white resembled a rabbit's tail). Early Texas women, however, saw a similarity to a sunbonnet and gave it the name bluebonnet. It was adopted as the state flower by the Texas legislature in 1901 at the request of the National Society of the Colonial Dames of America in the State of Texas. In recent years Lady Bird Johnson has promoted the spread of bluebonnets and other wildflowers along Texas highways.

The bluebonnet: state flower and a favorite subject of Texas art. Photograph by David G. McComb.

The Big Thicket

In southeast Texas north of Beaumont near the old sawmill town of Kountze is a tangled forest once 42 miles wide and 113 miles long. Nearly every variety of pine and hardwood native to this latitude is found there, along with rare six-foot-tall ferns, seven varieties of orchids, and palmettos ten feet high. Much of the thicket is dense with vines, creepers, shrubs, and other undergrowth to the extent that it is almost impenetrable. Cut into by lumber companies, there remains only the 84,550-acre Big Thicket National Preserve, established in 1974.

In early years even Indians hesitated to leave the well-established trails, and during the Civil War the area served as a refuge for draft dodgers and outlaws. Through the years the Big Thicket has been connected with tales of lost travelers, mysterious disappearances, and murder.

over half of the orchards. The trees that produced the sweet ruby Texas grapefruit had to be replanted, and it took four years for the valley to bear fruit again.

The vegetation pattern of the area, like that elsewhere, responds to the precipitation, temperature, and soil conditions. There are more than eight hundred soil types in Texas, and of the ten major soil orders, seven can be found abundantly in the state. They range from leached sandy soils to nearly impermeable clays to dark loams. Early settlers preferred the alluvial soils of the river bottoms and the black, waxy clay of the coastal prairie. Here, so it was said in early days, the soil was so good that Irish potatoes would turn into sweet potatoes.

The western end of a pine forest strip that runs to the Atlantic Ocean reaches into East Texas, and three prongs of the central hardwood zone thrust across the Red River into the north-central and northeastern part of the state. Oaks, pecans, hickories, and elms are a part of these three fingers known as the Western Cross Timbers, Eastern Cross Timbers, and the Post Oak Belt.

Scattered through and between these four forest areas in early Texas were corridors of prairie which served as natural passageways through the thick timbered regions, as well as glades of grassland which attracted farmers and planters. In the southeast in the midst of the pine woods stood a unique and almost impenetrable rain forest called the Big Thicket, while along the shoreline were

Swamp in the Big Thicket. Photograph by Campbell Loughmiller.

salt marshes. As the elevation rose, however, bunch-grass and bluestem took over. All of this impressed early travelers and attracted the earliest Anglo-American settlers, who tried to combine in their claims a combination of grassland and timberland.

To the west beyond the Balcones Escarpment and the ninety-eighth meridian, where the land becomes drier, the taller grasses and trees scatter and eventually disappear. Other species of grass, shorter in the more arid country, cover the west—Indian grass, bluestems, side-oats, buffalo grass, switchgrass, and others. Interspersed are various shrubs such as mesquite and sagebrush along with cacti, various thorny plants, and the tall spikes of yucca plants. William A. McClintock, a soldier in the War with Mexico, observed the brush in South Texas in 1846 and commented, "There is nothing of the vegitible world on the rio grand but what is armed with weapons of defence and offence . . . pricks, thorns, or burs."

Throughout the early land there flourished a rich wild-life, which included bears, wolves, roadrunners, alligators, rabbits, deer, turkeys, javelinas, and ducks. All four poisonous serpents of the United States lived in Texas—copperheads, rattlesnakes, coral snakes, and cottonmouth moccasins. The western diamondback rattler grew to seven feet in length. Buffalo ranging into the coastal prairie were also common in early days. Cabeza de Vaca reported them in the 1530s apparently in the vicinity of Austin. "They have small horns like the cows of Morocco; their hair is very long and flocky like merinos'," he wrote. "Some are tawny, others black. . . . The Indians make blankets out of the skins of cows not full grown; and shoes and shields from the full-grown." George W. Kendall, a Texas Ranger, rancher, and newspaperman, observed in 1842, "I have stood upon a high roll of the prairies, with neither tree nor bush to obstruct the vision in any direction, and seen these animals grazing upon the plain and darkening it at every point." No mammals with the exception of human beings have thronged together in such great numbers.

With settlement in Texas in the nineteenth century the bison all but disappeared. Some people drove them away because it was thought the buffalo attracted Indians. By the late 1850s they were rare enough in Mason County west of the Balcones Escarpment that when one lone animal appeared, several German farm children ran home screaming that the devil was into the cattle herd. Following the Civil War the systematic slaughter of the bison

Rattlesnakes

There are ten kinds of rattlesnakes in Texas, the largest and most famous being the western diamondback. It has a wedge-shaped head, a large diamond pattern of earth colors on its body, and a rattle which sounds like dry beans shaken vigorously in a tin can. An average size is four to five feet, but the largest ever measured is seven feet and five inches. At the 1970 Sweetwater Rattlesnake Roundup hunters caught one that measured seven feet.

The snakes have often figured in Texas literature. Pecos Bill used a rattlesnake for a quirt, and George W. Kendall on the Santa Fe expedition in 1842 recorded: "We had a troublesome and unwelcome visitor in camp on the night of the Fourth of July . . . The wet grass without probably drove a prairie rattlesnake to more comfortable quarters within our canvass, the first intimation we had of the vicinity of his snakeship being his crawling over one of us in an attempt to effect a lodgement under some of the blankets. . . . For myself, fearing to move lest I should molest the reptile, I rolled myself, head and all, under my blanket, and lay perfectly quiet until daylight."

Teddy Blue (E. C. Abbott), a Texas cowboy, told about a man who brought a live rattlesnake in a large glass jar into a saloon. He bet that no one could keep a finger on the outside while the angry snake struck on the inside. "To show you what a bonehead I was, I took him up. It was thick glass and I knew damn well the snake couldn't bite me, so I put my finger on it. The snake struck, and away came my finger. I got mad and made up my mind I would hold my finger on that glass or bust. It cost me seventeen dollars before I quit, but since then I've never bucked the other fellow's game and it has saved me a lot of money."

Rip Ford, a Texas Ranger and writer, claimed to have met a ten-foot diamondback in the Cross Timbers. He could hear the rattle one hundred yards away, and its

herds on the Great Plains removed them from the state.

Passenger pigeons, gray and red wolves, bighorn sheep, jaguars, elk, and greater prairie chickens disappeared. Black bears and ivory-billed woodpeckers were left only in remote areas, but alligators, brown pelicans, and pronghorn antelope have revived through conservation measures in the twentieth century. The fate of whooping cranes, peregrine falcons, and southern bald eagles remains to be determined.

The Spanish, on the other hand, contributed mustangs and longhorn cattle to the environment, and with time some ninety-two other species came from elsewhere in the world. Brown house sparrows spread after the release of a flock in Galveston in 1867, and the European starling, which landed in New York in 1890, made it to Texas in 1925. The grackle arrived in the twentieth century, and the armadillo swam the Rio Grande sometime in the 1840s. John James Audubon published a picture of one in the 1850s.

The fire ant, capturing five to ten miles per year, marched into East Texas in the 1950s from South America via Alabama. This painful threat to livestock and crops now infests 130 counties. The latest arrival of note, however, was the black- and white-striped Asian tiger mosquito, whose eggs can survive cold weather. With its lust for human blood and its potential to carry dengue fever, the Asian tiger mosquito arrived in used tire casings at the Port of Houston in 1985. In two years' time it spread to seventeen states.

The most important agents of change, also migrants, have been human beings, who moved to exploit the environment for their benefit. The first of these were ancient Indians. The popular image of the Indian, the mounted and feathered nomad of the plains, has been projected by western fiction writers, Hollywood, artists, and travelers. It was not necessarily a false image, but rather one that was too simple and narrow, too generalized.

The natives of Texas and their histories were more complex and sophisticated than the image. None of the various groups, however, possessed the ability to write, and most of what is known about them comes from Anglo observers and writers, archaeologists, and anthropologists. Unavoidably, there was an ethnic and cultural bias; there were few notations from the Indian side of the historical ledger to balance the account.

During the last Ice Age, some 12,000 years ago, maybe earlier, while the Bering Strait was a land bridge, primitive peoples migrated into North America. Following ice-free corridors, one along the eastern side of the Rocky Mountains, they traveled southward and occupied the open land. These Paleo-Indians appeared as early as 9200 B.C. in the Texas Panhandle, where they hunted mammoths with distinctive Clovis-style flint spear points. Later Ice Age hunters with spear throwers tracked large primitive straight-horned bisons. Near Langtry on the Rio Grande the bones of such animals, mixed with narrow, fluted Folsom projectile points, have been found. This was the result of a slaughter after hunters drove a herd over the edge of a steep canyon and butchered them below. The same sort of event occurred a thousand years later, in 7000 B.C., in West Texas, where archaeologists discovered a new style of spear tip called the Plainview point.

The skeletons of a man and a boy found under a rock ledge near Waco in 1970 and that of a woman at Leander in 1982 represent the earliest known burials in North America. The fossilized remains of a Folsom woman exposed in the sand by the wind at Midland in 1953 revealed a physical structure the same as that of modern human

head was waist high when the snake coiled. He left it alone, but other people eat rattlesnakes. The snake is prepared like fried chicken and tastes like pork. Arthur and Bobbie Coleman in *The Texas Cookbook* (1949) wrote: "To prepare, cut the head off the snake, let the body drain a while, slit up the middle and pull out the insides (they come out easily). Then slice the snake across in one-inch hunks, roll in corn meal, salt, and fry well done in lard."

A Texas rattlesnake, photographed by W. D. Smithers, San Antonio. Western History Collections, University of Oklahoma Library.

beings. There were no precursors to Homo sapiens in the New World.

At the time these first Paleo-Indians entered Texas, in the Middle East at Jericho other primitive peoples invented agriculture, established the first city, and started civilization. In Texas and most of North America the Indians remained at a stone-age level of technology until the coming of the Europeans. Yet, as George C. Frison, an anthropologist from the University of Wyoming, commented: "The Paleo-Indians were a proud people. Look at their weaponry. Look at the individuality and the perfection that went into their projectile points. It's just like a hunter today who has his favorite rifle, and he polishes it and engraves the barrel and takes care of it. These people knew what they were doing."

With the retreat of the Ice Age glaciers and the warming of the land to its modern climatic pattern, earlier game animals disappeared and the Indians had to depend more on plants for a food supply. The Paleo-Indian culture gave way to the Archaic period (5000 B.C. to A.D. I), during which Indians used a greater variety of stone tools—dart points, axes, choppers, picks, drills, mortars, and pestles. It was during this time that the Indians acquired dogs as traveling companions, but North American natives domesticated only one other animal, the turkey. At about the time of Christ, when the Romans were using catapults and steel-edged swords, Texas Indians learned about the bow and arrow and acquired a knowledge of agriculture.

It is a mystery how corn, a hybrid plant, developed and traveled, but the earliest form dates from 2500 B.C. and came from northern Mexico. This became the most valuable domesticated plant of the New World, and by the time the Europeans arrived it was cultivated to its environmental limits throughout North and South America. The agricultural revolution in America, which included other plants such as beans, squash, potatoes, and tobacco, had the same effect as in the Old World. People settled down to till fields, populations increased, communities developed, and the social organization became more complex. This was particularly true of the civilizations of Central and South America. Texas Indians, however, remained for the most part hunters and gatherers, with a few tribes giving part-time effort to agriculture.

It is assumed that the Jumano Indians, who lived in permanent settlements and farmed the Rio Grande and Rio Conchos valleys, were peripheral beneficiaries of the Pueblo culture of the Southwest. This whole area was close enough to have benefited through technological transfer from the high civilizations of Central America. The Jumanos, however, did not apply irrigation techniques and were known to hunt buffalo. They lived in flat-roofed rectangular adobe houses clustered together, organized their society under the leadership of chiefs, manufactured pottery, and possessed bows reinforced with bone and sinew. They are the least known of Texas Indians and because of changes in climate were declining at the time of Spanish colonization. Cabeza de Vaca in his escape from Texas in the 1530s reported drought conditions to the extent that the Jumanos refused to waste their corn by planting it. After experiencing slave raids by the Spanish and flirting with Christianity, the Jumanos were last seen riding in the hunting parties of the Lipan Apaches.

Across Texas in the eastern pine forests lived another Indian group, the Caddoes, who were also noted for their farming. For them the crops of corn, squash, beans, sun-

The Mockingbird

Found throughout the American South and Southwest, this medium-sized bird is about the size of an American robin but more slender and is distinguished by a gray body with large white patches on its wings and mobile tail. Its song is a long continued succession of notes of much variety. It repeats phrases a half-dozen times or more in quick succession and is known to be an excellent mimic. It lays blue-green, spotted eggs in nests located in dense shrubbery or trees and was adopted as the state bird in 1927 at the request of the Texas Federation of Women's Clubs.

The mockingbird, state bird of Texas. Barker Texas History Center, The University of Texas at Austin.

The Armadillo

The Spanish name translates "little armored one" and refers to a primitive group of mammals that probably originated in the New World. Their tough platelike shell, unique among mammals, accounts for 16 percent of the body weight. There are approximately twenty species, all of which except the nine-banded armadillo live in Central and South America. The nine-banded variety is the most numerous and can be found from Argentina to the southern United States.

Adults weigh about fourteen pounds and measure two and one-half feet. The nine bands are not rigid, but are connected by skin, which allows the animal to fold like an accordion. The Texas version is not flexible enough to curl into a complete ball like some of its cousins, and consequently it depends upon furious skittering

Armadillos. Barker Texas History Center, The University of Texas at Austin.

flower seeds, and tobacco provided the mainstay of life. Both men and women using crude bone or wooden hoes worked the fields, which had been cleared of debris by fire. Deer, buffalo, bears, ducks, rabbits, snakes, mice, and fish caught on a trotline supplemented their diet.

They played a game much like field hockey; ruled themselves with a hereditary bureaucracy; honored an omnipotent God; and lived in round huts constructed of poles covered with grass. They made clay pots, baskets, mats, flutes from bird bones, and superior bows of bois d'arc. The division of labor between men and women was much more equal among the Caddoes than among other Indian groups, and women at times acquired influence and property within the inherited male structure of authority. The tribes of the Hasinai division, part of the larger Caddo confederation, called each other Taychas, a word for "ally" or "friend." The Spanish used the word to refer to friendly natives, and from this came the name Texas.

Much of the Caddoan pattern of life, including the construction of rough temples on a foundation of raised earth, reflected the earlier culture of the Mound Builders of the Mississippi Valley. This civilization—noted for its large, flat-topped, square earthen mounds, agriculture, continental trade patterns, and large towns—flourished in A.D.

500, the time of the fall of the Roman Empire in Europe. The Caddoes at the moment of Spanish and French entry into Texas appeared to be a degenerating remainder, a shadow, of this earlier sophisticated people.

This raises a particular anthropological question about Texas Indians. The Caddoes in the east and the Jumanos in the west seem to have learned their agricultural techniques from others. The Indians who inhabited the area between them were much more primitive in their technology and did not rise above the level of hunting and gathering. If the high civilization from Central America had spread across Texas to the Mississippi, why did it not affect the people of Central Texas? Did technology transfer occur by boat travel along the Gulf Coast? Probably not, since there is little evidence of seagoing adventures by native Americans. Was it possible that the Mound Builders achieved their development on their own? Perhaps, especially if there was some contact through trade. Under any circumstance, the level of development was lower among the interior tribes than among those on the periphery.

Between the Caddoes in East Texas and the fierce nomads of the high plains lived the Wichita tribes, which served as intermediaries in trade and revealed a combination of cultural traits. Pushed southward by the military superiority of the Osages to the north, the Wichitas migrated into Texas in the seventeenth and eighteenth centuries. Their language was of Caddoan origin, and they lived in the same sort of round grass huts as their eastern neighbors. They believed in a variety of deities and thought that all objects possessed a soul. The Wichitas cultivated extensive fields of corn, beans, melons, and squash and hunted buffalo. They did not eat fish, however, and the division of labor was much more like that of Indians other than the Caddoes. As the eighteenth-century observer Athanase de Mézières noted: "The women tan, sew, and paint the skins, fence the fields, care for the corn fields, harvest the crops, cut and fetch the fire-wood, prepare the food, build the houses, and rear the children, their constant care stopping at nothing that contributes to the comfort and pleasure of their husbands. The latter devote themselves wholly to the chase and to warfare."

Most North American Indians painted and tattooed their bodies, but the Wichitas were unusual in the extent of their tattoos. This was accomplished by pricking the skin with a needle until it bled and then rubbing charcoal

through brush and quick digging to escape from enemies.

With its short, stubby feet and claws the armadillo feasts on earthworms, crayfish, lizards, insects of all sorts, and dead birds. There is some thought that they will also kill snakes and small rabbits. They construct deep burrows in river embankments for nesting purposes, and the young are born in the spring with their eyes open. By the fall the newborn are able to fend for themselves, although they are not sexually mature until the second year. Their chief enemies are wolves, mountain lions, bobcats, coyotes, dogs, and automobiles.

The armadillo crossed the Rio Grande in the 1840s, reached Nueces Bay in the 1890s, and waddled into Louisiana in the mid-1920s. The rate of spread has been two to six miles per year, which has carried the creature to Florida on the east and Oklahoma and Arkansas on the north.

Human beings have used the armadillo for food, baskets, pets, race animals, and as subjects for leprosy study. When grilled and basted with paprika, chili powder, salt, and catsup, armadillo tastes like pork. Hondo Crouch, longtime mayor of Luckenbach, once recommended a diet of armadillo for weight loss. "You eat nothing but armadillo for a month, and you have to run down and catch all the armadillos you eat—really takes the weight off!" The armadillo became a folk symbol for Texas in the mid-1960s and barely missed immortality in 1981 when a bill sponsoring it as the state mammal failed passage in the legislature.

The Mustang

The Spanish introduced the modern horse to North America, and the animals passed into the hands of Texas Indians from early seventeenth-century Spanish villages in the vicinity of Santa Fe, New Mexico. The spread of horse technology was slow until the 1680 Pueblo rebellion, which left the Indians heir to large herds of sheep, cattle, and horses. Although the sedentary Pueblos had little need for the horses, their nomadic neighbors with whom they traded were delighted. Horses allowed the Plains Indians to become more efficient nomads and ushered in a "golden age." Buffalo, their mainstay of life, could no longer outrun them, and the Indians now could easily follow the herds wherever they moved.

By 1700 all Texas Indians knew about horses, and when a few footsore Comanches arrived to trade in 1705 with the Spanish in New Mexico, they rode off with a stolen herd. Most Plains Indians could make crude saddles by stretching green buffalo hides over a wooden frame. They also used a "pad saddle," made like a pillow stuffed with grass with short stirrups and girth attached. They used a rawhide rein tied to the lower jaw of the horse and a loop around the neck to cling to while riding and using the horse as a shield.

dust into the wound. The men thus decorated their eyelids, drew lines from the outside edge of the eyes and downward from the corners of the mouth, put claws on the backs of their hands, and marked their arms and chest with symbols of victory in war. They also pierced their ears in as many as four places and hung ornaments from them. The women fashioned a line down the bridge of the nose and around the mouth to join with four parallel lines on the chin. They also placed a tattoo line along the chin and zigzags down the arms. Around each breast they drew three concentric circles, which were thought to prevent the pendulous conditions of old age.

To the west of the Wichitas on the Great Plains ranged the nomadic Comanche and Apache Indians. For settlers of the nineteenth century the Comanche was the principal enemy and the one who embodied the image of the Indian in the Texas mind. The Comanches were related to the Northern Shoshones of Colorado and Wyoming; from the mountains in small bands they followed the Arkansas Valley into eastern Colorado and Kansas. Early in 1700 they entered New Mexico, acquired horses, and by 1750 controlled the southern plains. Buffalo was their mainstay, which with horses they could follow at will, but they also hunted bears, antelope, and longhorn cattle. Along the way they gathered wild plums, grapes, mulberries, persimmons, the tunas of prickly pears, pecans, acorns, and various tubers. They traded or stole corn and tobacco, and when starving would eat almost anything, including their horses.

Always on the move, they learned to make and eat pemmican, a trail mix of dried buffalo meat mixed with nuts, berries, and tallow. They carried this in bags made from rawhide or intestines. They often ate their meat raw and delighted in uncooked liver flavored with the contents of the gall bladder. In addition, the Comanche drank the warm blood of a fresh kill, ate the curdled milk from the stomach of suckling fawns, and devoured broiled tripe, which they dragged over the grass to remove the worst of the filth.

Their homes, which were tepees made of poles and tanned buffalo hides, were easily moved and set up. They were circular, twelve to fourteen feet high, and tied with a leather rope at the top where the poles crossed. The entry hole as well as the vent at the top faced away from the prevailing wind, and inside was a fireplace for cooking and warmth. Women holding on to stakes driven into the ground and assisted by other women gave birth in the tepees or in special brush shelters. Skins were utilized for sitting and sleeping, and supposedly the Comanche tepee gave more protection from the weather than did the log cabins of Anglo pioneers.

The men fought and hunted with spears and short bows and arrows tipped at first with stone, later with iron or steel. They carried painted bison-hide shields which could turn away enemy arrows and sometimes a glancing bullet. The rim of the shield was decorated with feathers, scalps, horse tails, and bears' teeth. They hunted on horseback and could drive an arrow all the way through a buffalo. In warm weather boys and men wore breechclouts, leggings, and moccasins while girls and women wore skin gowns, skirts and blouses, and moccasins. In cold weather they put on leather shirts and buffalo robes. In earlier times the warriors wore headdresses of buffalo horns, and in the nineteenth century adopted feather war bonnets. The men plucked out their facial hair, including eyebrows, and wore an array of silver, brass, or shell rings in their pierced ears. Both sexes used a plenitude of body paint, the men even decorating their horses and the women accenting their eyes with yellow or red lines, their ears with red insides, and their cheeks with a circle or triangle of solid red-orange.

Decisions were made by the common consent of the male leaders in council, but they respected independence and freedom of action. Every band recognized a principal war chief, and warriors held the position of highest status. Anyone, nonetheless, could lead a war party, and individuals, often during a full moon, rallied camp mates to follow their lead. Like other Texas Indians, they struck in

Spanish horses, which in the wild became known as "mustangs," were a mixture of African, Arabian, and Spanish breeds. They were generally small, weighing about 700 pounds and measuring less than fourteen hands high; they could be of any color. They were not generally noted for beauty but were swift, tough, and enduring.

At Fort Chadbourne north of San Angelo some officers challenged a band of Comanches to a horse race. The Indians did not appear eager to go against the soldiers' thoroughbred Kentucky mare, but nonetheless brought out a longhaired, miserable "sheep of a pony" and placed bets. When the soldiers saw a 170-pound Indian with a club mount the pony, they substituted their third-best racehorse. The Comanches won, of course, and carried off the flour, sugar, and coffee that had been bet against their buffalo robes. The soldiers demanded a second race and put in their second-best racer. Again the Indian pony with its heavy rider won. The outraged soldiers then brought out the Kentucky mare, and the betting became hot. In the race the Indian jockey gave a yell, threw away his club, bolted into the lead, and fifty yards from the finish line turned around on the horse and gestured obscenely at the American loser.

Mustangs: statue by Alexander Phimister Proctor (1948) on the University of Texas campus in Austin. Photograph by David G. McComb.

The Buffalo

The American bison, popularly misnamed "buffalo," is a bovine ruminant related to European bison, domesticated cattle, and perhaps the huge extinct bison hunted by Paleo-Indians. When Europeans first arrived, bison roamed over most of North America east of the Rocky Mountains and north of Mexico. The greatest herds, however, were located on the Great Plains, where they wandered in erratic and unpredictable fashion. In Texas they were found mainly on the prairie lands and seldom in the pine woods of East Texas or the deserts of the Trans-Pecos area.

The dim-sighted animals were sluggish, mild in temperament, and possessed of "intense stupidity," as one observer put it. They were unafraid of gunshots, and at times whole groups were killed without a stampede. Dying animals did not arouse others. When disturbed, however, they were extremely dangerous, and with a slight lead they could outrun a horse. Once running, moreover, not much would stop them, and they would blindly rush over cliffs, into rivers, and even into railroad trains.

They were the largest of the big game animals in America, with bulls averaging 1,600 pounds and standing six feet tall at the shoulder. For Plains Indians buffalo provided the sustenance of life—food, hides for clothing and tepee covers, bones for tools. Although there were a few exceptions, buffalo could not be domesticated. Consequently, a systematic slaughter of the herds for their hides and tongues and for sport began in 1830 and continued until their near extinction in the 1870s. In the southern herd of the Texas Panhandle, hunters killed over 3 million animals in three years, from 1872 through 1874. When the slaughter was completed, the prairie was open to the cattle barons, and the Indian cultures that depended upon the buffalo collapsed.

Buffalo on the Goodnight Ranch, 1903. Barker Texas History Center, The University of Texas at Austin.

small groups to loot, kill, and withdraw. They divided their booty quickly and, if pursued, they split apart, each warrior fleeing alone. Their goal most often was the theft of horses, but after the Civil War they profitably sold stolen Texas cattle to New Mexicans. This brought them into permanent warfare with the ranchers and the state.

War was a necessity of life for the Comanches. It gave them command of the southern plains, and it was the only way for them to hold the rich bison country against the encroachment of settlers or other Indians. Stealing horses from an enemy camp, scalping an opponent under dangerous circumstances, and touching a live adversary were considered among the bravest of acts. A warrior could "count coup," similar to an award of merit, for these events at tribal meetings. With the advance of Anglo-American civilization and the destruction of the buffalo herds after the Civil War, however, the end was unavoidable. The Comanche moon rose no more. After years of sporadic outbursts, the exhausted and defeated Comanches left the plains in the 1870s for the reservations of Oklahoma. Their legacy, however, was an indelible image like that recorded in 1845 by German traveler Ferdinand Roemer, who once observed a Comanche tribe on the move: "According to Indian custom, they rode single file, the men in advance, dressed in their best, looking about, dignified and grave; the lively squaws following, sitting astride like the men, each usually carrying a black-eyed little papoose on her back and another in front of the saddle. At the same time they kept a watchful eye on the

pack horses which carried the skins and the various household goods."

The eastern tribes of the Apache nation, which lived in West Texas prior to the invasion of the Comanches, gave way to the fierce intruders from the north. The Jicarillas retreated westward to mix with Pueblo tribes, and the Kiowa Apaches along with the Kiowas became so much like the Comanches that they formed an alliance with their ferocious overlords in the last years of the eighteenth century. The Lipan Apaches, however, were pushed southward and crushed between the Comanches to the north and the Spanish in the south. Their gardening villages were but loosely linked, and the Comanches eliminated them one by one.

Kiowa boy. Western History Collections, University of Oklahoma Library.

Lipan Apaches wore simple buckskin clothing decorated with beads and brass ornaments. The men cut their hair short on the left side of the head in order to show off multiple earrings and tried to remove all facial hair, including eyelashes. Frederick Law Olmsted met Castro, a chief, in the 1850s and described him wearing a beaded buckskin shirt, a wreath of fresh oak leaves on his head, heavy brass earrings, and a vermilion stripe painted across his face. Olmsted thought "his face was not without some natural dignity and force, but the predominant expression was wily and brutal."

The Lipans depended upon buffalo, antelope, and turkeys more than the produce of the women's gardens or the wild agave and sotol plants they gathered. They suffered from lice, but took advantage of the condition. As an observer noted: "The lice laid their eggs, or nits, in the seams of their clothing. It was amusing to see them take a garment and fold it with the seam exposed and pass it between their teeth biting the nits. You could hear them pop, and from the greedy manner in which they would lick their lips it was evident that they liked the taste of the nits." By 1750 the Lipan Apaches had been forced into the more desolate parts of western Texas and northern Mexico where little agriculture was possible. Their poverty conditions reduced their numbers and changed them from once proud and independent people into beggars.

The Apaches believed in supernatural spirits, as did the Comanches, and it was the Mescalero Apaches who painted the pictographs on the rock walls near El Paso. Victorio, a Mimbres Apache, rallied the warriors of the Texas–New Mexico and Mexico borders to a fatal stand in the Tres Castillos Mountains of northern Mexico in 1880. That event, along with one more raid in 1881, gave

Kiowa woman. Western History Collections, University of Oklahoma Library.

the Apaches the honor of being the last Indian remnant to fight on the Texas frontier.

The Texas tribes to the south and along the Gulf Coast were the least developed of the Indians. They all hunted, gathered wild plants, and fished, but practiced no agriculture. The numerically weak Tonkawas searched for allies, even courting the Spanish by asking for missions. They ate almost anything, including rats, skunks, and rattlesnakes, but preferred buffalo when they could get it. Their family organization was matrilineal, and mothers after giving birth in special grass huts placed their babies in cradleboards in order to flatten their foreheads.

Like other Indians, the Tonkawas practiced ritual cannibalism. At one time John H. Jenkins, a soldier and writer, observed them celebrating with yells and dancing while cooking and eating the hands and feet of a Wichita warrior. Such action supposedly gave them the spirit power of the dead and served as an insult to the enemy. They also seemed to enjoy the feast; Europeans applied the label "cannibal" to such coastal groups.

Coahuiltecans, another tribe of South Texas whose focal point was San Pedro Springs, now a park in San Antonio, were so primitive in their skills that anthropologists speculate that they represent the remainder of an earlier Indian culture that was swept to the least habitable part of Texas by technically superior invaders. Cabeza de Vaca found them capable of running after deer for an entire day, protective of their territory, and willing to eat almost anything available, including spiders, ant eggs, rotten wood, and deer dung.

They were mainly vegetarians, however, who ate mesquite beans mixed with dirt and enjoyed an intoxicating drink, mescal, which they made from agave leaves. They existed in small family groups and, nearly naked, roamed their territory as various seasons made food available. They used peyote in religious ceremonies, responded well to Spanish missionaries, and readily died of European diseases. By 1800 most of the Coahuiltecans in southern Texas had disappeared, and by 1900 the acculturated groups in northern Mexico had also vanished.

Sharing the bottom of the technological scale with the Coahuiltecans were the Karankawas and Atakapans of the Gulf Coast. Little is certain about the Atakapans of southeast Texas, but the group extended across the Sabine into Louisiana, lived mainly by hunting, and ate their enemies on occasion. In the Choctaw language their name meant "man-eater."

The Karankawas, similar to their neighbors, wore few clothes and subsisted by frequent moves in search of food. They were tall and well built but often hungry. The men wore pieces of cane through their lower lips and nipples, and both sexes used tattoos and body paint. In addition, to fend off mosquitos they coated their bodies with shark or alligator oil, which gave them a particularly repulsive odor. They ate oysters, clams, turtles, fish, porpoises, the bulbs of underwater plants, berries, deer, bears, and bison if available. They used crude dugout canoes propelled with poles, nets to catch fish, and long cedar bows for hunting. They wove baskets and waterproofed them with natural asphalt that washed up on shore.

Because of the lack of food, they roved in small bands and allowed their children to suckle until twelve years of age, when they were declared self-sufficient. They were the first Texas Indians to meet Europeans, and they saved the lives of the shipwrecked Spaniards who first appeared on the shore. With disease from the newcomers and an example of Spanish cannibalism, however, the Karankawas turned away from the alien civilization. Hard experiences with the Spanish and others, including Jean Laffite's pirates, made them implacable enemies.

Mesquite

With the removal of the Indians from the prairie the mesquite tree, an indigenous plant of lacy, pale green leaves, half-inch needle-sharp thorns, and twisted branches, began to spread. The natives annually fired the grasslands, which inhibited the tree by burning it back to its roots. As the range deteriorated and Indians disappeared, cactus and mesquite took over, and the tree with its thin shade and its twenty-foot height prevented grass from growing. By 1872 it had advanced out of South Texas into the ranchland around San Antonio, and the U.S. Department of Agriculture in 1957 reported twice as much mesquite in Texas as in 1900. It is tough to remove from rangeland—cattle spread its seeds—and it has little commercial value except as a special firewood to lend unusual flavor to barbecued meat.

Photograph by David G. McComb.

Since this was the earliest point of settlement by Europeans, the Karankawas were among the first Indians eliminated. Although they were said to be cannibals, eyewitness reports were rare, and there was no one to tell the Indian side of the story. As their numbers thinned, the Karankawas drifted toward Mexico and in the 1850s became extinct. "The Karánkaways are gone," wrote Roy Bedichek, the Texas naturalist of *Karánkaway Country.* "Only bitter memories of them remain. In the minds of our people they are eternally damned, largely because they refused a culture we offered, resisting our proffered blessings to the last."

Such might well be the epitaph for all Texas Indians. At present there are no original Indian cultures left in the state, although there are two small reservations for tribes that came later—the Alabama-Coushattas in the east and the Tiguas in the west. Various other tribes—Shawnees, Delawares, Kickapoos, Seminoles, Cherokees—were refugees from the westward rolling Anglo frontier who sought sanctuary in Texas, but most of them failed in their quest. The Indians lost because of disease, destruction of the buffalo, fewer numbers, and the superior technology of the newcomers. This technology included not only the repeating firearms that came in the nineteenth century— weapons capable of matching the rapid fire of a bow and arrow—but also the technology of farming, communication, and transportation.

The Indians faced an informed, united, and determined opponent which in the long run overwhelmed them. The various Indian groups did not all work together like their enemies, nor did they possess the means of communication to take advantage of such situations as the Civil War. They lost to a stronger foe, just as earlier Texas Indian groups had lost to others who invaded the land. The Indian peoples were caught in the flood tide that carried Anglo-American civilization from the Atlantic Coast to the Pacific. It was an inevitable defeat.

2. The Spanish Legacy

Santiago!
BATTLECRY OF THE SPANISH
CONQUISTADOR

Unwilling, cold, defeated, and sick, the first consequential representatives of European civilization in Texas landed with a thump on the sands of Galveston Island in November 1528. They were the remnants of the ill-fated Narváez expedition sent to conquer Florida. Abandoned by their fleet and attacked by hostile natives, the four hundred starving Spaniards ate their horses, built crude barges, rigged sails from their shirts, and floated westward. The chill waves dumped eighty to ninety survivors on the beach at Galveston, and of these only four lived to see their countrymen again. The white men called the place Malhado, or the Isle of Doom.

There had been earlier investigations of the Texas coastline by Spanish explorers. In 1519 at the time Cortez began his adventure among the Aztecs of Mexico, Alonso Alvarez de Piñeda, a navy lieutenant, sailed from Jamaica and followed the northern Gulf Coast to the Rio Grande. There, a few miles upstream, he rested his sailors in a palmetto grove, replenished his supplies, and repaired his gear. After forty days in camp he continued down the coast for a while, then turned about and retraced his course back to Jamaica. Much later, in 1785, at the command of Bernardo de Gálvez, the viceroy of Mexico, José de Evia charted the Texas shoreline, but the first European to cross Texas was Alvar Núñez Cabeza de Vaca, the second in command of the Narváez expedition and one of the survivors.

Most of the Spaniards on Galveston Island shortly died from disease, malnutrition, exposure, and angry Karankawa Indians. The initial meeting of the two cultures, however, was friendly. The Europeans exchanged bells and beads for food, and after the Spaniards lost all of their clothing and gear to the surf in an attempt to continue their voyage, the Indians shared food, warmth, and shelter. The Karankawas, however, blaming the white men for a rash of dysentery and disgusted at an example of cannibalism among the starving Europeans, enslaved the Spaniards after this brief period of helpfulness and compassion.

Cabeza de Vaca survived by his wits for six years and then escaped with three others by walking into northern Mexico. His exact route across Texas is unclear, but he reported buffalo and the rumor of a rich native civilization somewhere to the north. Estevanico, a black slave from the west coast of Morocco who had escaped with Cabeza de Vaca, guided a return group. Ranging ahead and demanding women and turquoise from Indian villages, Estevanico overreached himself. The Indians killed him, but the expedition's leader, Fray Marcos de Niza, returned to Mexico City with the news that he had seen from a distance one of the golden cities of Cibola.

It was legend that seven Portuguese bishops fleeing Islam in the eighth century had gone westward and established seven cities of great wealth. Fired with the possibility of finding another Aztec or Inca empire, the viceroy of Mexico ordered a young alderman of Mexico City to march forth in conquest.

Glittering in golden armor, Francisco Vásquez de Coronado rode northward in 1540 leading over three hundred soldiers and several hundred Indian allies, along with supplies of sheep, cattle, horses, mules, and swine. The expedition discovered and ravaged the poor Pueblo towns, which included Fray Marcos's Cibola, and wintered in these Indian villages of the upper Rio Grande. In the spring the army marched through New Mexico onto the high prairie, which the Spaniards called the Llano Estacado ("staked plains"), supposedly after the spearlike stalks of the yucca plant, but perhaps also because of the rising wall of the escarpment. They reached the Cap Rock at Palo Duro Canyon in West Texas in search of a fabled Gran Quivira and saw nothing but rolling grassland stretching before them into the shimmering distance.

Pushing on with a small troop into what is now Kansas, Coronado discovered that Gran Quivira amounted only to the straw huts of tattooed Wichita Indians. Here under torture their impressed Indian guide, the Turk, confessed he had lied. They first baptized him and then killed him with a garrote, an iron collar that strangles the victim and crushes the spinal cord. Disillusioned, Coronado returned to his winter quarters, where his men nearly starved because the Indians had been driven out and the land despoiled.

In his report to the king Coronado concluded that Texas was a good land for agriculture but that there was little else to attract the empire. Through the explorations of Piñeda, Cabeza de Vaca, Coronado, and Hernando de Soto, who had led an expedition from Florida across the Mississippi to Arkansas and eastern Texas, the Spanish claimed a vast territory. Without the incentive of gold, however, there was no compulsion to explore farther. In 1543, moreover, one year after Coronado's discouraging report, the crown prohibited personal adventures that led to the killing of Indians. The day of the conquistador was over; slow northward settlement into the upper Rio Grande became the pattern.

To control settlement, the Spanish used a patriarchal bureaucracy that passed commands from the king to a viceroy in Mexico City. From there orders traveled to provincial headquarters and to the frontier outposts. Reports from parallel civil (pueblo), military (presidio), and church (mission) institutions moved upward through the chain of command, while special investigators checked complaints and the performance of officials. Little was left to chance, and rarely did anyone act without approval from above.

The prevailing economic theory of mercantilism maintained that trade should be kept as much as possible within the empire so that bullion would flow into the treasure vaults of Seville for the glory of the nation. The outlying province of Texas in the Spanish Empire, therefore, counted only as a poor and difficult frontier, significant primarily as a buffer to the ambitions of other nations.

The complacent Spanish attitude toward Texas was shattered by the energy of the French explorer René Robert Cavelier, Sieur de La Salle. He reached the New World in 1666, followed other Frenchmen into the Great Lakes, and descended the Mississippi River in 1682. He claimed by right of discovery the great river and its tributaries for Louis XIV, the Sun King. The Spanish respected that right, even though it created a rival claimant for the lands of the Gulf Coast. More disturbing was La Salle's proposal to establish a colony at the mouth of the Mississippi. He foresaw that the nation that controlled the river would also control the mid-continent.

La Salle received orders to move ahead, and he departed France in 1684 with 280 settlers on four ships. He left one

vessel in Haiti, skirted Cuba, and through faulty navigation landed on the Texas coast at Matagorda Bay. There is
some speculation that this landing was intentional, because La Salle planted his colony there rather than searching further. The settlement was unsuccessful. Syphilis,
hostile Indians, and poor management brought about its
demise. La Salle wrecked two ships, and the third returned to France. The remaining people perished except
for a few who embraced Indian life and some others who
journeyed overland to Canada. La Salle died, shot from
ambush by several rebellious men, and the Indians destroyed the settlement.

News of this venture, nonetheless, sent alarm bells
ringing through the Spanish bureaucracy. Spies in Paris
and Haiti had told of the expedition, and much to the as-
tonishment of the officials in northern Mexico, a Jumano
Indian carrying a piece of paper printed in French turned
up asking for missionaries for his people. In addition, a
bearded French deserter dressed in skins arrived to con-
firm the news. The Spanish sent out ten unsuccessful expeditions to eject the intruders, but the fort could not be
located. Finally, in 1689 the governor of the new province
of Coahuila, Alonso de León, with the aid of an "Indi-
anized" Frenchman uncovered the ruins of the French
encampment and three skeletons. While in Texas the
governor met with Caddo Indians, who also asked for
missionaries.

Throughout their days of conquest the Spanish carried
with them a zeal for Christianity and the salvation of
pagan souls. Priests trudged alongside the conquistadors,
and the Franciscan Order established seminaries for the
training of monks to evangelize the New World. They
were practical men with one eye on the soul and the other
on daily routine. Working in pairs or more, the priests,
commonly, would raise a chapel, plant crops, and start
some handicrafts. They would hand small presents and
rations to curious Indians and teach them not only about
Christ but also about the Spanish way of life. The state
paid the costs of the missions, and consequently, the location and administration of the installations often reflected a secular purpose. As the power of the empire declined, the church was used to forestall the advances of
foreign nations into Spanish lands.

In the late 1500s missionaries and settlers went into
New Mexico, and in the 1600s Franciscans explored and
probed into Texas—to the Edwards Plateau and the land
around the Nueces River. They contacted the Caddo and

Jumano Indians and in 1681 established Ysleta on the Rio Grande, now a part of modern El Paso. It is the oldest surviving settlement in Texas. To be sure, there were genuine conversions to Christianity, but the Indians of Texas were not easily subjugated. Many chose to fight and die rather than to submit. When they invited missionaries to live with them, the Indian motive in large part was to gain an ally against their traditional Indian enemies. This intent explains why the missions so often failed.

The Caddoes first met Europeans late in 1541, when Hernando de Soto's army marched through southern Arkansas and Texas, attacked their villages, and stole their grain. Their culture did not center on the warrior tradition, and their flint-tipped arrows clattered off the Spanish armor. Nonetheless, they resisted pillage and death. One of de Soto's men was attacked by five Caddo women who grabbed him by the arms, neck, leg, and penis. He was saved by a comrade who quickly discarded the Iberian code of honor, which forbade the slaughter of women. At the same time, ironically, three hundred miles to the west some friendly Caddoes met a patrol from the Coronado expedition. The Indians wept when the Spaniards robbed them of their hard-earned buffalo robes.

The Caddoes got along much better with the French, who began to arrive after the explorations of La Salle. These newcomers were interested in trade more than anything else and offered to the Indians the fruits of western technology. The eventual result was a balance of weaponry achieved by the mid-eighteenth century. At that point the Lipan Apaches, squeezed by the Comanches in the north and the Spanish in the south, asked for a mission at San Saba, to the northwest of San Antonio. The flattered padres quickly responded. The Lipans were hoping to get their two enemies to fight, and that is what happened.

Two thousand Comanches—painted red and black, mounted on horses, and armed with bows, lances, and several hundred French muskets—arrived in the springtime of 1758. The priests rushed to greet them with gifts of tobacco and beads only to be met with war whoops and death. In retaliation for the destruction of San Saba the Spanish government sent out a punitive army of six hundred soldiers and allied Indians under Colonel Diego Ortiz de Parilla. Their fate was the worst defeat for Spanish arms in Texas.

After obliterating a Tonkawa village on his march northward, Parilla attacked a Wichita village near the Red

River. The village was protected with a moat and a stockade, the horses were safely in a corral, and the Indians on the walls were armed with French guns. Parilla's Indian allies fled, and the Spaniards had to fight their way through an enemy encirclement. Parilla lost his supply train and two cannons during the precipitous retreat, which led him back to Bexar and a court-martial in Mexico City. The arrogant *entradas* of Coronado and de Soto, when the Spanish had the advantage of horses, lances, armor, and guns, were no longer possible when the Indians were equally armed.

The Europeans, however, had an invisible weapon which even they did not understand. There is no evidence in Texas history that the Spanish or French traders deliberately infected the Indians with disease organisms, but smallpox, measles, cholera, typhoid, and venereal diseases swept regularly through the Indian encampments. Smallpox struck the Caddoes in 1690, for example, and thereafter regularly decimated the bands of the Caddo confederacy. By 1800 the Caddo population, once the largest group in Texas, amounted to only a few hundred families. Contagious diseases seemingly hurt the more settled tribes worse—cholera with its 50 percent mortality rate, for example, was spread through sewage-contaminated water. Nomads such as the Comanches habitually moved their camp when someone died and thus avoided the pollution and death.

As the tribes weakened, they needed allies in order to resist their traditional enemies and, consequently, sought help from the Europeans. It was a downward spiral. Closer contact brought more disease, dependence upon trade goods, a taste for whiskey, and debilitation. This was the case on the Spanish and French frontier with the exception of the horse people of the plains, who adopted the warfare technology of the Europeans but not their lifestyle. For the oppressed Caddoes and others to request missions was understandable under such circumstances, but the priests were not invited for religious reasons. The Caddoes, with their own well-developed system of rituals, beliefs, shamans, and temples, had little theological use for white strangers in robes performing odd ceremonies.

De León in the late seventeenth century responded to the request of the Caddoes for priests, nonetheless, and followed the orders of the king that East Texas should be conquered through Christian love. The attempt, lasting from 1690 to 1693, failed due to disease, floods, famine, and hostile natives. Reportedly, however, de León and others abandoned cattle and horses to the prairies, where the animals found ideal conditions and formed wild herds. A range-cattle industry later became the principal economic activity of Spanish Texas. Cattle drives along the coast to New Orleans, even though illegal much of the time, justified the risk through high profits.

The French again inspired the Spanish when a group of French traders in 1714 arrived at the San Juan Bautista mission and presidio on the central Rio Grande under the leadership of Louis Juchereau de St. Denis. The French governor in Louisiana had received a letter from a Spanish Franciscan expressing concern for the Indian souls in East Texas. The governor then asked St. Denis, a successful trader on the lower part of the Red River, to contact the Spanish and encourage them to reopen their missions.

The Alamo

It began as the San Antonio de Valero Mission, authorized by the viceroy of Mexico in 1716 and started by Fray Antonio de Olivares in 1718. Priests located the site in 1724 and laid the cornerstone of the chapel in 1744. Its purpose was to bring Christianity to the Indians, but mission activity waned after 1765, and it was abandoned in 1793. The buildings became barracks for Spanish soldiers from Alamo del Parras in Coahuila, Mexico, during the Mexican War for Independence. It may have gotten its name from that source, or perhaps from a grove of cottonwoods nearby. *Alamo* is the Spanish word for "cottonwood."

The old mission was occupied by Mexican soldiers from 1821 to 1836, when they surrendered to Texan troops during the rebellion. The Alamo then served as a fortress for Travis and his men until its capture by Santa Anna. Following that, the structure and grounds were in ruins. The property passed at various times with some improvements into the control of the Roman Catholic Church, U.S. Army, and Confederate States of America. In 1883 the State of Texas bought the Alamo from the Roman Catholic Church and ordered it into the custody of the city. Another change in 1905 delivered the Alamo to the Daughters of the Republic of Texas, the organization that now maintains it.

The Alamo, a mission, citadel, and Texas shrine. Photograph by David G. McComb.

Since the French and Spanish embraced the same religion, it was not unthinkable, and, moreover, amicable relations all around would be good for the French Indian trade.

The charming St. Denis succeeded not only in carrying out the orders from his governor, but also in winning the hand of the Spanish commandant's granddaughter. He helped to lead a Spanish expedition to reestablish the missions of East Texas and blazed a trail that became the Old Spanish Road between San Antonio and Nacogdoches, now State Highway 21. In addition, with the aid of the Franciscans St. Denis reopened a mission, founded four more near modern Nacogdoches, and then crossed the Sabine River to start another one, Los Adaes, within fifteen miles of his trading post at Natchitoches in Louisiana.

To supply the missions the Spanish set up a depot on the San Antonio River, where they built the mission San Antonio de Valero, later called the Alamo, and a presidio, San Antonio de Bexar. Acequias, still-existing irrigation ditches for watering squash, pumpkins, corn, and beans, were a part of the effort. The Texas Indians, however, resisted conversion and were more interested in receiving presents. Worse, in 1719, as a distant ripple of a minor war between France and Spain over Sicily, six Frenchmen entered the mission near Natchitoches and terrorized the two Spaniards who occupied it. While the Frenchmen were stealing chickens, one of the Spaniards escaped to spread the alarm. Although there was no pursuit by the French, all of the Spanish people in East Texas fled in panic to the presidio at Bexar.

In 1721 they returned to replant, rebuild, and fortify under the lead of the provincial governor, the Marquis de San Miguel de Aguayo. The French and Spanish were once again at peace, but Aguayo strengthened the mission at Los Adaes with six cannon and one hundred soldiers. He constructed La Bahía, a mission and presidio, on Matagorda Bay near the site of the old French fort. Aguayo also requested the crown to send colonists from Cuba or the Canary Islands. After a long delay fifty-six people reached Bexar in 1731. These Canary Islanders set up their own community, parceled out town lots, established farms, and eventually welcomed soldiers from the presidio as husbands for their daughters. Villa de San Fernando, as it was called, became the first official municipality in Texas.

The San Antonio area was the most successful mission field in Texas while elsewhere the various far-flung missions shifted and changed. Three of the East Texas missions closed, but others were set up on the Rio Grande

and briefly in Tonkawa country on the San Gabriel River. The Spanish blocked an attempt by the French to erect a trading post on Galveston Bay in 1754, and in 1763, moreover, as a result of the French and Indian War, France transferred the Louisiana territory to Spain. With Spain's boundary now at the Mississippi the century-long competition with France ended.

Since the expensive missions had proved unsuccessful and were no longer necessary to hold the land against the French, the Spanish missionaries retreated. In 1800 the Spanish Texas frontier of some five thousand persons consisted of ranches on the northern bank of the Rio Grande; Laredo, founded in 1755; San Antonio de Bexar, the provincial capital; La Bahía, one hundred miles southeast of Bexar; and Nacogdoches, three hundred miles to the northeast. Except for the small presidio of La Bahía, which had been moved inland to Goliad, the Texas coastline was undefended. In the interior the fierce Apaches and Comanches, under an uneasy truce negotiated by the Spanish in 1780, roamed at will. Efforts to recruit Spanish colonists failed, and as a consequence the sparse population of Texas made the province vulnerable to land-hungry people from the east.

Mission Concepción in San Antonio, established as part of the Spanish attempt to settle Texas. Western History Collections, University of Oklahoma Library.

Jean Laffite, the "pirate of the Gulf," who established a base on Galveston Island. Barker Texas History Center, The University of Texas at Austin.

At the Peace of Paris in 1783 the triumphant United States gained British territory to the Mississippi River and above Florida to Canada. Florida and New Orleans were returned to Spain. In 1803, however, the sudden retrocession of Louisiana to France and its quick sale to the United States made Texas once more the eastern boundary of New Spain. The boundary lines were unclear because of La Salle's early colony, and for Spanish Texas that meant trouble was on the way.

During the American Revolution patriots had joined the armies of Spain and France to expel the British, and by the 1790s adventuresome Anglo-Americans arrived in Louisiana, where they engaged in ranching and Indian trade. In 1801 Spanish soldiers killed Philip Nolan, an American horse trader, in a skirmish on the Brazos River and sent his ears to the governor. Ostensibly, Nolan was capturing mustangs to sell in New Orleans, but the Spanish authorities suspected he was running contraband and fostering revolution. Several other Americans set up a trading post in Nacogdoches, and the United States sent exploring expeditions into their new purchase. Some of these, such as the one led by Zebulon Pike, wandered into Spanish territory, reinforcing Spanish nervousness about U.S. ambition.

Following the Louisiana Purchase, Spanish officials sent troops into Nacogdoches and Los Adaes to defend the unclear border, and after a flurry of skirmishes the frontier commanders agreed to a neutral zone between the Sabine and a dry creek bed west of Los Adaes. The boundary of the Sabine was confirmed when the United States purchased Florida in 1819. Meanwhile, without success, Spain tried to find settlers for southeastern Texas, a task complicated by the breakup of the Spanish Empire in America and the outbreak of the War for Mexican Independence in 1810.

By necessity, Spain had to concentrate its efforts in Mexico to the neglect of its frontiers. In 1811 revolutionaries seized San Antonio and held it for three months. In 1812–1813 a combined army of Mexican revolutionaries and Americans who wanted to make Texas part of the United States held the province until expelled by royalist forces. The War of 1812 offered a pause while refugee revolutionaries helped Andrew Jackson defend New Orleans. Then in 1815 Henry Perry began to gather mercenaries at Galveston Bay for yet another filibuster. He joined with Luis de Aury, a French privateer who had established a stronghold on Galveston Island, and with Francisco Xavier Mina, who favored the revolutionaries in Mexico. Aury ferried the troops to the Mexican coast in 1817 for an attack on the fort at Sota la Marina. Following a brief rebel success, the royalist troops rallied, killed Mina and Perry, and scattered the remainder of the army.

Aury, meanwhile, sailed back to his Galveston base only to find himself deposed by a stronger privateer, Jean Laffite. After destruction of his former port in the back bays of New Orleans and his aid to Jackson in the defense of the city, Laffite had returned to the business of smuggler and supplier of privateers. He was also a secret agent for Spain and at Galveston ruled a mixed community of desperadoes beyond the reach of any law. While occupying the island, a group of Napoleonic refugees passed through to establish a colony on the Trinity River under the lead of General Charles Lallemand. Supposedly they were going to become peaceful agriculturists, but they harbored a scheme to free Napoleon from his rocky prison in the South Atlantic and to make his brother Joseph, who was then in New York, a Mexican king. Before the Spanish could react, the Lallemand colony collapsed from disease, heat, and lack of supplies. Laffite helped them return to New Orleans.

The U.S. Navy forced the buccaneer to abandon Galveston in 1821 because of his smuggling operations in New Orleans. Laffite burned his base, boarded his ship, *Pride,* and disappeared into the Gulf of Mexico. James Long, another adventurer fishing in the troubled waters, had requested without effect that Laffite leave the buildings. In 1819 Long and about 120 followers had occupied Nacogdoches, declared Texas independent, and organized a government with Long as president. He then went to Galveston to invite Laffite to be admiral, but the pirate made no commitment while secretly informing his Spanish contacts.

Spanish troops from Bexar drove Long and his men back across the Sabine, but the insurgents reassembled on Bolivar Peninsula across from Galveston in 1820. Conflicting rumors reached Bolivar and New Orleans about the success of other revolutionaries in 1821, and Long with fifty-two men sailed to join the uprising at La Bahía. He left behind at the fort on Bolivar his pregnant wife, Jane, a servant girl, and some men for protection. The leaders at La Bahía thought Long was bent on independence for Texas, not just freedom from Spain, so they sent Long and his men to Mexico City. There a guard accidentally shot and killed Long. His death may have been ar-

Jean Laffite

The birth and death of the "Pirate of the Gulf" are shrouded. Jean Laffite was born in Bayonne, France, in 1780 or 1781 of a French father and a Spanish mother. The family migrated to the New World, and Jean with his brother set up smuggling operations at Barataria near New Orleans around 1808. In spite of the destruction of their base by the governor of Louisiana in 1814, Laffite and his pirates aided Andrew Jackson in the defense of New Orleans early in 1815.

Although pardoned for their past because of their support in the war, the Laffite brothers went back into business as brokers to pirates on Galveston Island in 1817. They sent captured goods overland by pack mule to the black market in New Orleans and sold captured slaves to the Bowie brothers for one dollar per pound. The pirate camp, called Campeachy, located on Snake Island, contained about one thousand people ruled by Jean. He hanged sea captains who plundered American ships and said that he attacked only Spanish shipping—even though he was also a Spanish secret agent. After his departure from the island, forced out by the U.S. Navy in 1821, he disappeared into the Caribbean on his ship, *Pride.* The circumstances of his death are unknown, but the best evidence suggests he died of a fever in the Yucatan in the 1820s.

His shadowy end inspired tales of buried treasure as well as a fake diary which claimed that he died in East St. Louis in 1854. One of the stories states that Laffite was overheard muttering before his departure from Galveston, "I have buried my treasure under the three trees." After he sailed, several men in the middle of the night went to the three trees, a landmark on the island, dug into the sand, struck a box, and pried it open. There in the moonlight appeared the pale face and rigid body of the pirate's dead wife.

ranged by a rival who had just been named governor of
Texas under the new government of Mexico.

At Bolivar, meanwhile, Jane Long stoically awaited the
return of her husband. After a month she could have left
with others, but she chose to remain. With the help of her
black servant, Kian, she gave birth to a daughter, Ann,
kept the Karankawa Indians at bay by firing a cannon,
flew a banner made from a red petticoat, and fished for
food with an old hammock. In 1822, after receiving news
of her husband's capture and death, she moved on with
the first of the Austin settlers. Since her daughter was the
first birth for Anglo-Americans in Texas, Jane Long became known as the "Mother of Texas" to the Anglo community. The sobriquet was also a tribute to her loyalty
and toughness.

In Mexico the politicians put together a constitution
which outwardly resembled that of the United States. It
included a bicameral legislature and an elected president,
but it lacked a Bill of Rights or a system of checks and
balances. The country, moreover, was split between cen-
tralists, who wanted a strong national government and
weak states, and federalists, who wished for a weak national government with strong states. Church officials,
major landholders, and the army favored the centralist
position, while small landholders and middle-class re-
formers wanted the federalist structure. The conditions
were disruptive, and only the first president served his allotted time in office. For the next fifty years Mexico suffered a series of coups and revolts that kept it in turmoil
and enabled its enemies to prevail.

The state governments reflected the same divisions.
Both Texas and Coahuila lacked sufficient population, so
the two were combined into one state with the capital at
Saltillo. The legislature, consisting of ten members from
Coahuila and one from Texas, agreed on little, particularly as the Texas population became increasingly Anglo-
American. The newcomers did not accept the Mexican
judicial system, which lacked trial by jury, bail, freedom
of speech, and freedom to assemble. Mexico also opposed
slavery and allowed immigrants to bring slaves into Texas
only for the improvement of the economy. Moreover,
there remained for Mexico the same problem of underpopulation in Texas. Settlement was needed to forestall
foreign takeover.

The empresario system was supposed to take care of
that difficulty. As it was worked out in the 1820s, the
state contracted with a person who agreed to bring in a

stated number of industrious, Roman Catholic families to a designated area within six years. Only the borders—fifty-two miles west of the Sabine and twenty-six miles inland from the coast—were forbidden to immigrants from the United States. In return, the empresario received 23,000 acres for every one hundred families. Each family was to get one league (4,428 acres) and one labor (177 acres) upon payment of $60 in fees to the state. This amounted to about one and one-third cents per acre at a time when the United States was selling public land at $1.25 per acre in 80-acre lots. This was a bargain at any time, but even more so to Anglo-Americans who had just suffered the depression of 1819.

Jane Herbert Wilkinson Long, the "Mother of Texas," who gave birth to the first Anglo child in Texas. Reproduced from the holdings of the Texas State Archives.

Moses Austin was such an impoverished man. The War of 1812, the subsequent depression, and the panic in 1819 had ruined him financially. In New Orleans he learned of conditions in Texas and applied in 1820–1821 for a grant to introduce colonists. Spain had earlier approved such activity in Louisiana, and the commandant at Monterrey gave him 200,000 acres for a promise of three hundred families. Many of the terms were vague, such as the location of the site and the size of individual allotments, but Austin moved ahead. Within a few months of approval, however, Moses Austin died. The grand project was then taken up by his son, Stephen F. Austin.

After gaining confirmation of the grant, Stephen F. Austin advertised for settlers from whom he could collect twelve and one-half cents per acre purchased. With the first colonists arriving by land and sea at sites on the coastal plain along the Colorado and Brazos rivers, the new government of Mexico refused to approve Austin's Spanish contract. Austin then had to pursue a new law for himself, first through the government in Mexico City and later through the state government at Saltillo. Under three contracts he agreed to settle 1,200 families in his tract.

He held almost complete civil and military control until 1828, when the new state constitution provided for local government. Meanwhile, he directed surveys, allocated grants, prepared titles, collected fees, corresponded with federal and state officials, and punished hostile Indians. By 1834 an estimated nine thousand people lived on the Austin grants.

Other empresarios followed Austin's lead. Some, such as Green DeWitt and Martín de León, a descendant of the founder of the eastern missions, fulfilled their contracts. Others only partially succeeded, while still others defaulted. The system attempted to control the immigra-

Stephen F. Austin

Stephen F. Austin was born in southwestern Virginia in 1793. His parents later moved the family to Missouri, but Austin went to school in Connecticut and then for two years at Transylvania University in Lexington. After the death of his father, he took up the Texas venture as an empresario and brought some 1,200 families to the area. He labored among the Mexican politicians to protect his own interests as well as those of the settlers. He personally thought, for example, that slavery was a "curse on posterity," but he worked to keep the institution in Texas to ensure a labor force. The prerevolutionary convention of 1833 selected him to deliver petitions to the Mexican government.

Santa Anna refused home government for Texas and arrested Austin at Saltillo. Mexican authorities shifted Austin from prison to prison without trial until late in 1834, when he was released on bond. A general amnesty in mid-1835 allowed him to leave Mexico City, and he returned to Texas via New Orleans. He sanctioned rebellion and went to the United States for six months to solicit support for the cause. He was defeated for the presidency by Sam Houston but served as secretary of state until his death from pneumonia in December 1836 at the age of forty-three. The "Father of Texas" died on a pallet in a two-room clapboard shack.

tion, but there was leakage. Some immigrants simply drifted westward across the border and took up residence. Farmers thinking that they were in Arkansas territory moved into the Red River Valley. Others occupied the so-called Atascosita District between the Austin colony and the Louisiana border in far southeastern Texas. There was little authority to stop them and the driftage was inevitable.

Land-hungry, aggressive Anglo-American pioneers, pushing the Indians before them, had been moving westward since before their revolution of the 1770s, and in less than fifty years afterward had gobbled the land between the Appalachians and the Mississippi. They went on into the best lands of eastern and southeastern Texas. In 1836 the population of Texas was estimated at thirty-five thousand, a sevenfold increase in two decades. Most of the immigrants were from the southern United States.

The newcomers were unused to Mexican law and Spanish customs; they expected local government; they remained Protestant under their professed Catholic skins; they continued to use English; and they carried black slaves with them for cotton cultivation. The Anglo-Americans were brash and quick to speak out, as was their accustomed right, were less respectful of authority, refused assimilation, and thought others should be like them. The logic of the Mexican policy of encouraging settlement by people from the nation it feared most can be questioned, but, then again, Mexico had little choice. The American westward movement could not be stopped, and the underpopulation of Texas created a land vacuum that drew into it these contentious pioneers. There was bound to be trouble.

The first major break came in 1826–1827 at Nacogdoches with the Fredonia Rebellion. Haden Edwards, an empresario from Mississippi, had agreed to settle eight hundred families in an area stretching from north of Nacogdoches almost to the coast. He squabbled with settlers already there, installed his son-in-law as alcalde, formed a loose alliance with the local Cherokees who had moved across the border, and with his brother declared the area the Republic of Fredonia.

The Indians, disgusted with the drunken behavior of Edwards's followers, shortly quit, and the Texas government called out the militia from the Austin colony and the Atascosito community. With government troops from Bexar they marched on Nacogdoches and the Edwards headquarters in the old stone trading post in the center of town. Before they arrived, however, loyal residents with the Indians routed the Edwards gang, which fled to the Sabine. As a result of this incident, the government cancelled Edwards's contract and placed a garrison at Nacogdoches.

What brought the Americans and Mexicans to a breaking point, however, came with disagreements over points of law. The president of Mexico, as a gesture on Mexican Independence Day in 1829, emancipated all the slaves. Austin's friends in government moved quickly, however, to exempt the colonies in Texas. In 1830, recognizing that the Americans in Texas outnumbered the Mexicans and that they resisted assimilation, the Mexican government banned further American immigration into the colonies and barred slave imports. Austin obtained, this time, immunity only for his and DeWitt's colonies. At the same moment, the Mexican government canceled the exemption from Mexican fees and duties which the colonists had enjoyed. With no income or land taxes, the government depended upon these duties and various licensing fees for revenue. Americans, however, traditionally opposed customs duties and looked upon the fees as a form of graft. The stage was set for a clash, and it took place at Anahuac.

Stephen F. Austin, the "Father of Texas." Barker Texas History Center, The University of Texas at Austin.

Under orders from the national government, Juan Davis Bradburn established a customs station and garrison at Anahuac in Trinity Bay. Bradburn ordered all ship captains trading on the Brazos (across Trinity and Galveston bays to the west) to clear their papers through Anahuac. This was an expensive inconvenience, and Bradburn neglected to explain that it was only temporary until the government placed another station on the Brazos.

Bradburn, meanwhile, arrested William Barret Travis, a hot-headed twenty-five-year-old lawyer recently arrived from Alabama. Travis was trying to regain for a client two runaway slaves who were part of Bradburn's garrison. Travis had pulled a prank—he sent a fake note indicating that an armed force threatened the garrison—and Bradburn retaliated by arresting Travis and his law partner, Patrick Jack.

The local people protested, and fighting broke out at Velasco, located at the mouth of the Brazos. Henry Smith and John Austin had gone to Brazoria to acquire a cannon to use against Anahuac, and while there attacked a Mexican fort which blocked the passage of the ship carrying their cannon. The Mexicans had to surrender after exhausting their ammunition, but seven Texans and five Mexicans died in the fighting.

Santa Anna, president of Mexico who fought against Sam Houston at the decisive battle of San Jacinto. Western History Collections, University of Oklahoma Library.

At Anahuac fighting also broke out, but ended when the ranking commander from Nacogdoches, Colonel José de las Piedras, who feared a general uprising, agreed to the demands of the rebels. He removed Bradburn and released Travis and Jack. For their part the insurgents issued the Turtle Bayou Resolutions, which insisted that they were not objecting to Mexican sovereignty but only to the despotic centralist commander at Anahuac. The new federalist regime in Mexico City accepted this explanation and shortly withdrew all centralist troops from Texas. Piedras, upon returning to Nacogdoches, ordered the colonists to turn in their guns, but the settlers from Ayish Bayou came to town with a different idea. They used their weapons to capture the Mexican colonel and exile him to San Antonio.

Hispanic control of Texas thus ceased in 1832. In that year and the one following, Texans met in illegal conventions to discuss grievances and request changes. They were never granted separate statehood—under the excuse that Texas lacked sufficient population—but the federalists allowed an exemption from the tariff, the use of English for some official business, and additional foreign immigration. In 1835, however, President Antonio López de Santa Anna, a former federalist, began concentrating power in his hands. He systematically reduced state power and changed the states to departments of the national government with appointed officials. The Mexican congress voided the Constitution of 1824 and placed control in the central government, which made Santa Anna a virtual dictator.

At Anahuac Captain Antonio Tenorio reinstated the collection of taxes and arrested several Texans on suspicion of smuggling. Travis, leading a small group, freed the men and captured the Mexicans. Momentarily, a peace group ridiculed Travis and honored Tenorio at a Fourth of July barbecue. Then General Martín Perfecto de Cós, who had been in Coahuila to settle a jurisdictional dispute between Saltillo and Monclova, demanded that the "criminals" who had attacked Anahuac stand at a court-martial. Although many Texans disliked Travis, they would not turn him over for a Mexican military trial.

A Texan meeting at Columbia issued a call to all citizens to gather in November at a larger gathering, the Consultation. At this juncture Stephen F. Austin arrived from Mexico City, where he had gone to plead the Texas case. He had been imprisoned during the Santa Anna takeover, and now he returned, saying, "War is our only resource."

Texan opinion remained divided, however, until the first shots of the rebellion.

Colonel Domingo de Ugartechea, in command at San Antonio, ordered a patrol to take control of a six-pound cannon used for Indian defense at Gonzales. The alcalde Andrew Ponton refused the patrol's request on the grounds that he required written orders. This gave the Texans a chance to prepare, and when a second patrol arrived, they found the loaded cannon pointing at them in the midst of an armed camp flying a flag that challenged, "COME AND TAKE IT." Under the lead of Colonel John Moore, the Texans fired first, on October 2, 1835, and the Mexicans, with one man killed and no orders to attack, retired to San Antonio.

Ugartechea wrote to Austin urging him to prevent bloodshed, but Austin joined the men at Gonzales and led them as their general to besiege San Antonio, where General Cós had arrived with eight hundred men. On the way an advanced contingent fought a thirty-minute battle with Mexican cavalry and infantry at Mission Concepción. Taking a defensive stand in the curve of a wooded river bottom, the Texans under James Bowie and James W. Fannin, Jr., avoided the feared mounted lancers and repelled three charges with a crossfire from their Kentucky long rifles. Mexican grapeshot, which ripped through the overhead pecan trees, provided the men with a meal of ripe nuts as the keen crack of their rifles answered the dull roar of the cannon. Although the rebels were untrained as soldiers, no one had to teach them how to shoot. The Texans lost one man, the Mexicans, sixty, before the Mexicans retreated to San Antonio.

Edward Burleson, a man with fighting experience who had come to Texas in 1830, replaced Austin so that "the general" could attend the Consultation. After a month of siege Burleson was ready to give up when a captive told the Texans that the Mexicans were ready to surrender. Forty-seven-year-old Ben Milam, a former Indian trader and scout, rallied the soldiers with "Who will go into San Antonio with old Ben Milam?" The attack lasted five days before victory, and Milam, killed by rifle fire, was one of four Texans to fall. Burleson paroled Cós and his men on the promise that they leave Texas and not return. It was a promise that was not to be kept.

The Consultation, meanwhile, endorsed the Mexican Constitution of 1824, sent Austin and others to the United States to solicit support, appointed Henry Smith to handle administrative matters, and assigned Sam Houston, an-

Antonio López de Santa Anna

Santa Anna was born of middle-class Spanish parents in Vera Cruz in 1794 and at age sixteen became a cadet in an infantry unit policing Indian tribes. After working through the ranks, he gained promotion to brigadier general by supporting Emperor Agustín de Iturbide. He became the military governor of Yucatan and, after retirement to civilian life, governor of Vera Cruz. In 1829 he defeated the Spanish at Tampico and four years later was elected president of Mexico. In 1834 he declared Mexico not ready for democracy and characterized himself as the "Napoleon of the West." He defeated the liberal Zacatecans in 1835 but lost Texas to Sam Houston the following year. After failing to negotiate an agreement between Mexico and the United States about Texas, he returned to Mexico.

He helped defend his country against the French in 1838 and lost a leg in battle. He became acting president of Mexico in 1839 and dictator from 1841 to 1845. Overthrown for his excesses, he went into exile in Cuba. Then, with the United States at war with Mexico, he reentered Mexico through American lines, supposedly to bring peace. Instead, he took command of the Mexican forces only to be defeated by Zachary Taylor at the Battle of Buena Vista and by Winfield Scott at the Battle of Cerro Gordo.

After the fall of Mexico City he returned to exile only to be recalled by conservatives to head the government from 1853 to 1855. This time he was overthrown for selling the Mesilla Valley to the United States as the Gadsden Purchase. He schemed unsuccessfully to return to power, and finally officials allowed the now harmless old man to return to Mexico City in 1874. Remarkably, Santa Anna died peacefully in obscurity in 1876.

Bowie Knife

James Bowie was born in 1795 in Tennessee. At the age of nineteen he moved to Louisiana, and after a brief association with James Long he formed a partnership with his brothers to buy slaves from Jean Laffite and smuggle them into New Orleans. In two years they made $65,000 in the trade. According to one story, Bowie designed his famous knife while recovering from a wound. Since it was more reliable than a flintlock pistol, the Bowie knife became the favorite side arm of the frontier until Colt's invention of the revolver.

The Bowie knife was like a butcher knife, but with greater weight in the blade and a heavier handle, usually made of horn. It was well balanced so that it could be thrown, and its thick, ten-inch steel blade resisted breakage. Some people described it as a small sword, and it was used for skinning, cutting up meat, eating, fighting, hammering, and sometimes for picking

Bowie knife, engraved "R. P. Bowie to H. W. Fowler, U.S.D." Daughters of the Republic of Texas Library, San Antonio, Texas.

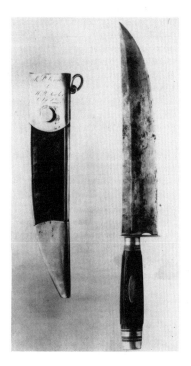

other man with fighting experience, to command the army. Still divided, the delegation postponed the question of independence until March 1836, when they were to reconvene. Then everything fell apart.

Houston withdrew from leadership after disagreements with others over strategy and traveled to East Texas, where he negotiated a treaty with the Cherokees to prevent an Indian alliance with Mexico. Smith quarreled with his council and was replaced with James Robinson. In San Antonio at the Alamo, Travis, who had mustered twenty-nine men, joined James Bowie, who with one hundred men had orders from Houston to destroy the place. Travis and Bowie worked out a joint command, but due to Bowie's illness with typhoid-pneumonia, Travis shortly assumed full leadership. There, contrary to Houston's orders, they waited, while in Goliad James Fannin with another gathering of volunteers likewise waited. This inaction proved fatal.

Fannin had been part of an attempt to march on Matamoros, but the northward movement of Santa Anna's soldiers prevented it. The Mexican dictator had gathered forces to crush a revolt in Zacatecas and afterward with six thousand men—young, old, criminals forced to serve, and peasants—continued toward Texas to rid the land of Anglo-American residents. His soldiers, many from southern Mexico, suffered in the winter cold, and a February norther froze six of the men to death.

Part of his army under General José Urrea overwhelmed the thirty-four Texans at San Patricio, part of the aborted Matamoros army, and then turned on Goliad. Fannin, after a hesitant retreat toward Victoria, was caught in open prairie, subjected to cannon fire, and forced to surrender. Fannin gave up under the condition that his army would be treated honorably and paroled to the United States. Santa Anna, however, had earlier decreed that all foreigners in rebellion would be shot as pirates. This was to discourage American mercenaries from helping the rebels; twenty-eight had been executed earlier in Tampico. At dawn, under direct orders from Santa Anna, firing squads at Goliad executed 342 men of the Texas garrison. However, 28 managed to escape to tell this bloody story of atrocity.

Hermann Ehrenberg, a German who was part of a volunteer group from New Orleans, for example, became suspicious when he and other prisoners were marched onto a field by silent Mexican soldiers and ordered to kneel. He heard musketry and wails, a shouted warning, and shots. Uninjured, Ehrenberg and the company dog bolted through the thick smoke, ran over a Mexican lieutenant, and reached the bank of the San Antonio River. With bullets zipping around him he shouted, "The Republic of Texas forever!" and leaped into the water. The dog jumped also, but was killed by a bullet. Reaching the other side, Ehrenberg could still hear shooting and yelling on the killing field. He was among the few who eluded pursuing horsemen and lived to tell the tale.

Shortly before this massacre Santa Anna marched with the main Mexican army into San Antonio and laid siege to the Alamo. A few more Americans attracted to the revolution had drifted into the town of two thousand people, notably Davy Crockett, a frontiersman from Tennessee and former U.S. congressman. Travis had moved his soldiers inside the thick-walled compound of the mission and asked "the People of Texas and all Americans in the world" to come to their aid. In this famous letter of February 24, 1836, Travis proclaimed, "I shall never surrender or retreat," and signed the appeal with "Victory or Death." He answered Santa Anna's demand for surrender with a cannon shot.

There could be no aid from Fannin, of course, but the entire male population of Gonzales, 32 men, arrived as reinforcements on March 1. This brought the count to over 180 when Santa Anna, refusing to wait for the arrival of

the teeth. The Bowie knife on display in the Alamo museum is inscribed "R. P. Bowie to H. W. Fowler." This presentation knife is a little over fourteen inches long with a nine-inch blade that has no curve. Later versions, made by others, often had a clipped point and a false edge on the top part of the point.

In another version of the origin of the Bowie knife, Jim's brother Rezin gave him the knife after Jim had been shot at by an adversary named Norris Wright. Jim's pistol had misfired. Afterward on a sandbar in the Mississippi near Natchez in 1827, an arranged duel between others turned into a brawl, and Jim Bowie was wounded. His enemy, Wright, charged him with a cane sword as the muscular Bowie lurched to his feet. Wright lunged. But Bowie grabbed the sword, jerked Wright in close, and gutted his opponent with the knife, "twisting it to cut his heart strings."

The Bowie knife thereafter became a popular frontier weapon, and Jim Bowie became a legend. When told that her son had died at the Alamo, Bowie's mother said, "I'll wager no wounds were found in his back."

The attack on the Alamo as painted by Theodore Gentilz in 1885. It is considered an accurate portrayal. Reproduced from the holdings of the Texas State Archives.

Sam Houston

Samuel Houston was born in Rockbridge County, Virginia, in 1793. After the death of his father in 1807, his mother moved the family to Maryville, Tennessee. He had only a few terms in neighborhood schools and found that working in a village store had little appeal for him. As a young man he spent three years living with neighboring Cherokee Indians; he learned to speak their language and respect their customs. From 1813 to 1818 he served in the U.S. Army under Andrew Jackson and then resigned to study law.

After a few months of study he opened a law office in Lebanon, Tennessee, where he quickly gained the respect of his frontier neighbors. He was successively selected as district attorney, adjutant general of the state, state congressman, and, in 1827, governor of Tennessee. He married Eliza H. Allen in 1829; after three and one-half months, she returned to her parents and Houston resigned from his position as governor. No one knows what happened between them. Houston drifted westward and for six years lived as a trader among the Cherokees. Like others in the business, he took an Indian wife and became a member of the tribe.

He traveled into Texas in 1832 to report on Indian affairs to Andrew Jackson, attended a prerevolutionary convention in 1833, and was counted as a resident of Nacogdoches in the census. He signed the Texas Declaration of Independence and was elected commander-in-chief of the armies.

his siege guns, attacked the mission with scaling ladders on March 6. There was no mercy, as the Mexican trumpeters announced before the assault. Travis fell early in the fighting with a bullet in his brain; Bowie died in his sickroom; Crockett suffered capture and execution. All Americans were slain except Susanna Dickinson, her daughter, and Joe, Travis's black servant. These were allowed to live to carry the news of the defeat; the Mexicans burned the bodies of the vanquished. Santa Anna, however, needlessly lost 600 soldiers and gave his enemy a cause for ferocious revenge. Forever afterward the war cries of "Remember the Alamo" and "Remember Goliad" have echoed through the corridors of Texas history.

The defense of the Alamo can be considered an unnecessary, even foolhardy, act from a military viewpoint. It was not needed for the success of the rebellion. Yet, of all the battles in the Texas Revolution, this defeat is most widely recalled. The reason is that the Alamo gives a clear instance of chosen heroism. Even today, to the

Sam Houston. He led the revolutionary forces, helped govern the Texas Republic, and led Texas into the United States. Barker Texas History Center, The University of Texas at Austin.

tourists walking through the cool interior of the mission building, the ghosts of history whisper a personal question: for what cause would you give your life?

Consider the case of James B. Bonham. He was born in South Carolina, where he was a classmate and friend of Travis. He was practicing law in Montgomery, Alabama, in 1835 when Travis asked him to come share in the struggle for Texas independence. He arrived in December and was commissioned a lieutenant of cavalry. In January he traveled to the Alamo, probably along with James Bowie. During the siege Travis sent him through the lines to seek aid from Fannin. He made it and then returned to report to his commander. As the situation turned desperate, Travis again sent him for help. He rode to Goliad and Gonzales to no avail but returned through enemy fire to the citadel to die with his companions three days later. He was twenty-nine years old.

Although the men in the Alamo and at Goliad did not know it, on March 2 the Consultation had met again and declared the independence of Texas. The delegates used Thomas Jefferson's great declaration as a model, went on to write a constitution, and selected David G. Burnet, a man who had been involved with South American independence, as president of the ad interim government. Again, they designated Sam Houston commander of the rebel forces, and as he galloped toward San Antonio he found at Gonzales nearly 400 men awaiting direction. There he learned from Susanna Dickinson the fate of the Alamo and shortly thereafter about the loss at Goliad.

Houston ordered Gonzales burned and with his ragtag army retreated eastward to the Colorado River. There he rested briefly and drilled the men, then retreated to the Brazos River, where again he paused and trained the soldiers. The restless army wanted to fight, but still Houston moved eastward in retreat. The civilian population, hearing of Goliad, the Alamo, and the advance of the Mexican army, rushed from their homes, cursed Houston, and fled over the chill muddy roads and the swollen streams to the east in the so-called Runaway Scrape. Slaves took advantage of the confusion to escape, and pioneer Mary Rabb recorded, "We was all drove out of ouer houses with ouer little ones to suffer with cold and hungry and little Lorenzy not three months when we started died on the road."

President Burnet, who moved with the government first to Harrisburg and then to Galveston Island in preparation for escape to New Orleans by sea, taunted Houston

After being strongly criticized for his retreat across Texas, he defeated Santa Anna at the Battle of San Jacinto. Wounded in the ankle, he went to New Orleans for treatment and upon his return was elected president of the new republic.

Against opposition he secured Santa Anna's release in order to send him to Washington, D.C. He maintained peace with Mexico and served a term that was relatively calm. Prohibited by law from seeking a successive term, Houston was replaced by Mirabeau B. Lamar. Houston kept up his political activity by election to the fourth and fifth congresses.

He married Margaret M. Lea in 1840, and she proceeded to persuade him to reduce his level of drinking and join the Baptist Church. He was elected to a second term as president, a time troubled by Mexicans, Indians, and finances. He favored annexation to the United States and served Texas as a senator for nearly fourteen years. Increasingly, he took nationalistic stands on the sectional issues dividing the North and South. After losing the race for governor in 1857, he won in 1859. He opposed the secession of Texas, argued after the fact that Texas was again an independent republic, and quietly yielded his office when deposed by the secession convention. He refused the aid of Union forces to retain his position and retired first near Houston, then to Huntsville, where he died in 1863. His last words were "Texas! Margaret! Margaret!"

The Yellow Rose of Texas

According to folklore, the reason that Santa Anna did not respond quickly to the Texas charge at San Jacinto was that he was being entertained by a beautiful slave woman in his tent during siesta time. The twenty-year-old Emily Morgan, a Texas patriot, was a mulatto, and thus referred to as a "high yella gal" in the slang of the time. Since then, in song and fable she has been called "the Yellow Rose of Texas." There is little historical evidence to support this story, but there is also no other explanation except arrogance for Santa Anna's incredible carelessness at San Jacinto.

to give battle. Still Houston retreated. Santa Anna concluded that Houston would withdraw across the Sabine River, and so with a smaller force he moved to trap the Texan government at Harrisburg. He missed Burnet but burned Harrisburg. The two armies, now of comparable size, went into camp south of Buffalo Bayou, opposing each other on a small prairie called San Jacinto.

After a skirmish on April 20 Houston led his troops into action at siesta time on April 21. At this point the Texan army numbered about 900 men; the Mexican army, recently reinforced, about 1,400. With one drummer and three fifers playing the tune of a popular love song, "Will You Come to My Bower I Have Shaded for You?" the single rank of the Texan army, screened by trees and a rise in the ground, advanced on the run. Santa Anna had posted no guards. The Texans overran the Mexican camp and won the battle in eighteen minutes.

The rout and carnage, however, went on for several hours as the rebels took revenge for their fallen compatriots at the Alamo and at Goliad. Later, Mexican skulls could be found at the battlefield with star-shaped cracks, the result of clubbing during the rout. A rider, meanwhile, overtook the desperate refugees of the Runaway Scrape and shouted, "Turn back! Turn back! The Texian army has whipped the Mexicans! Turn back!"

Two Texans died and Houston was shot in the ankle. The Mexicans suffered 630 killed, 208 wounded, and 730 captured, including Santa Anna, who was identified by his own men the next day in the uniform of a private. The Texas soldiers wanted to execute the Mexican dictator, but Houston kept him alive and extracted an order from him to General Vincente Filisola to withdraw the remaining Mexican troops from Texas. Filisola, who had more than enough men to continue fighting, nonetheless obeyed and slowly departed from the new nation.

While still in the flush of victory Houston faced Peggy McCormick, who owned the battlefield and who wanted the dead soldiers removed. "Madam," Houston said, "your land will be famed in history as the classic spot upon which the glorious victory of San Jacinto was gained! Here was born, in the throes of revolution, and amid the strife of contending legions, the infant of Texan independence! Here that latest scourge of mankind, the arrogantly self-styled 'Napoleon of the West,' met his fate!"

"To the *devil* with your glorious history," she replied. "Take off your stinking Mexicans!"

Houston had to travel to New Orleans for medical help

for his ankle, and, subsequently, Burnet cleared the battle-field and signed the Treaty of Velasco with Santa Anna. The dictator publicly consented to end hostilities, not take up arms again against Texas, withdraw soldiers south of the Rio Grande, and release all prisoners. Privately he agreed to work within the Mexican government to secure recognition of Texas' independence as well as a treaty of commerce between the two nations. For his part, Burnet agreed to release the Mexican prisoners and to set Santa Anna free in Vera Cruz.

The Texas army, reinforced with fresh recruits from the United States, refused to release the Mexican leader, however, and worse, the Mexican senate annulled the treaty and vowed to continue the war. For the senators the war was unfinished. Since they did not actually re-new the fighting, however, Texas achieved a de facto independence.

The Mexican prisoners, including Santa Anna, mean-while, languished in captivity for the remainder of the year. In January 1837 Texas officials sent Santa Anna to Washington, D.C., to negotiate an agreement whereby Texas would be free to become part of the United States and Mexico would accept the Rio Grande as its northern boundary. Although it was not a bad idea and might have prevented a future war, neither Washington nor Mexico City was agreeable. Santa Anna had no power. The former dictator then returned to Vera Cruz, free but discredited, to await another turn on the stage of history. Thus ended Hispanic power in Texas, but the influence of the Spanish heritage continued.

In the years that followed, Texans adopted the style and equipage of the range-cattle industry from the early

Longhorn Cattle

The Spanish brought cattle to the New World, beginning with Columbus, who left stock in Santo Domingo in 1493. In 1521 the Spanish transported cattle to Mexico, and wherever they placed missions and settlements, they took cattle and horses with them. Some animals escaped; others were turned loose. Several breeds inter-mixed, and the multicolored long-horn evolved into a superb open-range cow. By the time Stephen F. Austin reached Texas in the 1820s, they were running wild from the Red River to the Rio Grande.

Thin-flanked and flat-sided with horns stretching as wide as eight feet, the tough longhorn could for-age for itself, protect its young from wolves, go for days without water, withstand blizzards and heat waves, resist tick fever, and if nec-essary eat prickly pears and brush. Its large horns sometimes made the animal wobble when it walked and forced cowboys to twist its head in order to get the 1,200-pound beast through the five-foot-wide door of a rail car. The main defect of the longhorn was too much bone and horn in relation to meat—it was said that you could pack all of the steer's roasting meat on one of its horns. But the longhorn became the basis of the range-cattle indus-try, the long drive, and the creation of the American cowboy. With the closing of the open range, better beef breeds came into the state, and the longhorn almost disappeared.

Longhorn steers. Barker Texas His-tory Center, The University of Texas at Austin.

Lone Star Flag

The expression "six flags over Texas" refers to the flags of the different sovereign nations that have ruled the land—Spain, France, Mexico, the Texas Republic, the Confederate States of America, and the United States. The "Lone Star" flag resulted from the work of a committee which designed a new standard for the republic in 1838. It was approved by an act of the Texas congress, which was signed by President Mirabeau B. Lamar on January 25, 1839. The law said that the flag should have a blue perpendicular stripe of the width of one-third of the length with a five-pointed white star in the center. The other part would have two horizontal stripes of equal breadth, the upper white, the lower red. When Texas joined the United States, it was represented by the twenty-eighth star in the U.S. flag; the Lone Star flag then became the state standard.

The tradition of a lone star reaches back to James Long, who acclaimed independence by raising a red and white flag with a lone star at Nacogdoches. During the Texas Revolution several other lone star flags appeared. Sarah Dodson fashioned a flag at Harrisburg in September 1835 which featured a white star as a symbol of the only rising star of liberty in the Mexican provinces.

ranches and continued the irrigated farming around San Antonio. Spanish architecture remained popular and endured into the twentieth century in well-to-do homes and on the campus of the University of Texas at Austin. Mexican cuisine became a part of the culture. Spanish place-names were kept—San Antonio, Gonzales, El Paso, Rio Grande, Nueces, Brazos. The Roman Catholic religion endured, and the Alamo, originally a Spanish mission, eventually became a shrine of Texas liberty. For the Mexican people of Texas, however, the war cast seeds of prejudice that still bear bitter fruit. Hispanics became a despised and distrusted minority.

Juan N. Seguín, for example, was born in San Antonio, joined the cause for Texas independence, recruited soldiers, escaped the slaughter at the Alamo when he went through the Mexican lines to seek help, fought at the battle of San Jacinto under Houston, and took over San Antonio as the military commander. While in that position he reverently buried the ashes of the men killed at the Alamo and brought order and confidence to the Mexican population of the town.

He worked for amicable race relations while a senator in the Texas congress and urged the printing of laws in both languages. Seguín was elected mayor of San Antonio in 1841 and 1842, but after he warned the city to evacuate in the face of a Mexican invasion people turned against him. The leader of the invading forces called him a friend, and Seguín shortly had to move to Mexico. There he was given the choice of prison or service in the Mexican army, and so when he returned to Texas he unfortunately came as a Mexican soldier. Texans branded him a traitor, and it was not until after the War with Mexico that he could go back to the land of his birth.

The terms *spik* and *greaser* became a part of the Texas vocabulary in the 1850s as Hispanics became lower-class citizens. To be sure, the highest wall of prejudice in Texas, one buttressed with segregation laws, was that between whites and blacks. The Hispanics, nonetheless, frequently lived in barrios, remained impotent in politics, and became almost faceless in Texas society until the middle of the twentieth century. The Spanish imprint, however, was indelible, even though it was scarcely noticed in the new dominion of the Anglo-Americans.

3. Texas and the United States

With Sam Houston attending to his wound in New Orleans, the Texan army became a problem. Hundreds of mercenaries continued to arrive to join the Texas cause, aching for a battle in order to participate in the generous land rewards offered to those who served. A group of them under General Thomas J. Green prevented Burnet from sending Santa Anna back to Vera Cruz. They removed him from the warship *Invincible*, and Burnet had to keep the fallen dictator under guard for his own safety. Isaac Burton's horse marines, who patroled the coast, captured a Mexican ship at Copano Bay in June, and there was talk once again of marching on Matamoros in search of plunder. Mirabeau B. Lamar, whom Burnet appointed to head the army, could not control it, and the ad interim president feared fighting would flare up again through some rash act of the unruly soldiers.

In advance of the convention's timetable, consequently, Burnet called for an election of permanent officials in September to bring the republic into being. Henry Smith declared immediately for the presidency, and soon Stephen F. Austin joined the roster. Eleven days before the election Sam Houston assented to run for the top position, and out of the 6,640 votes cast on election day, Houston won 5,119. The electorate overwhelmingly endorsed the constitution and voted 3,277 to 91 to seek annexation to the United States.

Houston hoped that annexation would solve his problems of dealing with Mexico, disbanding the revolutionary army, and establishing a viable economic system. The army enlarged daily, and for each three months of service the Texas congress promised a bounty of 320 acres in addition to the headright of 640 acres for any immigrant. The men remained restless while they waited, and the

There's a yellow rose in Texas,
That I am goin' to see.
No other soldier knows her,
No soldier, only me.
She cried so when I left her,
It like to broke my heart.
And if I ever find her,
We nevermore will part.
CONFEDERATE MARCHING
SONG BASED ON A NORTHERN
MINSTREL BALLAD

government gave away so much territory—1,162,240 acres between 1837 and 1841—that it could produce no revenue from land for several years.

Houston appointed Albert Sidney Johnston, the adjutant general, to head the army, but the soldiers preferred Felix Huston, the current commander. Huston then wounded Johnston in a duel over the issue, and the president, like Burnet earlier, began to fear he would lose control of the military. Houston, therefore, put all but 600 men on furlough—which turned them loose, kept them available in case of renewed warfare, and avoided the cost of mustering-out pay. There was no money and no income for the government, so the congress issued "star money," so-called because of a star printed on the paper. The first limited amount held its value, but subsequent issues depreciated. By the end of Houston's term star money was worth about twelve cents on the dollar in U.S. currency.

In sympathy with the Indians and also in an effort to save expenses, Houston urged the congress to ratify the treaty he had made with Chief Philip Bowles of the Cherokees during the war. The treaty reserved lands in East Texas for these Indians, who had crossed the Sabine into Texas about 1819, but the Convention of 1836 had not ratified it and, now that the war had ended, the congress refused to honor it. As Houston commented, "If I could build a wall from the Red River to the Rio Grande, so high that no Indian could scale it, the white people would go crazy trying to devise means to get beyond it." The settlers in East Texas wanted to drive them out, and, unfortunately, the Cherokees gave them an excuse in the Cordova Rebellion.

Vicente Córdova tried to rally loyal Mexicans along with the Cherokee Indians to oppose the rebels in 1835. Because of the turn of events his scheme was delayed, but in 1838 he tried again. With an estimated one hundred Mexicans and three hundred Indians Córdova established a camp on an island in the Angelina River of East Texas and declared in a letter to Houston their lack of allegiance to the republic. Leading the militia, Thomas J. Rusk, one of the heroes of San Jacinto, marched on the camp and dispersed the rebels. Chief Bowles denied any personal connection with the plot and Córdova escaped to Mexico. All the rebels arrested, even though charged with treason, eventually went free, but distrust of the Cherokees remained.

Houston's effort to resolve all these problems by an-

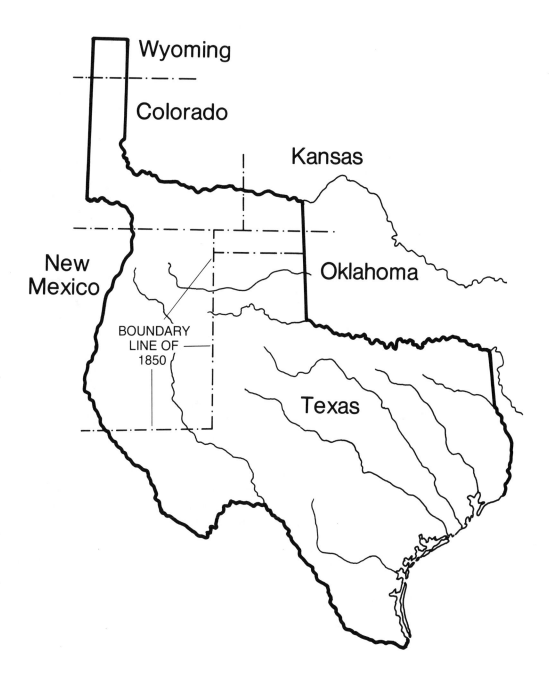

Map 2. The Republic of Texas, 1836–1846

nexation to the United States failed. Agents in Washington, D.C., worked for it, the people in Texas supported it, but former president John Quincy Adams denounced the victory of San Jacinto from the floor of the House. He argued that the triumph had established slavery in a land where it had been banned by the Mexican government. The annexation proposal thus became entangled with the slavery question. In desperation and at some political cost Houston even sent Santa Anna to Washington to argue the case. It was to no avail, and on his final day in office President Jackson, Houston's old friend, signed a bill recognizing Texas independence. At midnight Jackson raised his wine glass to the Texans he had invited to the White House for his final hours and said, "Gentlemen, the Republic of Texas." After the toast he added another for his old companion in arms, "The President of the Republic of Texas."

The incoming leader of the United States, Martin Van Buren, likewise rejected Texas because it would be a slave state and also because it might mean war with Mexico. The mood of the United States was not favorable, and Texas had to wait for a shift in attitude, which came in less than a decade. To avoid further embarrassment, Houston instructed Anson Jones, who was representing Texas in Washington, to withdraw the offer. This helped the popularity of Mirabeau B. Lamar, a wartime hero.

By law, Houston could not succeed himself in office, and Lamar won easy election. Lamar cared not a fig for annexation and turned a hard face toward the Indians. He supported the Córdova campaign, ordered the Cherokees out of the country, and authorized companies of Texas Rangers to secure the frontier against Apaches and Comanches. The Indians resisted. At the Battle of the Neches in 1839, near Tyler, the Cherokees lost and were driven northward into Indian territory. Both Vice-President David G. Burnet and Secretary of War Albert Sidney Johnston participated in the fighting.

The aged Chief Philip Bowles, wearing the handsome sword and sash presented to him by Sam Houston, died on the battlefield. The victors scalped the body, tore the skin off the back, and left the remainder to rot. As the last of the Cherokees crossed the Red River, a group of hunters shot and killed four of them. That was their farewell and East Texas was now cleared for settlement. This was the first instance of Texans pushing a tribe across a border to get rid of it. In general, however, this action was typical of the nineteenth-century Anglo-American treatment of

Indians. The natives were forcibly removed from the land so that it could be occupied by others.

This episode is the result of a long-running Indian migration of shattered tribes moving ahead of the frontier line in advance of Anglo-American settlement. Before 1800 a part of the Alabama tribe moved west of the Sabine and was joined seven years later by their kinfolk, the Coushattas. These were followed in the succeeding decades by Choctaws, Shawnees, Delawares, Biloxies, Kickapoos, Quapaws, and Cherokees, most of whom were peaceful, agricultural Indians who had taken up Anglo farming techniques. Some had their own alphabet and schools; others owned slaves and planted cotton; some attended Christian churches. They were the cultural equal of most Anglo-Americans, and they wished to settle in northeast Texas, as did other pioneers. Only the Alabama-Coushatta were allowed to stay. In 1854 Texas gave them a 1,300-acre reservation in Polk County, where they have persisted to the present.

There was, of course, little love between the Indians and Texans, and each side stereotyped the other. From the point of view of the whites, "The only good Indian is a dead Indian" or, as "Rip" Ford put it, "If savagery is right, civilization is wrong. There can be no middle ground." All had tales to tell. Mary Rabb, a young wife living in the wilderness of the Colorado River bottoms in the 1820s, for example, recorded the nuisance of Indian theft of tools and animals. When left alone, she kept her spinning wheel whirring at night to "drownded" the sounds of Indians outside "hunting mischief," and for comfort she invited young pigs indoors to eat cracked corn under her bed. That trouble was mild.

There were hundreds of small bloody fights. In 1835 near Belton the Taylor family—mother, father, and four children—was attacked by a raiding party of eleven Indians. Their dog barked a warning and died, but it gave Mrs. Taylor time to hustle her children across the open space of their dogtrot cabin so the family was in one room. They shot two Indians who charged the cabin, but the warriors set the roof on fire. Mr. Taylor wanted to surrender, but Mrs. Taylor refused and climbed to the ceiling where she quenched the fire with buckets of milk and vinegar handed up by her daughters.

The fight ended with the death of another Indian and injury to two others. One had rushed the cabin and was peering through a large hole when Mrs. Taylor threw a shovelful of hot coals in his face. "Take that, you yellow scoundrel," she said as the blinded Indian staggered away. After that the Indians gave up the attack.

In another early episode in 1836 a band assaulted Parker's Fort near the headwaters of the Navasota River, a tributary of the Brazos. While most of the men were in the fields, a hundred Comanches, Kiowas, and a few Caddoans rode up and demanded a cow to eat. When the settlers refused, the Indians attacked. They killed seven people, including John Parker, who suffered the loss of his scalp and genitals before death. Granny Parker they stripped, pinned to the ground with a lance, and raped. She survived, but the Indians rode off with two adult women and three children. The women were stripped and repeatedly ravaged at a victory dance on the plains, but four of the captives lived long enough to gain freedom through ransom. The fifth one, nine-year-old Cynthia Ann Parker, grew up among the Comanches. Later she provided one of the most poignant stories in the history of the American West.

From the Indian point of view they were experiencing an invasion. Noah Smithwick, an early Texas blacksmith, recalled a conversation with an aged Comanche chief:

> We have set up our lodges in these groves and swung
> our children from these boughs from time imme-
> morial. When game beats away from us we pull down
> our lodges and move away, leaving no trace to frighten
> it, and in a little while it comes back. But the white
> man comes and cuts down the trees, building houses
> and fences, and the buffalos get frightened and leave
> and never come back, and the Indians are left to
> starve, or, if we follow the game, we trespass on the
> hunting ground of other tribes and war ensues. . . .
> No, the Indians were not made to work. If they build
> houses and try to live like white men they will all die.

From the Anglo view the Indians were in the way and had no right to the land. President Lamar's aggression, however, was not limited to Indians. In 1841, without approval, he sent an expedition of military people, merchants, and adventurers to New Mexico to claim the Santa Fe trade for Texas. Lamar thought the people there would welcome the opportunity to join Texas, but instead they supported the Mexican troops, who captured the Texans without firing a shot and marched them off to prison.

Lamar further stirred the Mexican pot by sending

twenty-nine-year-old Commodore Edwin W. Moore and the Texas Navy to harass the Gulf coastline. Moore swept the waters clear of Mexican shipping, made a de facto alliance with the rebels of Yucatan who were trying to gain independence from Mexico, and captured the town of Tabasco.

Within the Republic Lamar supported the idea of universities sustained with public land set aside for their maintenance. In addition, while on a buffalo hunt he discovered a hilly site in central Texas near the frontier village of Waterloo, which he thought perfect for the capital of an empire. He disliked the temporary location in the City of Houston, which was named for his chief adversary, and he urged the Texas congress to move to the new site—which could be foreseen as a crossroads for trade from the Red River to Mexico and from Santa Fe to the Gulf. Houston and others objected to the move because it was subject to Indian depredations, but in 1839 the congress approved of the new capital at Austin.

Lamar, moreover, carried out all of these activities without proper financing. There was no revenue—the congress had given away the lands normally used for income by a North American state—and Lamar failed to gain loans from abroad. He thereupon resorted to deficit financing by printing "redback" dollars, so-named because of the color of ink on the reverse side. They were aptly named and quickly worthless. As a consequence of wild expenditures and unsuccessful belligerence, Sam

Texas Navy

To protect supply lanes to the United States, the provisional government of Texas on November 25, 1835, provided for the purchase of four schooners and the organization of a navy. In January 1836 the purchase of the *Liberty, Invincible, Independence,* and *Brutus* brought the navy into existence, with Captain Charles E. Hawkins appointed commodore by President David G. Burnet. By 1837 all the ships had been lost to battle, storm, or nonpayment of repairs.

In 1838 the republic bought the brig *Potomac* as a receiving ship at the Galveston Navy Base, and then in 1839 purchased the *Zavala, San Jacinto, San Antonio, San Bernard, Wharton, Austin,* and *Archer.* President Mirabeau B. Lamar appointed Edwin W. Moore as commodore of this second navy. Cuts in appropriations and the opposition of Sam Houston reduced the navy, but Moore kept some ships sailing with personal credit and subsidies from Yucatan rebels. In 1843 the congress ordered the sale of the last four ships, *Austin, Archer, Wharton,* and *San Bernard,* but the outraged citizens of Galveston prevented the auction. After annexation the ships of the Texas Navy were transferred to the U.S. Navy, but only the *Austin* was fit for service.

The *Independence,* war vessel of the Texas Navy, 1836–1837. Painting by Fred Toler. The San Jacinto Museum of History, Houston, Texas.

Houston and the "Old Peace Party" returned to power. He inherited over $5 million in debt and a foreign policy in turmoil. His predecessor had released demons which proved hard to recapture.

In order to curtail expenses, Houston withheld the appropriations for the navy, but Moore kept his fleet afloat through personal loans and subsidies from the Yucatan rebels. When Moore refused to sail home, Houston proclaimed the commodore a pirate and invited other nations to capture the Texas ships and send them to Galveston. With that, Moore returned at once—to be greeted as a hero by Galvestonians and dishonorably discharged by Houston.

The congress ordered a court-martial to try Moore for disobedience, contumacy, mutiny, piracy, and murder among other violations. He was acquitted, however, on all but four minor charges and allowed to remain in the navy. Houston meanwhile put the fleet up for sale. The incensed people of Galveston prevented the auction, but the fleet did not sail again until it was absorbed into the U.S. Navy at the time of annexation.

In response to Texas aggression in the Lamar administration, Mexico mounted three predatory raids in 1842. One was stopped at the Nueces River, but the two others briefly held San Antonio. When the Mexican forces under General Adrian Woll withdrew from San Antonio on the last foray, they took with them sixty-seven hostages. Houston ordered Brigadier General Alexander Somervell to raise the militia and to pursue the raiders into Mexico if reasonable and necessary. Somervell reached the Rio Grande and took Laredo and Guerrero, but lacked the supplies and support to penetrate further. He ordered the men home. Some of the army refused and formed the Mier expedition under the command of William S. Fisher, a leader of revolutionary troops and former secretary of war.

Dreaming of plunder, the men crossed the Rio Grande twice, first to demand supplies from the town of Mier and then to fight the Mexican army that had invested the town. After hard combat the Texans surrendered as prisoners of war, but Houston said that the men had acted without authority. After an unsuccessful attempt to escape, Santa Anna, again in charge of Mexico, ordered their execution.

The foreign ministers in Mexico were able to gain a modification in the decree so that only 10 percent faced the firing squad. The choice for the decimation was made by having each man reach into an earthen jar and draw out a bean. There were 176 beans, one for each, including 17 black beans to designate death. William A. A. (Big Foot) Wallace, a Scotsman who had come to Texas to avenge his relatives' execution at Goliad, figured that the black beans were bigger and successfully pulled out a white one. The doomed men were then unshackled, blindfolded, and shot at dusk. Later, others escaped, a few were released, some died, but most of the remainder worked as prisoners on Mexican roads until finally freed by Santa Anna in 1844.

To further control expenses Houston curtailed Ranger activities against the Indians, which brought charges that he was an "Indian lover." Houston did have the expense of calling out the militia in East Texas, however, to suppress the Regulator-Moderator War. On the eastern border, which had a long-standing reputation for lawlessness, a feud flared between two factions, the Regulators and the Moderators. They operated as vigilante groups, attacked one another, prevented the courts from working, and terrorized the residents of Shelby County. The militia arrested the leaders, brought them before Sam Houston, and remained in the county for four months to enforce the peace agreements that Houston had negotiated.

Through all of these difficulties Houston still hoped for annexation to the United States. John Tyler, who inherited the presidency of the United States after the death of William Henry Harrison, fashioned a pro-Southern administration. Texas agents worked out an agreement with Secretary of State John C. Calhoun for annexation as a territory, but it was rejected by the Senate. The issue, however, became a part of the election campaign of Democrat James K. Polk, who urged the "re-annexation of Texas and the re-occupation of Oregon." The drive of Manifest Destiny, given force by the meddling of Britain and France, won this time. The U.S. Congress offered acceptance as an equal state in February 1845.

Anson Jones, the new president of the republic, however, moved slowly and laid before the Texas congress the choice of recognition by Mexico as an independent nation or annexation to the United States as a full-fledged state. Britain and France had brought Mexico to the position of accepting Texas, but the Texas congress voted overwhelmingly to become a part of the United States. It was something that Texas-Americans had wanted all along. A state constitution was written and accepted. Jones signed the final papers, and on December 29, 1845, he pronounced, ". . . the Republic of Texas is no more."

As the Lone Star flag slipped down the flagstaff for the final time, it was clasped into the waiting arms of Sam Houston.

The citizens of the new state elected James Pinckney Henderson as the first governor, and the legislature selected Sam Houston and Thomas J. Rusk as the first senators. Politically, as it had been in spirit all along, Texas became a part of a larger fate, the destiny of the United States. Still, the unique experience of ten years as an independent republic gave Texans an element of pride that has never been forgotten.

The act of admission to the American union brought to the Lone Star State a period of economic growth, prosperity, and warfare. Four days after annexation President Polk sent John Slidell to Mexico with instructions to solve the differences between the two nations. At the same time he sent General Zachary Taylor with 1,500 troops to the mouth of the Nueces River, and then on to the Rio Grande when the Mexican government refused to receive Slidell. Taylor thus entered disputed territory. General Mariano Paredes y Arrillaga, the head of state in Mexico, declared a defensive war against the United States and ordered Mexican troops to cross the Rio Grande. A skirmish on the north bank on April 24, 1846, resulted in several American deaths, and the fighting started.

Taylor then won two quick battles on May 8 and 9 at Palo Alto and Resaca de la Palma near Brownsville. Polk asked Congress for a declaration of war, and Congress approved on May 13. Texans, along with most of the nation, embraced the war enthusiastically. Over eight thousand

The Walker Colt six-gun, the famous gun of the Texas Rangers, which was an improvement over the five-shot gun. Connecticut State Library, Museum of Connecticut History.

Texans enlisted, and the governor took a leave of absence in order to command Texas troops. Former President of the Republic Mirabeau B. Lamar participated along with Texas Rangers, future governors, and Albert Sidney Johnston, who later became one of the best generals of the Confederacy. Taylor was of this opinion: "On the day of battle I am glad to have Texas soldiers with me for they are brave and gallant, but I never want to see them before or afterwards, for they are too hard to control."

Taylor moved inland, captured the city of Monterrey in September, and defeated Santa Anna, again in control of Mexico, at Buena Vista in February 1847. General Winfield Scott, in charge of another American army, landed at Vera Cruz and then struck overland at the Mexican capital. After bloody fighting Scott took Mexico City in September, and the fighting stopped. In the Treaty of Guadalupe Hidalgo Mexico recognized the Rio Grande boundary of Texas; ceded New Mexico, Arizona, and upper California; and received from the United States $15 million plus U.S. payment of some $3 million in suits against Mexico by American citizens.

Texas still claimed land as far west as Santa Fe, and in March 1848 the state legislature created Santa Fe County, which included the eastern half of New Mexico. Neither the U.S. military authority nor the residents, however, recognized Texas jurisdiction. The citizens in New Mexico wanted their own territory, and the next President of the United States, Zachary Taylor, agreed. The issue continued at a low boil as Texas representatives in Washington pushed their claim.

After Taylor's death in office, his successor, Millard Fillmore, presided over a compromise that included solutions to additional questions. Part of this Compromise of 1850, which also held the slavery question at bay for a decade, permitted the formation of the New Mexico territory, a redrawing of the western boundary of Texas along its present line, and compensation of $10 million to Texas from the federal treasury. At a special election Texas voters endorsed the agreement by a two-to-one margin.

The United States held half of the $10 million for the payment of revenue debts—principal and interest on Republic of Texas securities. As it worked out, in 1858 these bondholders were paid about seventy-seven cents on the dollar. State authorities argued that this was fair because Texas had not received par value for the bonds when they were issued and the bonds had passed at a discount into the hands of speculators. This echoed the same logic used

Walker Colt

Samuel Colt invented the revolver in 1831, but its success as a military weapon came after the suggestions of Captain Samuel H. Walker of the Texas Rangers. Walker wanted a weapon useful for a rider on horseback. The pistol needed a trigger guard and enough weight to be used as a club when empty. Together Colt and Walker designed a .44-caliber, six-shot, four-pound nine-ounce weapon, which Colt manufactured in Connecticut and shipped to Texas in 1847. After an earlier failure, sales of the Walker Colt revived Colt's fortunes in firearms manufacture.

The new revolver was based upon the lighter five-shot Paterson Colt, which proved its usefulness in 1844 when sixteen Rangers, including Walker, defeated eighty Comanche warriors at Nueces Canyon. The Indians were accustomed to single-shot rifles and would use a feint to exhaust rifle fire before charging in for close combat with lances and tomahawks. Discharging arrows, the Comanches swept by the dismounted Rangers on both sides. The Texans replied with rifle fire and then sprang into their saddles to charge the Indians.

Said one of the old Rangers: "Never was a band of Indians more surprised than at this charge. They expected the Rangers to remain on the defensive, and to finally wear them out and exhaust their ammunition. . . . In vain the Comanches tried to turn their horses and make a stand, but such was the wild confusion of running horses, popping pistols, and yelling Rangers that they abandoned the idea of a rally and sought safety in flight." In their panic the Indians dropped bows, shields, and lances all along a three-mile route.

by states after the American Revolution in respect to state debts.

Part of the $5 million that the state received went to pay old nonrevenue debts—claims from participants in the revolution and from suppliers of military materials. Texas spent the remainder on education, public buildings, and internal improvements. An education bill in 1854 used $2 million of this money for a permanent education fund.

Following statehood Texas began to adopt the political party organization of the United States. Before this, Texas politics had revolved around personalities, with a particular focus on Sam Houston. Citizens were either pro-Houston or anti-Houston, and to a degree this division continued as long as Old Sam remained as a U.S. senator. Houston was a Jacksonian Democrat. Most Texans also considered themselves Democrats because this was the national party that supported annexation.

In 1853 the Whig Party and in the following two years the Know Nothing Party made enough of an impact to tighten Democratic Party organization in the state. In the late 1850s, however, the polarization of the national parties, the Democrats in the South and the Republicans in the North, brought confusion. Houston, whose nationalistic tendencies found scant support in his home state, ran as an independent candidate for governor in 1857 against the Democratic Party nominee, Hardin R. Runnels. Houston lost by nine thousand votes, but in 1859 in a rematch Houston won by the same margin. Shortly thereafter, Texas slipped into the vortex of the Civil War.

Texas, meanwhile, experienced unprecedented growth and economic expansion. The population increased a little over seventeen times in the twenty-five years between the Republic and the Confederacy. In 1836 the estimated count was 35,000. It was 212,000 in 1850 and 604,000 in 1860. Filling in the open spaces, people settled mainly in the eastern and southeastern portions—on the coastal plains, in the pine forests and the river valleys, and on to the Balcones Escarpment, where they confronted the double barrier of high-plains aridity and the Comanches.

The flow of immigrants came primarily from the South. The roots of people from the upper South were in the middle Atlantic states. They were yeoman farmers of German, English, and Scots-Irish descent, praised by Thomas Jefferson, who practiced subsistence agriculture without slaves. They grew corn and wheat and bred mules, horses, and pigs. They settled the backwoods of Maryland, Virginia, North Carolina, and southeastern Pennsylvania and formed the image of the typical American pioneer with a log cabin, covered wagon, and isolated family farm. They burst across the Appalachians into Kentucky, Tennessee, Missouri, and Arkansas. They were the sharpshooters of the backwoods who came to Texas during the Mexican period and fought with their flintlock long rifles and Bowie knives against the Mexican peasants of Santa Anna.

From the lower South came the immigrants who carried the slave-cotton-plantation culture. This developed, generally, in the states of Virginia, Maryland, South Carolina, and Georgia, spreading westward through the Gulf Coast states. These people were of English and African descent with some mixing among the Creole, sugar-cane people of Louisiana. At the time of the Texas Revolution people from the lower South had settled in the Atascosita District in the southeastern corner of Texas, and afterward into areas capable of supporting cotton cultivation. At the time of the Civil War the numbers of people from the lower South were about equal to those from the upper South. East and southeastern Texas thus became the western border of the Cotton Kingdom.

With the heavy influx of people from the lower South also came an increase in the number of Afro-Americans. At the time of the revolution slaves numbered about 14 percent of the Texas population, around 5,000 people. In 1860 one-third of the population, 183,000 people, was black, with their distribution and origins similar to those of other immigrants from the lower South. There was some illegal smuggling, and the census of 1870 revealed 318 blacks of African birth living in Texas.

Texans defended slavery with the same arguments used in the older South and claimed that slaves in Texas were better treated than those elsewhere. Frederick Law Olmsted from New York, who toured the state in the 1850s, thought otherwise, but there are no social statistics to prove the claim on either side. As a measure of discontent, slave attempts to escape to Mexico were common. Newspapers carried advertisements for the return of runaways, and Olmsted recorded this conversation with a white man searching for a judge's escaped slave:

"What made him run?"
"The judge gave him a week at Christmas, and he made a good deal of money, and when the week was up, I s'pose he didn't want to go to work again. He got unruly, and they was a goin' to whip him." ". . . He

might have just worked and done his duty, and his
master'd 'a' taken care of him, and given him another
week when Christmas come again, and he'd 'a' had
nothing to do but enjoy himself again. These niggers,
none of 'em, knows how much happier off they are
than if they was free. . . ."

Most of the twenty-two thousand slave owners of 1860
possessed ten or fewer blacks, often a family. Only fifty-
four owners possessed more than one hundred. After the
Civil War the immigration of blacks to Texas dropped
sharply, and since 1865 the percentage of blacks in the
population has declined.

The number of Hispanic inhabitants, as might be expected, declined after the revolution, and only 5 percent
of the population had Spanish surnames in 1850. This
changed dramatically in the twentieth century, but in the
nineteenth century the Texas population was largely of
U.S. origin. Anti-Hispanic prejudice continued, and Mexicans in Texas (Tejanos) along with blacks were often
treated with much less than equal rights. As a new judge
in Brownsville in the 1850s expressed it in a toast to his
fellow Anglo-Americans, "To justice modified by circumstances!" Ethnic strife flared in the Cart War of 1857, the
Cortina War of 1859, and the Salt War of 1877.

The Cart War involved the intimidation and murder of
Mexican teamsters who hauled freight from San Antonio
to the coast at a cheaper rate than Anglo competitors. In
this instance the poor Mexicans found protection from
U.S. military escorts who ended the difficulty. More significant was the "war" two years later.

Red-bearded Juan Nepomuceno Cortina was heir to a
large ranch on the U.S. side of the Rio Grande, a ranch
which had to be ransomed with a square league to prove
his mother's ownership after the War with Mexico. In
Brownsville the city marshal roughly arrested one of Cortina's former servants for drunkenness. Cortina saw this
and protested, and the marshal snarled an insult. They
drew their guns, and in the gunsmoke the marshal fell
with a wounded shoulder. Cortina and his rescued friend
then galloped out of town.

Several months later unpunished Cortina returned
with some eighty men, took over the town, hoisted the
Mexican flag, released the prisoners in jail, and killed four
men—three Anglo-Americans and one Mexican who
tried to shield a gringo friend. He shortly abandoned the
town, but issued a proclamation stating that he was a

Mexican wood hauler and ox team with a two-wheeled cart. Western History Collections, University of Oklahoma Library.

Texas citizen protecting the rights and property of Mexicans. Hispanics on both sides of the river rallied around him, and when Texas Rangers lynched one of his lieutenants, he threatened to invade Brownsville again. After some fighting a combined force of U.S. soldiers and Texas Rangers forced Cortina to retreat into the Burgos Mountains of Mexico, and the rebellion ended.

During this conflict Cortina sacked small Anglo settlements, and Captain John "Rip" Ford of the Texas Rangers crossed the Rio Grande several times to engage the outlaw on his own ground. Cortina afterward continued to live in northern Mexico, a hero to the common people. But to the Anglos on the Texas side of the river Cortina was a bandit and horse thief. The bloodshed on both sides—about 245 dead—merely served to deepen the distrust and hatred between the two peoples.

Later, in 1877, after attempting to assert claims to free salt deposits one hundred miles east of El Paso, Charles Howard used a shotgun to murder Louis Cardis, the leader of the Mexican opposition. Although Howard was protected by Texas Rangers at San Elizario, a Mexican mob forced his surrender, placed him and two companions before a firing squad, killed them, dragged the bodies behind horses, and dumped them into an abandoned well. In re-taliation an Anglo posse descended upon the town, killed five men, and forced others to flee across the border. No one was arrested for the Salt War, but U.S. troops sup-pressed the communal anger, and people began to pay for their salt.

There were other notable ethnic groups in Texas, par-ticularly the Germans, who at a later time were also to receive a bitter dose of prejudice. Before 1844 German im-migration was unorganized, with only a modest accumu-lation between the lower Brazos and Colorado rivers. A society of German noblemen, the Adelsverein, however, sent 7,400 immigrants to Texas between 1844 and 1847— at first under the leadership of Prince Carl of Solms-Braunfels and later under John O. Meusebach. In addition, Henri Castro, a French empresario, settled 2,100 people mainly from Alsace in Medina County west of San An-tonio. These immigrants formed a fragmented band of German-speaking settlers stretching west from Houston and curving northward into the Hill Country. Their main towns were Galveston, San Antonio, Houston, New Braunfels, Fredericksburg, and Castroville.

Mexican-American women making tortillas in San Antonio in the 1870's. Western History Collec-tions, University of Oklahoma Library.

The Lutheran and Roman Catholic religions, German language, Gothic church buildings, homes of stone and half-timbered construction, and folk festivals such as Oktoberfest still linger in these communities. In the nineteenth century the German farmers seemed to fare better than their Anglo-American counterparts. A higher percentage owned their land, they reported higher incomes and production, and they spent more money on fences and equipment. In comparison with Anglos, the Germans farmed more intensively with a feeling for the conservation of the land. They tended to remain in the same place and did not use slaves.

Scattered elsewhere could be found pockets of Czechs, Poles, Swedes, Norwegians, Danes, Italians, and Irish—all a part of the greater immigration pattern of the United States. These ethnic groups left their individual imprint—some more, some less—on the Texas character, but they all had in common the trauma of migration and their interest in agriculture. By the 1850s the immigrant trade from Europe had become highly organized and an important part of trans-Atlantic commerce.

Immigrants secured government documents; sold their farms and excess personal property after harvest; packed clothes, food, household goods, and tools in chests; bought tickets from a broker; and traveled by rail to the nearest embarkation point. These points included Liverpool, Bremen, Hamburg, Le Havre, and Naples. Their broker purchased the tickets and usually tried to gain the maximum number of people for the space allotted. It cost twice as much to travel by steamship as by sailing vessel, but it was three times faster—two weeks instead of six.

The voyage was none too pleasant and might take longer than expected. Augustine Haidusek, a Czech who came to Texas as a child in 1856, recalled: "This sailboat was about one hundred feet long and had only two masts. . . . The very first night we ran into a storm, the waves tossed our boat as if it were a piece of wood, and to my dying day I will not forget the suffering and seasickness of the travelers, especially the women. This lasted a whole night and a day; after this the sailing was fair, but it was fourteen weeks before we reached Galveston harbor."

The immigrant ships to Texas sometimes touched at New York or New Orleans before dropping anchor at Galveston or Indianola. Upon arrival most of the newcomers moved inland as quickly as possible, not only to take up their new land but also to avoid the sickness of the port cities. Jesse A. Ziegler, who lived in Galveston from 1857 to 1883, remembered the immigrants trudging up the middle of the street to the train depot—Russians in fur coats, Swiss in knee breeches, Scots with bagpipes, women and children burdened with pots, pans, and utensils.

Ninety-five percent of the Texas population was involved with agriculture—livestock breeding and grain cultivation in the north-central area, cotton cultivation on the eastern and southern coastal plains. Farming acreage doubled in the decade of the 1850s, as cotton production increased seven and one-half times and corn two and one-half times. The cotton economy was vigorous and slave productivity increasing. These thinly scattered farms, with a density of only three people per square mile in 1870 (this statistic from the *Texas Almanac* is somewhat distorted in that it includes all of Texas, even the Indian country), were supplied by a network of towns, dirt roads, and a few railroads.

The discovery of gold in California and the acquisition of new territories accelerated the westward movement, and Texans began to reach out into their own west. Robert Neighbors, an Indian agent, and John "Rip" Ford explored the land between San Antonio and El Paso to blaze a trail called the Upper California Road, which went from San Antonio to Fredericksburg and across Guadalupe Pass to El Paso. More popular for pioneers, however, was the Lower California Road laid out by U.S. Army Captain Wilt C. Whiting, which went from San Antonio to Fort Clark (Brackettville), across the Pecos near Ozona, and then on to El Paso. Captain Randolph B. Marcy established at the same time a third route farther north. The Marcy Trail left the Red River at Preston, went through present-day Henrietta and Big Spring, crossed the Pecos, and went over Guadalupe Pass to El Paso. This route was used by the Butterfield Mail Line in the late 1850s.

The gold rush turned El Paso, five loosely joined settlements, into a hustling frontier town of commerce. The area had a long Spanish heritage, but this was when it changed into an Anglo community with an assortment of soldiers, outlaws, merchants, debtors, wife deserters, and the "Great Western," supposedly the first Anglo female in El Paso. She was six feet tall and was reputed to be as quick with a gun as she was with her affections.

A bizarre experiment occurred at this point in the westward thrust. Secretary of War Jefferson Davis used $30,000 to purchase seventy-three camels from North Africa and Asia to test their usefulness in the American West. To the great curiosity of bystanders they were landed at Galveston and Indianola and driven to Camp Verde, south of present-day Kerrville. From there the army carried out various experimental excursions, and the soldiers discovered that the camels could carry heavier loads and travel farther than mules. Even with this proof, others remained skeptical, and the army gave up the effort. Some of the camels were sold to freighters and others simply turned loose. Years afterward western travelers reported camel sightings, but, unlike longhorns and mustangs, the camels did not proliferate and eventually died off.

The blazing of trails and even the camel experiments were a part of the continuing westward movement, and with that came pressure on the Indians. In 1849 the U.S. War Department placed a string of eight military posts from Eagle Pass on the Rio Grande to Fort Worth west of Dallas in north-central Texas. In 1852 they moved their line one hundred miles to the west and later built a third defensive line between the Concho River and the Rio Grande. In 1855 the army set up two reservations, one near the present city of Graham on the Brazos River for sedentary tribes, and the other on the Clear Fork of the Brazos in Throckmorton County for Comanches.

Despite this, Indian conditions became worse in the late 1850s. The Comanches began raiding into settled Texas, and there was fighting along the Texas-Oklahoma border. At the Battle of Pease River the Rangers, led by Sul Ross, captured Cynthia Ann Parker (Naduah) and her eighteen-month-old daughter, Prairie Flower. Comanches had kidnapped Cynthia Ann Parker at age nine during the raid on Parker's Fort. Five years later an army officer unsuccessfully tried to buy her back from the Indian family which had adopted her. Later she married Chief Peta Nocona and bore two sons, Pecos and Quanah Parker. She told Indian traders that she was happy and had no desire to return to her Texas relations. She was seen again at the Battle of Antelope Hills in 1858 and then captured with her daughter in 1860.

She was then thirty-four years old, had forgotten the English language, and looked like a Comanche woman except for her blue eyes and fair complexion. Interrogators established her identity after she heard her name and burst into tears. Although she still had kinfolk in Texas and the legislature granted her a pension and league of land, she made several attempts to escape to the prairie. In 1864, shortly after the death of her daughter, Naduah starved herself to death. Her Comanche husband never

Cynthia Ann Parker, long-time captive of the Comanches and mother of Quanah Parker, with her baby Prairie Flower soon after their recapture by Texas Rangers. Western History Collections, University of Oklahoma Library.

took another wife and died of an infected wound. Her son Pecos died of a disease, but Quanah, her remaining child, lived to complete the final chapter in the history of the Comanche nation.

Texans by and large believed reservation Indians participated in the periodic raids on farms and ranches. There was little way to prove this, but the result was the removal of the Indians to the Washita River of Oklahoma in 1859. This officially ended Indian life in Texas with the exception of the Alabama-Coushattas in East Texas and the Tiguas at El Paso. It did not stop, however, the raids of the Comanches and Kiowas, which continued on into the 1870s.

The control of Indians and the blazing of trails westward were frontier problems. Meanwhile, people were moving into the eastern and southern portions of the state with farms, plantations, ranches, and towns. The frequent travelers through the countryside expected free lodging and meals of coffee, pork, and cornbread from earlier settlers. It was expensive for those living on frequently traveled routes, and some turned to innkeeping in self-defense. Lydia Spencer Lane, an army wife who had to entertain frequent and sometimes ungrateful guests, commented: "We are told to take in the stranger as by so doing we 'may entertain an angel unawares.' I do not think that class of guests often traveled in Texas and New Mexico, at least while I was out there; if they did, their visits were few and far between, and their disguise was complete."

The focal points of Texas society were the towns. There were the older Texas places established during the Spanish period—San Antonio, Nacogdoches, Laredo, El Paso, Gonzales, Goliad—along with newer ones founded before the Civil War—Galveston, Houston, Dallas, Marshall, New Braunfels, Castroville, and Austin. New Braunfels and Castroville started as a part of colonizing activities; Austin for political purposes; Galveston, Houston, Marshall, and Dallas for commercial reasons; and Fort Worth for military reasons.

It was in these cities that the seeds of the culture were most deeply planted. They were the centers not only for business but also for theater, education, law, newspapers, and religion. When the Reverend James Huckins, for example, sailed into Galveston Harbor in January 1840 as an agent for the American Baptist Home Mission Society, he saw no reason to go ashore, for surely no Baptist would be found in such a dark, forlorn, chill place. But he changed his mind the next day, disembarked, and founded the First Baptist Church within the week. Others did likewise, and from their urban headquarters to the backcountry such people transferred the religions of western civilization.

Methodists and Presbyterians used circuit riders, while the Baptists tried to obtain a resident pastor for each congregation. They stressed piety rather than ethics, emphasized self-reliance, and defended slavery by defining the role of blacks as one of servitude and labor. The Baptists, nonetheless, offered their faith to the black community. In addition, these religions promoted literacy, sobriety, and lawful behavior. At the time of the Civil War the Methodists, the leading religion, possessed 410 church buildings; the Baptists, in second place, had 280 places of worship.

Shapley P. Ross, an Indian fighter and the father of future governor Sul Ross, provided another example of town significance. When Ross took his family into Texas, one of his relatives commented, "Ah well, let him go. In a few years he will come back from Texas in an old cart drawn by a crop-eared mule, and he will be followed by a gang of yellow dogs covered with mange. In that cart, and walking behind it, will sit a set of ignorant boobies, who would not know a schoolhouse from a hog pen or a schoolmaster from a Hottentot."

Ross decided to trade his wilderness land and move to Austin in order to educate his children. When informed of the decision, his wife laconically said, "You have been a long time coming to that conclusion."

The towns flourished as settlement continued. On the coast Michel B. Menard noted the natural harbor of Galveston Island and decided to exploit it. Menard, of French heritage, had been an Indian trader who wandered into Texas in 1829 and became involved in the fight for independence as a funding agent for Texas in the United States. Following the war he acquired a site on the eastern end of the island, laid out a town, and began to sell lots in 1838. Menard possessed the best harbor between New Orleans and Vera Cruz. It was on the landward side of the island and opened into Galveston Bay, through which small steamships could navigate. Galveston shortly became the most important port for Texas and its largest city during the 1870s and 1880s.

Working with Galveston in the cotton trade was Houston, founded in 1836 by John K. and Augustus C. Allen. They purchased land along Buffalo Bayou, which emptied into Galveston Bay, laid out a town in gridiron form, and named it after the hero of the moment, Sam Houston. They successfully persuaded the congress to designate their town as the capital and busily went about selling lots and building a meeting place for the politicians. The bayou was barely navigable, and the first arrivals had difficulty recognizing the site.

Francis R. Lubbock, a politician, traveled to the site by boat, missed the landing, floated back downstream, and finally found a road laid off from the water's edge with stakes and footprints. On shore he discovered several tents, one of which was a saloon, and several small houses under construction. That was the beginning of Houston, currently the largest city in Texas and the fourth largest in the United States.

Located inland about fifty miles from Galveston, Houston served as a transshipment point to Galveston. Cotton along with hides, sugar, molasses, cattle, pecans, and

cottonseed rolled into Houston on ox wagons, dockwork-
ers transferred the materials to small river steamers, the
steamships took the items to Galveston, and the Galveston factors placed them on oceangoing vessels for sale
in places like New Orleans, New York, Liverpool, and
Bremen.

In reverse manner Galvestonians shipped to the inland
farmers household goods and farming equipment. Buffalo
Bayou was the most heavily traveled stream in the state.
The value of the exports from Galveston was ten to twenty
times that of the imports. It was essentially a "colonial"
economy whereby Texas shipped out raw or semifinished
products for the use of manufacturers elsewhere. In return Texas received finished items for consumer utiliza-
tion. It was an economic pattern from which Texas never
entirely escaped.

To avoid the misery of the muddy and rough roads,
Sidney Sherman along with some Boston investors built
the first railroad in Texas—the Buffalo Bayou, Brazos and
Colorado Railway. With its terminal downstream on Buffalo Bayou it was meant to tap the cotton fields of the Brazos Valley and bypass Houston. Sherman, who had raised
a company of volunteers in the United States and fought
through the Texas Revolution, created a sensation when
he off-loaded a thirteen-ton locomotive in Galveston in
1852. Houstonians shortly followed his example and by
the time of the Civil War possessed a spiderweb of rail
lines reaching out into the hinterland. The boom of a cannon in 1860 announced the first train from Houston,
across a two-mile trestle, into the island city of Galveston.

Until the coming of railroads in the 1870s the northern
inland towns remained small retail points supplied by
wagon trains from the coast. Dallas began at a ford on the
Trinity River with John Neely Bryan's trading post in
1842, acquired a post office in 1844, and became the
county seat in 1846. When John B. Billingsley arrived
from Missouri in 1844, he wrote: "We soon reached the
place we had heard of so often; but the town, where was
it? Two small log cabins—this was the town of Dallas,
and two families of ten or twelve souls was its population." Grasshoppers and mismanagement defeated a
nearby community of French socialists (a Fourier colony)
in the mid-1850s and contributed some 200 skilled and
sophisticated Europeans to Dallas, but still the population was only 1,200 in 1870.

Dallas and other such places suffered little from the
Civil War, a cataclysm that had a much greater effect on

the coastal areas and the cotton economy. Although the majority of Texans did not own slaves, they had come from the South and their sympathies were with the slaveholding states. A states' rights delegation represented Texas at the national Democratic convention in Charleston in 1860 and bolted with seven other states when the platform did not contain a plank protecting slavery. The delegates participated in a subsequent meeting that nominated John C. Breckinridge of Kentucky, the Southern rights candidate.

Amid rumors of abolitionist activity—fires, assassinations, poisonings, and slave uprisings—and with vigilante groups roaming city streets, Texas voted for Breckinridge in the four-man race for the presidency. South Carolina had already determined that it would secede if Abraham Lincoln, the Republican candidate, gained the White House. Lincoln won and South Carolina voted to leave the union. This started the secession movement and Texas had to make a decision.

Governor Houston ignored the clamor for a state convention, but prominent state leaders called a meeting which the legislature endorsed. Within two days the delegates approved of a secession ordinance by a vote of 166 to 8, issued a declaration of causes, and before adjournment selected representatives for the convention of Southern states in Montgomery, Alabama. While the people discussed the secession ordinance, a committee on public safety arranged with U.S. General David E. Twiggs, who later sided with the Confederate States of America, for the peaceful surrender of federal property and the evacuation of federal troops from the state. Shortly, the electorate gave overwhelming approval to secession in a vote of 46,000 to 15,000.

Opposition was greatest in the frontier counties of central and north Texas, where there was a fear of Indian raids, sympathy for the Unionists, a larger non-Southern population, and small-farm agriculture. Support was strongest in East Texas and along the coast, where there existed large slave populations and plantations. In March a state convention canvassed the vote, adopted an ordinance joining Texas to the Confederate States of America, and asked Houston to take an oath of allegiance to the new government. The old man refused, and the convention declared vacant his office of governor. "Texas is lost," Houston muttered as Lieutenant Governor Edward Clark took over his chair. President Lincoln offered to send troops to help Houston hold on, but the deposed governor refused this, too.

Houston traveled to Galveston to explain his position and spoke to a hostile crowd from a balcony at the Tremont Hotel. "Will you now reject these last counsels of your political father," he pleaded, "and squander your political patrimony in riotous adventure, which I now tell you, and with something of prophetic ken, will land you in fire and rivers of blood?" His foresight and courage were to no avail. Texas continued on its reckless course, while Houston quietly retired to a home near Houston, then to Huntsville. His loyalty to Texas endured, however, and he wrote to his son, who had joined the Southern army, "If Texas demands your services or your life in her cause, stand by her." He died in July 1863 before the outcome was certain.

Former Republic of Texas president David G. Burnet and former governor Elisha M. Pease also withdrew from public service and attempted to remain neutral. Other dissidents tried to leave. Edmund J. Davis, a state judge, escaped and organized a Union cavalry regiment, which served in Louisiana and the Rio Grande Valley. Representative Andrew Jackson Hamilton, who was in Washington when the conflict started, moved to New Orleans for the duration of the war. Sixty-five German Unionists attempted to flee to Mexico, but were caught at the Nueces River by state troops. Thirty-five of the Germans were killed, and in the Hill Country several weeks later another 50 Union sympathizers were hanged. North of Dallas in Cooke and Grayson counties a court at Gainesville tried 150 people for Unionist activity and executed 39 of them. In the federal army, nonetheless, were to be found 2,200 Texans.

Fighting between the North and the South commenced with the bombardment of Fort Sumter in Charleston Harbor in April 1861. Lincoln called for troops, and four additional states from the upper South seceded to join with the other seven Southern states.

Most white male Texans greeted these events with enthusiasm and rushed to join military units, while the women began to make flags, tents, uniforms, and other war equipment. In Galveston, interestingly enough, about one-quarter of the eligible men rushed to the foreign consulates to claim citizenship and avoid conscription.

Estimates of the numbers of Texans in the service of the Confederacy reach sixty thousand, or about two-thirds of the white male population between the ages of eighteen and forty-five. When Texas soldiers arrived in Richmond, Virginia, in 1861, Jefferson Davis greeted them with these words: "Texans! The troops of other states have their reputations to gain; the sons of the defenders of the Alamo have theirs to maintain! I am assured that you will be faithful to the trust."

The state effort was poorly coordinated, and most of the men spent their time in home defense or in futile efforts to expand into the Southwest. A cavalry unit crossed the Red River and captured three forts in Oklahoma, and another kept the Comanches temporarily at bay with several engagements. In the summer of 1861 John R. Baylor, a former politician and Indian agent, led a force of three hundred into southern New Mexico to set up the territorial government of New Mexico. He was followed by Brigadier General Henry H. Sibley with three regiments. Sibley won a battle at Valverde and captured Santa Fe and Albuquerque but met defeat at Glorietta Pass and lost his supply train. He retreated into Texas with Baylor, and again the Texas dream of westward expansion failed.

War came to Texas with the appearance of the *U.S.S. South Carolina* off the port of Galveston in July 1861 to carry out Lincoln's order to blockade the Southern coastline. Business in Galveston ceased, and the Confederates erected several small forts on the eastern end of the island. They also posted a watch on top of the brick Hendley Building of the Strand to watch ship movements through spyglasses. Blockade runners using small gray sailing vessels began to run cotton to neutral ports in the Caribbean, and every once in a while a Union ship would bombard the city.

With commerce at a near standstill, the dependent towns and farms of South Texas began to suffer. Some cotton was sent out through Matamoros on ships of British registry—Charles Stillman, the merchant who established Brownsville, made a fortune this way. The editor of the Houston *Telegraph*, however, urged people to plant corn, not cotton, while housewives began experimenting with coffee made from okra seeds. The price of slaves, interestingly, remained high during the war.

As citizens abandoned Galveston, General Paul O. Hebert ordered an evacuation, and the governor recommended burning "every spear of grass." The scorching did not occur, and federal troops landed in 1862 to occupy the city. There were too few to control the island, and the soldiers retreated to a dock at night for safety. Confederate scouts crossed the railroad bridge in the darkness to roam at will through the nearly empty city.

A new Confederate commander, General John B. Magruder, determined to take back Galveston, worked out an elaborate plan whereby federal ships in the harbor would be attacked by steamboats armored with cotton bales while soldiers assaulted the outpost on the wharf. The Rebels quietly rolled siege guns across the bridge, and the steamers, armed at Houston, slipped down Buffalo Bayou into the bay. At five o'clock on New Year's morning of 1863 the Battle of Galveston opened with the boom of a Confederate cannon.

The fighting in the city around the wharf became a standoff after the Confederates discovered that their scaling ladders, which they carried into the water around the dock, were too short. The federal ships in the harbor, yet unengaged with the cotton-clads, moreover, poured canister and cannon balls into the city to hold back the Confederate troops. One Southern lad darting from the shelter of a brick wall across open ground was sent sprawling as a Yankee cannonball plowed a furrow under his feet. Uninjured, he slowly got up, bowed to the U.S. ship, and casually strolled the rest of the way to safety.

Just as the rebels were about to give up, the two cotton-clad steamers arrived and attacked the ships in the harbor. The federal sailors were able to sink one of the Confederate ships and disable the other, but the damaged one swung into the *U.S.S. Harriet Lane*, allowing a boarding party to seize control. The Northern command ship ran aground, and the captain by error blew himself up when he tried to destroy the vessel. The remaining Northern gunboats retreated down the channel and fled all the way to New Orleans. The abandoned federal troops on the wharf had no choice but to surrender, and thus the Confederates won the battle.

In one of those poignant episodes typical of this war, which split families along ideological lines, Lieutenant Commander Edward Lea of the U.S. Navy fell mortally wounded during the fighting on the *Harriet Lane*. Major Albert M. Lea, his father, served as an engineer under Magruder. The father knew that his son was on the *Lane*, and when it was brought to shore, he hastened aboard. He found the young man shot through the stomach with no chance to live. When Magruder heard of the situation, he exclaimed, "Good God! Lea, I had no idea of this. Take

Harriet Lane

Named for the niece of President James Buchanan, the *Harriet Lane* was built in 1859 as a revenue cutter with two masts, two side paddlewheels, and a low-pressure steam engine. At full sail and steam power it could move at eleven knots. It was a beautiful 180-foot copper-sheathed ship that could carry one hundred sailors. It was involved in the futile attempt to take relief to the soldiers at Fort Sumter at the start of the Civil War, became a part of the fleet that captured New Orleans, and served in the Western Gulf Squadron, which fought in the Battle of Galveston.

Following its capture, the Confederates stripped the *Lane* of its armaments and sold it to T. W. House of Houston for use as a blockade runner. House sent the ship through the blockade at Galveston with a load of cotton to Havana, where it remained for the rest of the war. Afterward the vessel went through a series of owners and finished its existence as a lumber freighter rigged as a barque with the engine removed. During a storm in 1884 the crew abandoned the water-logged ship, and it sank at sea.

Hood's Texas Brigade

The unit later known as Hood's Texas Brigade formed in the winter of 1861 and originally consisted of the First, Fourth, and Fifth Texas Regiments, the Eighteenth Georgia Regiment, and the infantry from Wade Hampton's South Carolina Legion. In March 1862 Brigadier General John Bell Hood, a Kentuckian who had adopted Texas, replaced the first commander, Brigadier General Louis T. Wigfall. Because of Hood's daring leadership and the heavy Texas component, the unit received its name. It served in Lee's Army of Northern Virginia and participated in at least twenty-four battles, including Antietam, Gettysburg, and Chickamauga, where Hood was wounded and left the command. During the Battle of the Wilderness Lee tried to lead the brigade in a charge, but the men forced him back with the cry of "Lee to the rear!" At its height it contained about 4,500 men, but heavy casualties reduced that number to 617 at the time of surrender. The brigade was highly

him to my quarters." As the father desperately searched for an ambulance, his son died while murmuring, "My father is here."

Nine months later a federal invasion of Texas was stopped at Sabine Pass. At this strategic point where the waters from Sabine Lake empty into the Gulf of Mexico, the Confederate forces had thrown up earthworks and installed six cannons and forty-two men. The soldiers, mainly Irish Houstonians, under the command of Lieutenants N. H. Smith and Richard W. Dowling, a gregarious barkeeper in Houston, faced an invading force of five thousand on twenty vessels protected by three gunboats. The Northern idea was to have the gunboats silence the fort before the troops landed.

As two of the boats approached, the Confederate battery opened fire. Shortly, the rebel guns knocked out one gunboat and then concentrated their fire on the second. In forty-five minutes the second boat went aground and both of the ships surrendered. The Confederates took the two gunboats and 315 prisoners. With that, the invading force retreated to New Orleans, and its leader, General William B. Franklin, got the reputation of being the only American general who managed to lose a fleet in a contest with land batteries. The rebel loss was "strictly and positively, nobody hurt."

The North tried once more to invade Texas, this time through Louisiana and the Red River. General Nathaniel P. Banks assembled twenty-five thousand soldiers supported by a flotilla of gunboats. He moved up the river, but was stopped by Southern soldiers below Shreveport in early April 1864. At the battle of Mansfield General Richard Taylor with many Texans sent by Magruder bloodily routed the advance troops. Banks retreated fifteen miles to Pleasant Hill and successfully defended his position the following day. After this, Banks retreated downriver to New Orleans, and there occurred no further attempt to invade the Lone Star State.

The larger and decisive battles of the war were fought outside the borders of Texas beyond the Mississippi River. Thousands of Texans took part and gave their lives to the Confederate cause. Albert Sidney Johnston, a veteran of the Texas Revolution, the War with Mexico, and the Indian wars, led the Confederate army at Shiloh against Ulysses S. Grant. The fighting was so deadly and intense that it was said a person could cross clearings on the wooded battleground by walking on the corpses, without touching the ground. Johnston himself was killed leading a charge.

Elsewhere, Hood's Texas Brigade, Terry's Texas Rangers, and Ross's Brigade fought with Confederate armies and won respect for the quality of Texas' fighting spirit. The war was lost, nonetheless. Captain Benjamin F. Sands, who was commanding the federal blockading squadron off Galveston, heard the news of the fall of Richmond and the surrender of Robert E. Lee. He sent the news to Galveston, and Magruder agreed to give up. With Kirby Smith, Magruder boarded a federal ship and signed the surrender papers on June 2, 1865. Sands landed at the port on June 5 and raised the U.S. flag over the courthouse. On June 19 Union occupation troops under General Gordon Granger landed, and Granger announced that Lincoln's Emancipation Proclamation was in effect. The slaves were free and the war was over.

The state, however, was in chaos. There was no civil government, and when the disbanded Confederate soldiers started home, they looted the commissaries and took what they could. Young blacks, freed from bondage, crowded into the cities only to be met by entrenched prejudice and little sympathy for the difficulties of their transition to freedom. In East Texas federal soldiers discovered that the plantation owners, needing their field hands for the harvest, had told the blacks they were not free until after Christmas.

Worse, with all of the unacclimatized people, including Yankee soldiers, yellow fever ravaged the coastline. In 1867 when the fever struck Galveston, some five thousand people fled and carried it with them to destinations as far as 125 miles inland. About three-fourths of the Galveston population caught the disease and over a thousand died, at a rate of twenty per day. Major General Charles Griffin, the head of military affairs in Texas, caught the fever and died. So did Dick Dowling, the Confederate hero of the Battle of Sabine Pass.

Amelia Barr, who later became a nationally famous writer, lost all the male members of her family, her husband, and two sons. Even the baby boy she bore a month after the fever subsided had a skin "yellow as gold" and died three months later. Having burned up most of its fuel, the contagion began to subside in November and ended with the first major frost. It was misery compounding the chaos of defeat.

President Andrew Johnson, who took office following

praised by Robert E. Lee, Stonewall Jackson, and James Longstreet.

Hood was generally well liked by the men, but he was never noted for his brilliant strategies. On one occasion the general berated a soldier for remaining by a warm fire and said, "I don't know why you are loitering here, so far behind your command." The man replied, "Yes, and what you don't know, General Hood, would make a mighty damned big book." Hood led his army to near destruction in Tennessee, and the brigade, serving elsewhere, added the following verse to its marching song, "The Yellow Rose of Texas." In the verse "Uncle Joe" refers to General Joseph E. Johnston, who knew how to make a judicious withdrawal from battle.

And now I'm goin' southward,
   For my heart is full of woe,
I'm going back to Georgia,
   To see my Uncle Joe.
You may talk about your Beauregard,
   And sing of General Lee,
But the gallant Hood of Texas,
   Played hell in Tennessee.

Juneteenth

Emancipation Day for Texas blacks occurred on June 19, 1865, when General Gordon Granger of the federal occupation forces landed at Galveston and proclaimed Lincoln's Emancipation Proclamation in effect. Since then, June 19, referred to as "Juneteenth," has been a time of picnics, parades, and parties for blacks in Texas. It was eventually recognized as an official state holiday.

Lincoln's death, announced a plan to bring the disaffected states back into the Union. Under a provisional government the state could rewrite its constitution to abolish slavery, repudiate secession, and cancel Confederate debts. Voters, excluding high-ranking Confederate officials and people with over $20,000 in taxable property, could take an oath of allegiance to the United States, approve the new constitution, and elect new state officers.

Johnson appointed former Texas congressman Andrew Jackson Hamilton as the provisional governor, and Hamilton called for elections to send delegates to a constitutional convention. The majority selected were ex-rebels, and they worked for two months to amend the 1845 constitution. They accepted the required changes but did not give blacks the right to vote. The electorate approved the changes in June 1866 and selected the conservative James W. Throckmorton as governor by about the same margin as the vote for secession. Not much had changed. Throckmorton took office in August, and in the same month President Johnson declared the Texas insurrection at an end.

Texans thought Reconstruction was over, but unhappy Radical Republicans in Congress disapproved and instituted their own Reconstruction plan. They divided the South into five military districts, placed state governments in a provisional status subject to military control, and ordered new state constitutions that gave blacks full political privileges. States, moreover, had to ratify the Fourteenth Amendment to the U.S. Constitution, and voters had to take an "iron-clad oath" that they had not voluntarily served in the Confederate army nor given aid to the rebel government. This disfranchisement along with military support and vigorous recruitment of black voters gave strength to the Republican Party in Texas.

Military authorities removed Throckmorton and replaced him with former governor Elisha Pease, who was given little power. Army officials in the summer and fall of 1867, in addition, set up public schools, protected the civil rights of blacks, provided emergency relief, and replaced dozens of local and state officials.

In Houston, for example, General J. J. Reynolds arbitrarily replaced six aldermen and the assessor and collector. In 1868 Thomas J. Scanlan, an Irish immigrant who had come to the Bayou City in 1853, was appointed alderman. His career is typical of the Reconstruction municipal governments. From 1870 to 1874 he worked as mayor to extend sidewalks and sewers, construct roads and bridges, erect a new market house, and welcome several blacks to the city council and police force. Scanlan was elected mayor in 1872 with a Republican slate, and when he left office he was accused of running the city into debt far beyond its means of repayment.

This is a traditional assessment of Radical rule in cities, but it does not consider the inflation in the early 1870s nor the rapid deflation and depression which struck in 1873. This sort of pattern of expansion followed by a debt problem during the depression was common in American cities, North and South. In Scanlan's case corruption was never proven, and it seems that he acted for the benefit of his city in most instances.

In February 1868 Texans qualified to vote selected delegates to a constitutional convention. Only six men from the prior convention appeared at this second one, which met in June. The majority were former Unionists, and nine of the ninety were black. The new constitution provided for a greater centralization of authority by giving the governor a four-year term and the power to appoint most executive and judicial officials. It also provided for greater support of public education and suffrage for adult, male blacks. Ratification and the gubernatorial election of Edmund J. Davis, the former Unionist Texas cavalry officer, took place in late November 1869. The newly elected state legislature quickly approved the Fourteenth and Fifteenth Amendments to the U.S. Constitution as required, and on March 30, 1870, President Grant proclaimed Reconstruction in Texas at an end.

Even with that, most Texans did not feel that Reconstruction was over until Governor Davis left office. On a state level he acted much like Scanlan on the municipal level. He extended the public roads, strengthened frontier defenses, supported a new homestead law, reformed the public schools, and encouraged the construction of railroads by issuing state bonds. He antagonized people with the creation of a state police force that was 40 percent black, the use of martial law in four counties to suppress lawlessness, increased taxes, and a larger state debt.

The Democratic legislature elected in 1872 moved to limit his powers, abolish the state police, and modify the school program. Davis found himself waging "a slow civil war" of criticism fought with bitter and truculent words. In 1873 Richard Coke defeated Davis in the general elections. Davis appealed to President Grant and barricaded himself with his followers in the basement of the capitol. Coke and his men took over the first floor. It was tense,

Yellow Fever

Yellow fever or yellow jack is a contagious, mosquito-borne viral disease with a mortality rate of about 20 to 25 percent. Symptoms are fever, red eyes, headache, quick pulse, jaundice, and "black vomit" caused by internal bleeding. Survivors gain lifelong immunity, and during the Spanish-American War Galveston provided a unit known as "the Immunes." Infected people unknowingly brought yellow jack to the Texas coast, and then mosquitoes spread it among those susceptible.

Physicians used various treatments—mustard baths, cold compresses, confinement to bed, moderate food, warm tea—but no one knew the etiology until it was proven by Walter Reed with his courageous experiments in Cuba in the early twentieth century. People did know that the disease ended with cold weather, but they did not realize that it was because frost killed the mosquitoes. There were epidemics in Texas in 1839, 1844, 1847, 1853, 1854, 1859, 1864, 1867, 1870, and 1873. After this, the use of quarantines prevented the spread of the fever.

with everyone armed to the teeth, but Grant refused to interfere and Davis gave up. There was statewide celebration, and in Galveston the Galveston Artillery Company fired a one-hundred-gun salute to "Coke and the Fourteenth Legislature to celebrate the triumph of the people."

The new governor and the legislature quickly moved to take away the vestiges of Reconstruction rule. They banished Republicans from office, curtailed expenses, and arranged for yet another constitutional convention. In 1875 ninety delegates met in Austin—seventy-six Democrats and fourteen Republicans, including five blacks. Thirty-eight belonged to the Grange, an agrarian organization dedicated to reducing taxes and to helping farmers by restricting corporate power. By vocation thirty-three were lawyers and twenty-eight were farmers.

The 1875 constitution, containing many provisions usually left to a legislature, was long and complex. It reduced the governor's term to two years; limited debt to $200,000; prohibited state bonds, but allowed land grants for railroad construction; authorized laws for the regulation of railroads; set a maximum tax rate; reserved more public lands for a permanent school fund, but reduced tax support for education; abolished the position of state superintendent of schools and the requirement of compulsory attendance; and made elective the positions of lieutenant governor, comptroller, treasurer, land commissioner, district and Supreme Court judges, and attorney general. The convention reiterated that the right to vote could not be restricted because of race, but it shunted aside a petition for women's suffrage.

There was some opposition to the reduction of support for education, but in February 1876 voters approved the new document by 137,000 to 57,000. It was passed in reaction to Reconstruction and the abuses people felt at the time. The Constitution of 1875, however, despite numerous amendments and thoughts of constructing a new one, has remained in force as the constitution of Texas to the present. At least Texas was back in control of its affairs, equal to the other states of the union.

4. Settlement

Following the Civil War, people took up the move to Texas at the earlier pace. Between 1870 and 1880 the population almost doubled, and in the next decades the rate slackened but slightly. By 1900 this confluence gave the Lone Star State a population of over three million and a ranking of sixth largest in the United States. During these thirty years the cities, following the national trend, attracted people at an even faster rate, and the urban population increased from 7 to 17 percent of the total state population. Density became greater, from three to twelve persons per square mile. As a result, the empty spaces in the eastern and southern portions filled up, and pressure was brought on the western part of the state. This was the home of the Comanche.

The attraction of Texas was still the same—land. When it joined the Union, the state retained its public domain, 150 million acres. It used 32 million acres to subsidize railroad construction and sold nearby property to individuals for $1.50 per acre beginning in 1874. Five years later the land office lowered the price to $1.00 for acres to support schools and $.50 for others. In 1883 a state land board classified the remaining public domain into agricultural, timber, and pastoral areas. The first two categories sold for $3.00, the pasture land for $2.00. Payment periods lasted from ten to forty years, and interest rates ranged from 5 to 10 percent. Until 1899 a married man could claim a 160-acre homestead with proof of three-year residence; a single man could obtain half that amount. Land in Texas was a bargain. There was no consideration of Indian claims to the country.

During the Civil War, after troops left for the campaigns of the East, the frontier defense weakened. Exploiting this debility, Indians out of Mexico and the high

A country where a man can switch his tail.
TEXAS COWBOY EXPRESSION, 1880s

Texas Rangers

The term "ranger" was used in Texas within two years of Anglo-American settlement to refer to a special law officer who could restore order when the situation was beyond the control of local authorities and yet not large enough to warrant the use of military force. In early days the Rangers rode against Indians and border bandits, in later times against outlaws, rustlers, fence-cutters, rioters, and striking workers. Well mounted and armed, they earned a reputation of being able to "ride like a Mexican, trail like an Indian, shoot like a Tennessean, and fight like a very devil."

In the nineteenth and early twentieth centuries the Texas Rangers dressed as they chose, lacked discipline, and occasionally stepped across the boundaries of human rights and law. After investigations for excesses in 1919, the Ranger force was cut from 1,000 men to 76, and after a period of overused patronage under Governor Miriam Ferguson the group merged with the Highway Patrol to become part of the Department of Public Safety in 1935. They were still utilized for special tasks, however, such as suppressing illegal gambling on Galveston Island during the 1950s and suppressing farm laborers of the Rio Grande Valley in 1966. Their reputation for violating civil rights and performing as strikebreakers led to reorganization in the late 1960s and early 1970s. Since then, the Rangers have operated as a more neutral law enforcement unit. Although many Hispanics had been on the force, Lee Roy Young, Jr., became the first black in 1988.

The most enduring myth of the Texas Rangers involves a worried Dallas mayor who sent to the statehouse for aid in stopping an illegal prizefight. When the anxious official met the train, Ranger Bill McDonald stepped off, and the disconcerted mayor asked about the rest of the men. The officer replied, "Hell, ain't I enough? There's only one prize-fight." This apparently did not happen, but the story retold

plains raided and burned isolated ranches and farms. In north-central Texas, particularly Wise and Young counties, over half the settlers abandoned their homes. In Tarrant County, the location of Fort Worth, the population declined from six thousand to one thousand. The state authorized a Frontier Regiment of Rangers in 1862 for Indian defense, and then reorganized it twice in the next two years. It was ineffective, and people either fled or "forted up" in stockades while awaiting a resolution of the war.

The soldiers sent west after 1865 were ill prepared for the hit-and-run tactics of nomadic warriors who could shoot their arrows from galloping horses. The Indians were able to string their bows fast enough to keep an arrow flying at all times and with enough force to drive the shaft through buffalo or man. The soldiers fought with the single-shot muzzle-loaders of the Civil War and expected to engage in set battles against a stationary foe. The army, moreover, assumed the defensive policy of protecting settlements while the national government adopted a humane but ineffective Quaker plan to place the Oklahoma reservations under the control of church people.

This was ideal for the Kiowas and Comanches, who raided as they wished and used the reservations as a sanctuary. The only way for the Texans to win this guerrilla war, as with any such war, was to attack and destroy the supplies and equipment of the enemy. In 1864 Kit Carson

Texas Rangers, 1918. Barker Texas History Center, The University of Texas at Austin.

led a group of New Mexico volunteers against the Plains Indians at Adobe Walls, an abandoned trading post on the South Canadian River in the Texas Panhandle. Although intimidated by Carson's mountain howitzers, the Indians forced his retreat. For the most part, the Indians pillaged at will and killed about one hundred Anglos each year. There was little to stop them, and although Texans complained loud and long, they found little response until 1871.

That year General William Tecumseh Sherman, who knew the ways of marauders, visited Texas. He doubted that the situation was as bad as the complaints implied and with a small escort visited Fort Richardson, the most northern in the Texas line of forts. While he was there, a wounded wagoner staggered in on foot to report an attack at Salt Creek. The Indians had burned the wagons, stolen the mules, and killed seven of the twelve teamsters. They had scalped one man, cut out his tongue, and roasted him face down tied to a wheel. Soldiers tracked the raiders to a reservation where one of the leaders was bragging about the attack. Sherman learned that he personally had barely escaped capture by the same war party. That did it, and the general unleashed soldiers on horseback to defeat once and for all the nomads of the plains.

The Indians were no longer safe. Between 1865 and 1881 there were 846 clashes in which sixty-one soldiers won Medals of Honor. The horse soldiers pursued the tribes even onto reservations to arrest renegades; they crossed the Pecos to harass the Apaches in the deserts and mountains; they violated the Rio Grande boundary to strike the Kickapoos in Mexico; they burned villages outside the reservations; they slaughtered captured ponies; they destroyed food supplies; and they killed Indians.

The turning point came again at Adobe Walls. Buffalo hunters had moved into the Texas Panhandle in 1874, and Dodge City merchants established a supply point near the old ruins. In June that same year about 250–300 Cheyenne, Comanche, and Kiowa Indians, under the leadership of Lone Wolf and Quanah Parker, attacked the twenty-eight men and one woman at the camp. The hunters held off the attackers with their powerful breech-loading Sharp's rifles, and on the second day of the siege Billy Dixon knocked an Indian off his horse 1,500 yards away. After five days and four men dead in the camp, the Indians withdrew.

In response the army dispatched forty-six companies, three thousand men, from five directions to flush the Indians from their secret winter camps in the Cap Rock re-

in many versions resulted in the myth of sending only one Ranger per mob. A statue, entitled "One Riot, One Ranger," in the lobby at Love Field in Dallas enshrined the fable, but the legend is not too far from reality. Rangers at times faced unfavorable odds.

Ranger John Armstrong, for example, in 1877 tracked killer John Wesley Hardin to Pensacola, Florida, and captured him while fighting off four gang members. Armstrong spotted Hardin, a man with thirty notches on his gun, seated in a passenger car at the train station. Armstrong pulled his Colt revolver, came down the aisle, and commanded the gang to surrender. Hardin, who recognized the weapon as being a favorite of the Rangers, exclaimed, "Texas, by God!" and reached for his own pistol.

Hardin's gun became entangled in his suspenders, but a gang member shot off Armstrong's hat. The Ranger killed that man with a bullet through the heart and reached for Hardin's encumbered revolver. Hardin kicked him into an empty seat, but Armstrong lunged back to whack Hardin on the skull with his six-gun. Hardin slumped unconscious for two hours, and Armstrong disarmed the rest of the intimidated gang. Hardin thus returned to Texas to stand trial and receive a twenty-five-year sentence.

Texas Rangers at Shafter Mines, Big Bend, 1890. Left to right, standing: Bob Speaker, Jim Putman; sitting, Lon Odom, Capt. John R. Hughes. Western History Collections, University of Oklahoma Library.

Adobe Walls

William Bent built a trading post about 1843 on the South Canadian River in Hutchinson County in the northern Panhandle. The original structure was a fort eighty feet square with adobe walls nine feet high. It was abandoned because of Indian hostility, but the ruins became a landmark for the area. Adobe Walls was the site of two major battles between Anglos and Indians in 1864 and 1874. Following the first engagement, Kit Carson said that it would take 1,000 fully equipped troops to hold the fort against the Kiowas and Comanches.

gion of the plains. Colonel Ranald Mackenzie—cold, taciturn, a "monk in boots," but the best Indian fighter in the West—found a hidden Comanche encampment in Palo Duro Canyon through the work of his scouts. He sent his troopers on foot leading their horses down the steep canyon trail at dawn, stampeded the Indian horse herd, and charged the tepees. The Comanches fled down the canyon and up the walls with only four killed, but they left behind their winter supplies. Mackenzie burned flour, blankets, smoked meat, new repeating rifles, and ammunition; and, most important, he killed their horses.

Earlier, in 1872, he had captured some Indian horses only to have Quanah Parker steal them back again. He vowed thereafter to eliminate all captured animals. The herd from Palo Duro, over one thousand horses, was driven to nearby Tule Canyon and shot. It was brutal, but a way to win the war. The Comanches were left afoot in winter on the exposed prairie without supplies. Agents cut reservations to half-rations to force Indians there to eat their horses while Mackenzie and others continued their unrelenting pursuit.

In June 1875 after a winter of starvation Quanah Parker surrendered and submitted to life in Oklahoma. This cleared the high plains of Texas. After the 1878–1881 defeat of the Apaches in northern Mexico by Mexican troops and in the Diablo Mountains of West Texas by black "Buffalo soldiers," all Indian resistance ended. It was the end of the native culture that had greeted Cabeza de Vaca on the sands of Galveston Island.

The Plains Indians were vanquished not only because of the effort of the U.S. Cavalry, but also indirectly through the bloody work of the buffalo hunters. Hides became worth $3.75 in the 1870s, and hunters like Billy Dixon at Adobe Walls ventured forth to make their fortunes. Bison were unafraid of gunfire and thus incredibly easy to kill. Using a .50-caliber Sharp's rifle, which fired a 600-grain bullet, hunters calmly stood in the midst of a group and began shooting. The record for a single stand was 90 animals; 250 was the buffalo-hunter record for a day. For the fun of it Sir St. George Gore, who toured the West in the 1850s, ordered his servants to hand him loaded guns and killed 1,000 bison in one day.

The hunters stripped off the hide, cut out the delicate tongue, and left the remainder to rot. They exterminated the vast southern herd between 1874 and 1878, and slaughtered the northern herd by 1884. It was estimated that 100 million buffalo existed in the beginning; by 1887

Quanah Parker

Quanah Parker, the last war chief of the Comanches, was born between 1845 and 1852 to Chief Peta Nocona and Naduah (Cynthia Ann Parker), an Anglo woman captured during childhood. He led raids against the Texas line of defense on the Llano Estacado and befuddled the soldiers sent against him by stealing their horses. In 1874 he helped lead five tribes in the second battle of Adobe Walls, and barely escaped death when buffalo hunters shot his horse from under him. After this the U.S. Cavalry units of Ranald Mackenzie so hounded the Comanches that Parker surrendered in 1875. With his people Parker retired to a reservation in Oklahoma, but later he made several trips to Texas and Mexico to visit his mother's relatives. He died in 1911.

Quanah Parker, Comanche chief, son of Cynthia Ann Parker. Western History Collections, University of Oklahoma Library.

only 1,091 animals still lived. A brief concern was expressed in the Texas legislature for the preservation of bison, but General Sherman pointed to the necessity of destroying the Indian "commissary." With the herds gone, the Indians became truly dependent. It also meant that the plains were empty, ready for exploitation by ranchers.

The range-cattle industry began essentially in the brush country south of San Antonio. Its roots were Spanish, but the industry had declined in the eighteenth century. It revived somewhat in the early nineteenth century under Anglo ranchers such as James Taylor White, who migrated to Texas from Louisiana in 1819. He gathered some eight to ten thousand longhorns in the lower Trinity River region, drove herds to the New Orleans market, and registered his JTW brand around 1830. More significant for the industry, however, was Richard King, who purchased an old Spanish land grant of 75,000 acres in south-central Texas in 1852. With Mifflin Kenedy he expanded in 1860, utilized Mexican vaqueros, and made famous the

King Ranch

Richard King began with 75,000 acres in Nueces County in South Texas in 1852. Mifflin Kenedy joined the enterprise for a while in the 1860s, and later Robert J. Kleberg married King's youngest daughter, Alice, thus becoming a part of the business. Richard King died in 1885, but Henrietta King, his wife since 1854, and Kleberg expanded the operations. In 1895, when Kleberg took complete responsibility, the ranch encompassed 650,000 acres. By 1925, the year of Henrietta King's death, it had grown to 1,173,000.

The ranch benefited from the discovery of oil and went on to expand into timber, banking, and horse racing. In 1946 a King Ranch horse, Assault, won the Triple Crown and for a time was the top money-winner in racing. Kleberg and his son Robert Kleberg, Jr., developed a new breed of cattle, the red-colored Santa Gertrudis, an ideal beef cow for the Southwest, and spread the running W brand to Australia, Brazil, and Argentina.

The Kings used Mexican families (Kineños) for labor on the ranch, and Henrietta King took a deep interest in them. At her death some two hundred mounted vaqueros in their working clothes waited respectfully until "La Patrona" was lowered into the ground. Then, single-file with hats off they rode once around the open grave and from there back to the pastures and cattle that were her life.

After the death of Robert J. Kleberg, Jr., in 1974, the ranch fell into the difficulties of family quarrels and the oil depression. In 1988 the ranch consisted of 825,000 acres in Texas with branches in Florida, Kentucky, Brazil, and Australia. Lands in Pennsylvania, Venezuela, Spain, and Argentina had been sold.

running W brand. The King Ranch went on to become one of the largest cattle operations in Texas and the world.

Longhorns were plentiful and cheap, even free for the taking if you could catch them. There were an estimated five million mavericks (a name attributed to Samuel A. Maverick, an early politician and rancher who let his cattle wander unbranded) in Texas at the end of the Civil War. Some early efforts at driving cattle to Louisiana, Missouri, Ohio, Illinois, and California occurred, but they were experiments. During the Civil War the U.S. agents in New Mexico needed beef for the Navajo reservations, and after the war the growing populations of the North and East demanded meat.

Chicago slaughterhouses were willing to pay almost any price—longhorns were worth three to four dollars each on the Llano Estacado while in Chicago a steer was worth ten times that amount. It cost about a dollar per head to drive a herd northward to a railroad, and thus with these simple economics the long drive and the cattle bonanza got its start.

During the spring and summer of 1866 some 260,000 head followed the trail to Sedalia, Missouri, the terminus of the Missouri Pacific Railroad. The trail cut through settled land, however, and Missouri farmers complained of trampled crops and the spread of Texas tick fever to local stock. The irate settlers set up "shotgun quarantines" to turn away the drovers, bandits extorted bribes for safe passage, and Indians found steer a tasty substitute for buffalo.

Joseph G. McCoy, a cattle buyer, solved these various problems. He took over the remote prairie village of Abilene, Kansas; arranged an extension of the Hannibal and St. Joe Railroad to the village; built pens, barns, and hotels; and marked the Chisholm Trail beyond the settlement line through Oklahoma and Kansas. He sent out the news of this first cattle town and awaited the result. About thirty-five thousand longhorns reached Abilene in 1867, but over the next two decades Texas cowpunchers drove six million into Abilene and other Kansas cattle towns.

Trail-driving became a profession. Contractors sup-

plied the manpower and equipment to move the herd and sold the animals when delivered. This saved the ranchers from a time-consuming effort and allowed them to keep their ranch hands at home. The drovers tended to be young men, although a few women went up the trail, too. They risked Indian attacks, bandits, blizzards, stampedes, dust storms, and drowning in river crossings. The cowboys sometimes remained in the saddle for thirty-six hours at a stretch and received for this work fifteen to twenty dollars per month plus board. Teddy Blue wrote in *We Pointed Them North*:

> But when you add it all up, I believe the worst hardship we had on the trail was loss of sleep. There was never enough sleep. Our day wouldn't end till about nine o'clock, when we grazed the herd onto the bed ground. And after that every man in the outfit except the boss and horse wrangler and cook would have to stand two hours' night guard. Suppose my guard was twelve to two. I would stake my night horse, unroll my bed, pull off my boots, and crawl in at nine, and get about three hours' sleep, and then ride two hours. Then I would come off guard and get to sleep another hour and a half, till the cook yelled, "Roll out," at half past three. So I would get maybe five hours' sleep when the weather was nice and everything smooth and pretty, with cowboys singing under the stars. If it wasn't so nice, you'd be lucky to sleep an hour. But the wagon rolled on in the morning just the same.

The trail boss picked the route, made work assignments, and carried the responsibility. A chuck wagon with food, spare equipment, and cook traveled along to prepare meals of beans, cornmeal, molasses, coffee, beef, and wild game. The drovers also herded along with them a remuda of saddle horses for periodic changes of mounts—the men worked longer than the horses. A dozen men could manage several thousand cattle. The longhorns would eat along the way, and if grass or water was scarce, there would be trouble.

Cattle Brands

Burning the hide of an animal to give it lifelong identification is a practice that goes beyond written documents. The Spanish, who often used a pictograph, brought the practice to the New World and to Texas as early as 1762. In 1848 Texas provided for the registration of brands with the county clerks. Texans used mainly initials or numerals, sometimes modified with stylistic changes. A leaning letter was "tumbling," and a letter on its side was "lazy." Short curved strokes at the top made it "flying" or "running," as in the case of the King Ranch "W," and a quarter circle at the bottom made it "rocking." There were also "bars," "stripes," "rails," "slashes," and "chains"—which created unique brands difficult to alter.

One of the more unusual stories involving brands comes out of the Big Bend country in 1891. Two men had a gunfight over an unbranded yearling. One of the combatants died in the fight, and the other was killed later by Texas Rangers. Cowboys branded the bad-luck maverick in block letters from shoulder to flank with the word "murder." Although there is some evidence that the animal was driven northward to Wyoming, legend holds that it became a ghost in the Big Bend, a lonely outcast, prematurely gray, with the brand a coarse red color.

Early ranchers usually bought or claimed land along a good stream and then assumed control of the surrounding range even though they did not own it. When Texas offered the land for sale, the ranchers acquired as much as they could and then leased the rest. In this manner the stock raisers took possession of West Texas.

In 1876 within two years of the defeat of the Comanches, for example, Charles Goodnight, a former Texas Ranger, and his wife, Mollie, moved into Palo Duro Canyon. With a financial partner in the 1880s he took over one million acres and handled 100,000 head of cattle. Goodnight also played a role in stocking the northern ranges by blazing a cattle trail into Colorado. Mollie Goodnight, the first Anglo woman on the plains, charmed the cowboys with her good nature and her home remedies—"coal-oil for lice, prickly pear for wounds, salt and buffalo tallow for piles, mud for inflammation and fevers, and buffalo meat broth for a general tonic."

During the depression of the 1870s, rather than sell their herds at a low price, ranchers left their cattle on winter pasture where the tough range cows could scratch down through the snow to eat the nutritious grass that had dried in the late summer sun. It is estimated that over half the herds driven northward were used to fill the empty spaces of Colorado, Wyoming, Montana, and the Dakotas. The end result was overstocking and overgrazing with little concern for the consequences.

An agent for the Department of Agriculture met with Texas producers about this problem in 1898, but the ranchers passed a resolution without any dissent: "That none of us know, or care to know, anything about grasses, native or otherwise, outside of the fact that for the present there are lots of them, the best on record, and we are after getting the most out of them while they last." For this foolishness their sons and daughters would reap a whirlwind of dust.

At the moment the cattle business helped Texas recover from the expense of the Civil War. Sales brought gold into the state for the improvement of breeds, the purchase of land, and acquisition of windmills. In addition, this episode in history provided the world with one of its finest frontier characters, honored in literature, art, music, theater, and motion pictures. The cowboy, as often depicted, in truth led a self-reliant life of adventure and hardship. Established religion had little place on the Texas frontier, as was true from the start of Anglo-American migration. Teddy Blue commented about his fellows: "Ninety percent of them was infidels . . . after you come in contact with nature, you get all that stuff knocked out of you—praying to God for aid, divine Providence, and so on—because it don't work. You could pray all you damn pleased, but it wouldn't get you water where there wasn't water. Talk about trusting in Providence, hell, if I'd trusted in Providence I'd have starved to death."

There were also gunfights. Old Tascosa, a cow town located at an easy crossing of the Canadian River, had its share. In trying to civilize this town, noted for its liquor, gambling, and fast women, Sheriff Cape Willingham in 1880 banned guns within the city limits. Fred Leigh, the foreman of the nearby LS Ranch, refused to comply, and the sheriff met him as he dismounted in front of a saloon. Willingham demanded Leigh's gun and raised a blunt, sawed-off, double-barreled shotgun to emphasize his order. Leigh jumped back on his horse without his foot in the stirrup, closed his hand around the handle of his six-shooter, and was blown out of the saddle by the sheriff. Leigh became the second man buried in Tascosa's boot hill.

The Cowboy

Developing from Spanish and Mexican roots, the American cowboy became one of our most distinctive and colorful frontier types. The cowboy's equipment, although romanticized by writers and moviemakers, served useful purposes. The broad-brimmed hat shaded the face and neck from the fierce sun and could be used as a temporary bucket to haul water. In cold weather the brim could be tied over the ears with a bandanna. The neckerchief served as a washcloth and could be pulled over the mouth and nose to filter out the dust of a trail herd. The leather chaps protected the legs from thorns, and the high-heeled boots prevented the foot from slipping through the stirrup. The high-horned western-style saddle could carry a lariat, canteen, blanket roll, and rifle as well as provide comfort enough to sit on all day and half the night.

Most cowboys were of medium to small stature (big men were too heavy on the horses), quick, wiry, and Southern. They selected a "string" of horses suited for different sorts of work—a calm horse for night riding, a quick one for working cattle, an animal with a barrel chest for swimming rivers. The cowboys were usually in their mid-twenties in age and came in all colors—black, white, and brown. They had to be self-reliant and adventuresome for their work. "In fact," said Teddy Blue, an experienced drover, "there was only two things the old-time cowpuncher was afraid of, a decent woman and being set afoot."

In addition to the blood and hardship, an expressive humor became part of cowboy life:

"Surprised as a dog with his first porcupine."
"Like a fifth ace in a poker deck, it is so unexpected."
"Grass as scarce as bird dung in a cuckoo clock."
"He couldn't hit a bull's ass with a banjo."
"They came pilin' out of that saloon like red ants out of a burning log."
"Wide spaces of the plains don't breed chatterboxes."
"Might as well been talkin' Chinese to a pack mule."
"He lets his ears hang down and listens."
"He called him names that'd peel the hide off a gila monster."
"A brand of booze a man could get drunk on and be shot through the brain and it wouldn't kill him till he sobered up."
"Likker that made you see double and feel single."
"Next mornin' I had a taste in my mouth like I'd had supper with a coyote."
"He acts like he was raised on sour milk."
"Whining lead is a hint in any man's language."
"Leave it to a female to put flavor in your grub."
"He's as popular as a wet dog at a parlor social."
"As ugly as galvanized sin."
"Happy as a flea in a doghouse."
"As wise as a tree full of owls."
"I figure I've been with this spread long enough to be entitled to a warm corner."

For some unexplained reason the sheepherder never caught the popular imagination like the cowboy, despite a life equally difficult. The shepherd spent solitary months looking after flocks of unbelievably stupid animals and protecting them from predators. The industry paralleled the cattle business and shared a common Spanish origin. The first sheep were Chaurros, lean and gaunt but blessed with stamina. Anglos crossed them with the Spanish Merino, producing a hybrid suited for the rugged Southwest. Contrary to popular belief, some of the larger ranchers, such as Richard King and C. C. Slaughter, ran sheep as well as cattle.

In Kerrville Charles Schreiner popularized sheep raising on the Edwards Plateau. He was a former Texas Ranger and cattleman who became a merchant and banker. Schreiner forced borrowers to use half their money raising sheep, and the Schreiner Company in 1900 utilized 600,000 acres from Kerrville to Menard for sheep production. He also recognized the value of mohair and the possibilities of mixing goats with sheep on the same range. So did William H. Haupt, an early enthusiast of Angora goats who commented: "In fine, the goat never butts you like sheep. With kind treatment, he is sensible, intelligent, docile, 'a thing of beauty,' and even a companion with whom one can spend a social hour." Indeed.

Kerrville became the "Mohair Center of the World," but the greatest promoter of goats was William L. Black, a Confederate blockade runner who became a cotton dealer after the war. He acquired a 30,000-acre ranch in Menard County, where he first tried cattle and then sheep. Because of the brushy nature of his land he decided to run goats and accumulated eight thousand head. He went into the slaughtering business, set up a tannery, and in 1893–1894 canned seven thousand goats. Goat meat did not sell well in the United States, but his legacy lingered. The Edwards Plateau today produces 90 percent of the nation's mohair.

On occasion the sheep and cattle people clashed because the animals they tended and their methods of work were so different. The nearly wild cattle needed long grass, plenty of water, and a rider on horseback to keep up with

Gambling in a saloon in Pecos, Texas, in the 1880's. Western History Collections, University of Oklahoma Library.

them. The thoroughly domesticated sheep fed on short grass and found enough water in the morning dew. They required a herder on foot, sometimes with a dog, to look out for them. The differences led to derision, especially of the sheepherder. Frequently there were ethnic differences, but the basic arguments centered on grazing rights, water, and fences.

After the spread of the cattle and sheep domains across West Texas, farmers, so-called sodbusters, took their turn with the country. An early visitor around Lubbock observed, "What a clean stretch of land. Why I could start a plow point into the soil and turn a furrow two hundred miles long without a break." By 1890 the first farmers entered the Panhandle, and, like others on the Great Plains, they lacked rainfall and timber. Early settlers grubbed roots for firewood and hauled water in barrels. One young housewife who spilled a bucket climbing down from a water wagon was heard to exclaim, "Oh God, how I hate a country where you have to climb for water and dig for wood."

The farmers constructed houses from prairie sod which were warm in winter, cool in summer, fireproof, and capable of lasting about six years. Sod houses also attracted rodents and rattlesnakes and fell apart in rainstorms. Farmers cleared the brush in a circle around their homesteads, a practice which gave them the nickname of "nester" from the derisive cowboys. Since there was little wood to burn, the early sodbusters used hay, cornstalks, roots, buffalo dung, and cow chips. A passing trail herd could well leave behind a winter's fuel supply, but there was no way to keep a determined longhorn out of a cornfield.

Photo made at the Burke Ranch in La Salle County, 1888. John R. Baylor and little daughter (later Mrs. Jim Bell) at left; Jack Baylor (young boy) at right. Western History Collections, University of Oklahoma Library.

Public school under a brush arbor, Live Oak County, 1887. Photo by Brack. Western History Collections, University of Oklahoma Library.

There were other problems—drought, grasshoppers, prairie fires, and blizzards. In 1874 grasshoppers chewed a barren swath from the Dakotas to Texas, and then returned in the two years following to eat what was left over. This was a warning to farmers about the periodic plagues of grasshoppers, which would bring whirring disaster upon them until the development of insecticides during World War II. The Great Plains was the most difficult section of North America for farmers to subdue— which explains why it was also the last. Only the windmill gave them a technology to hold on with; it produced enough water for family and stock. Mounted on squat towers, the olive-green Eclipse windmills, facing their fourteen-foot-diameter daisywheels defiantly into the wind, became symbols of hope and landmarks of settlement on the barren horizon.

With the occupation of the land, everyone began to fence—ranchers, farmers, townsfolk—in order to protect and proclaim their property. Joseph F. Glidden, an Illinois farmer, invented a popular form of barbed wire in 1874 and mass-produced it two years later. This was the answer for fencing in a treeless country. In 1879 Charles Goodnight rescued some harmless Pueblo Indians from a group of newcomers who thought that they were Comanches. The Pueblos had gone to trade with Kiowas and had tried to take a shortcut back to New Mexico when they were captured. Goodnight said to the chief, "You surely know the way back to Taos. Haven't you lived in this country all your life?"

Along with barbed wire, the wind-mill made possible the settlement of West Texas. Photograph by David G. McComb.

"Alambre! Alambre! Alambre! todos partes," the chief answered. "Wire! Wire! Wire! everywhere."

The large ranchers strung the wire across their pastures. The XIT in the Panhandle, for instance, put up six thousand miles of barbed wire, and the nesters fenced off their grain fields. They tended to cut one another off. Fences sometimes blocked roads and schools and interfered with mail delivery. People fenced public lands and sometimes boxed in another ranch or farm. Sheep could not get through to new pasture and cattle could not get through to water. As a result, everyone cut fences and trespassed.

Headlines in 1883 proclaimed a range war in which fence-cutting incidents occurred in half of the counties in Texas. The "war" was exacerbated by drought and the frustration of landless cattle owners who wanted the continued largess of a free and open range. But it also amounted to the illegal destruction of private property. Nipping became indiscriminate and was often done secretly at night by armed groups calling themselves Owls, Javelinas, or Blue Devils. They threatened fencers and burned pastures. Three people died, and damage was estimated at $20 million.

Governor John Ireland finally called a special session of the legislature. The lawmakers made it a felony to cut a fence and a misdemeanor to put up an illegal one. Ranchers who built across a public road, moreover, had to place gates every three miles and keep them in good repair. Following this and investigations by Texas Rangers, the fencing war subsided. It was a prelude to disaster, however, and evidence of the end of an era.

All over the West during the severe winters of 1884–1885, 1885–1886, and 1886–1887 cattle died by the thousands. It was estimated that on the southern ranges in 1885–1886 about 85 percent of the cattle died by freezing or starvation. Drifting with the storms, their tails to the wind, the cattle walked up to the fence lines, ate the remaining grass, waited, and died. The bodies stacked up, and other cows walked over the fences on the bodies to drift on to the next barrier. The "die-up" took the heart out of the cattle industry. Investors became much more cautious. The cattle trails were closed, and there were no more long drives. The Indians were on reservations, and the cowboys were ranch hands. The land was under private ownership. It was over. The Texas frontier was gone.

County government, an instrument of civilization, followed the settlers westward. Political organization reached the Panhandle and Big Bend in the 1880s, and by 1900 only 24 of the 254 Texas counties were yet unformed. At the same time perceptions changed about the role of the farmer. The myth in Texas, like that elsewhere in the nation, was that all persons depended upon the farmer because it was the farmer who fed them. The myth also held that people of the soil were self-sufficient and needed few others. In 1870 farmers lived the myth and by and large worked to produce what their families needed with perhaps a sale of surplus corn to raise enough cash to pay for the few items not manufactured at home. It was considered a virtue to live in such a manner. In 1878 W. W. Lang, the leader of the Texas Grange, damned the cities as "plague centers of the social system" where "depravity finds friendship."

By 1900 the foundation of the myth had crumbled because farmers had shifted to a position of greater dependence and production for larger cash sales. The railroads gave the agriculturalists this chance for a better living standard through access to city markets. In 1870 Texas farmers hand-planted one million acres of corn, which was the leading grain crop. In 1900, using mechanical devices, farmers sowed five million acres. The production of other grain crops—oats, sorghums, wheat, rice—reveals a similar pattern, but the most important commercial crop was still cotton.

Cotton was fairly resistant to drought, did not deplete the soil excessively, was adaptable to mechanization, and returned the best cash reward. Cotton advanced from

Barbed Wire

Fencing commenced in Texas with rocks and rails, and then osage orange (bois d'arc), briars, cactus, and smooth wire. None worked well in a dry land of prairie and longhorns. "Thorny fence" first appeared in 1867, and there were many experiments—401 patents and 1,600 variations. Joseph F. Glidden of Illinois, however, in 1876 began to mass-produce a practical double-strand barbed wire which became the wire that fenced the West. Texas ranchers were skeptical that it could stop their cattle, but the twenty-one-year-old salesman for Glidden, John W. Gates, built a corral with the wire in San Antonio's Military Plaza and issued a challenge: "This fence is the finest in the world, light as air, stronger than whiskey, cheaper than dirt, and all steel and miles long. The cattle ain't born that can get through it. Bring on your most ferocious steers, gentlemen, and see how this barbed wire corral will hold them."

The local ranchers herded in some twenty-five or more ornery longhorns and waited. The steers charged the fence once and then became satisfied to bellow defiance from the center of the enclosure. Glidden sold 5 tons of wire in Texas in 1874, 40,000 tons in 1880, and 200,000 in 1900.

Cotton picking near Terrell, Texas, 1941. Reproduced from the holdings of the Texas State Archives.

Cotton being hauled to market.
Barker Texas History Center, The
University of Texas at Austin.

351,000 bales in 1870 to 2,500,000 bales in 1890, and after 1880 the state led all others in production. Cotton gins, compresses, and oil mills for the seeds followed the railroads inland to the fields. It was the great money crop of Texas, and in terms of people employed, cotton was the state's most important product. Mechanical planters, stalk cutters, and walking cultivators came into use in the 1880s, but hand picking remained common into the 1950s.

Texas farmers planted as early as possible and started harvesting in July, if they could, to avoid damage by the boll weevil, an insect pest that had arrived in 1892 from Mexico. Dragging eight-foot sacks which would hold twenty-five pounds of cotton, the pickers, often families, worked their way through a field. Diligent laborers could harvest 250 pounds per day, but it was.hard work. Their backs would ache from bending over the twenty-inch-high plants, and people would try crawling on knee pads. The only relief came at lunchtime or when a sack was weighed and emptied into the cotton wagon. Perspiration left white lines of salt on shirts and blouses, but the work was hardest on the hands. As a retired engineer in Beau-

mont recalled from his youth, "You got up in the dark, ate your breakfast and got to the field by daylight. The cotton could be wet with a chilly dew, which could wet your clothes, but worst of all it softened your fingers so the sharp point on the cotton burrs pricked your fingers until they might bleed, but you kept on picking. In a little while the sun would come up and drive the dew away. Then the burr points would get sharper, but you kept on picking."

The shift to commercial agriculture brought dependence upon national markets, capitalization, and vulnerability to business cycles. The independence of the farmer became only a cruel illusion as the connective strands of interdependence with the greater United States and its cities tightened. Before the Civil War the richest people in Texas were planters and farmers. After the war they were merchants and bankers. During the depression of the 1870s across the nation, including Texas, there arose a full-throated rural protest against the hardship of the new order. It was also a cry of social despair.

Oliver H. Kelley, a federal employee, on a tour of the South noticed the distress and organized the Patrons of

Dock workers loading cotton, Galveston. Cotton was shipped from Galveston to mills in the eastern United States or Europe. Rosenberg Library, Galveston.

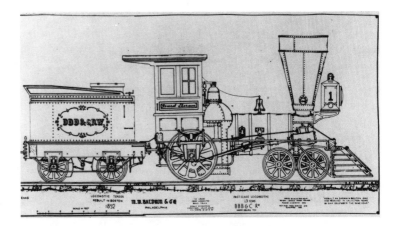

The railroads provided the necessary transportation link between the cities. Drawing shows the first engine in Texas, the *General Sherman*, 1852. Barker Texas History Center, The University of Texas at Austin.

Husbandry in 1867. The Grange, as it was commonly called, reached Texas in 1873 and organized fairs, social events, lectures, experimental farms, cooperative stores, and a program to regulate transportation facilities. It reached its peak of 40,000 members in 1876, when the Texas Constitution was rewritten, but then declined to 473 members in 1904. It failed because it promoted the myth of the self-sufficient farm while the economic truth led toward commercial agriculture.

Lewis Chavose and John R. Allen were more realistic when they organized the Texas Farmers' Alliance in 1877. They had been inspired by S. O. Dawes, a traveling lecturer, who attacked monopolies and middlemen and discussed political solutions. In the mid-1880s, as the Grange collapsed, 200,000 farmers joined the new organization. Internal divisions and the failure of an Alliance cotton exchange, however, shifted the disillusioned members into third-party politics. Disgruntled farmers became the backbone of the state's Populist Party (officially known as the People's Party), which participated in state elections from 1892 to 1904.

The party—advocating transportation regulation, an increase in the money supply, and protection from alien land purchasers among others items—gained only limited success and declined after the elections of 1896. This wandering of rural groups in the thickets of politics and business generally failed, but did serve to make farmers more politically aware and politicians more sensitive to farmers.

An example is the regulation of the state's railroads. The new railways were the key technological change that had disturbed the nature of farming and upset the rural-urban balance. At the time of the Civil War, Houston was the rail center of Texas with lines stretching 50 to 100 miles in five directions. In 1870 the state possessed 583 miles of track; in 1900 there were 10,000 miles. Texas granted over 700 charters and by 1904 had more trackage than any other state. In general, the railways built from the Gulf of Mexico northward in imitation of the earlier trade routes from the coast, or from east and west, which was the result of the national effort to construct transcontinental lines.

The Houston & Texas Central, using the first Chinese laborers in Texas, connected with the Missouri, Kansas and Texas at Denison in 1873. After the conversion to standard gauge in 1876 a boxcar could roll all the way from New York City, through St. Louis, Denison, and Houston, to the Port of Galveston. The Texas & Pacific Railroad, meanwhile, built from Texarkana to Eagle Ford near Dallas; paused to reorganize during the depression of 1873–1876; moved on to Fort Worth; and in 1880–1881 reached Sierra Blanca, ninety-two miles east of El Paso, where it joined the Southern Pacific from California. Branches filled in a spiderweb of railroads across the state—Austin welcomed its first line in 1871, San Antonio in 1877, Abilene in 1880, and Amarillo in 1887. Both Abilene and Amarillo got their start as railroad boom towns.

The continuing importance of the railroads is shown by this view of rails with the modern Dallas skyline in the background. Photograph by David G. McComb.

James Stephen Hogg

James Stephen Hogg was known as "the People's Governor" during his terms from 1891 to 1895 because he was the first governor born in Texas and because he championed some Populist issues, most notably the control of railroads and support of higher education. At six feet and three inches, with a weight that varied between 250 and 275 pounds, he was also one of Texas' largest governors, a fact witnessed today by his extra-wide desk chair preserved at the Barker Texas History Center in Austin. He and his wife, Sarah Ann Stinson, had four children—Will, Ima, Mike, and Tom. His daughter was named for a heroine in his brother's epic, *The Fate of Marvin* (1873), and contrary to popular jokes there were no siblings named Ura, Heza, and Sheza.

Following his work as governor, Hogg became involved in the oil business and amassed a fortune. Mike and Will became principals in the development of River Oaks, a wealthy suburb of Houston, and "Miss Ima," as she was affectionately known in Texas, became the grande dame of fine arts in Houston.

Governor James S. Hogg. Barker Texas History Center, The University of Texas at Austin.

A love-hate relationship developed between Texans and their railways. Immigrants used them to move westward, and the lines became involved in colonizing efforts in order to sell their land subsidies. Farmers and ranchers used them to move products to market and to receive supplies. At the same time the railroads were a symbol of desirable modernity and unwanted change. They were highly visible and audible, and thus a target for frustration. The HE & WT (Houston East and West Texas Railway) was nicknamed "Hell Either Way Taken," and the I & GN (International and Great Northern) was called "Insignificant and Good for Nothing." People spoke about "railroad abuses" while clamoring for more service.

Through the influence of the Grange, representatives at the constitutional convention in 1876 inserted all sorts of railroad regulations, including one that required railways to have an office in the state. This forced the interstate carriers to set up redundant bureaus. The Missouri, Kansas & Texas, for instance, duplicated its St. Louis headquarters in Dallas. The demands for rate regulation, furthermore, gave James S. Hogg a victory in the governor's race of 1890.

In 1891 Hogg established the Texas Railroad Commission and persuaded John H. Reagan to resign from the U.S. Senate to become its chairman. Hogg won election again in 1892 and with the support of Populists expanded the power of the commission to oversee the sale of railroad stocks and bonds. In 1894 the U.S. Supreme Court upheld the constitutionality of the commission, and in 1899 the legislature made rebates illegal. In defending the work of the commission Reagan claimed that lower cotton rates had saved farmers $800,000 in 1897.

In this latter part of the nineteenth century, farming and ranching fueled the economy and set the tone of politics. Industry played only a small role. As in other Southern states, non-agricultural production increased, but did not keep pace with that in the northeastern United States. Flour milling was the leading industry in Texas in 1870, but in 1900 it slipped to third place behind lumbering and cottonseed milling, two industries closely related to agriculture.

Lumberjacks entered the pine forests of East Texas in 1870 and sent their logs floating down the Sabine and Neches rivers to sawmills in Beaumont and Orange. At first coastal steamers carried the lumber to the port towns for transshipment, but the expanding railroad network provided lower shipping costs and opened up a market on

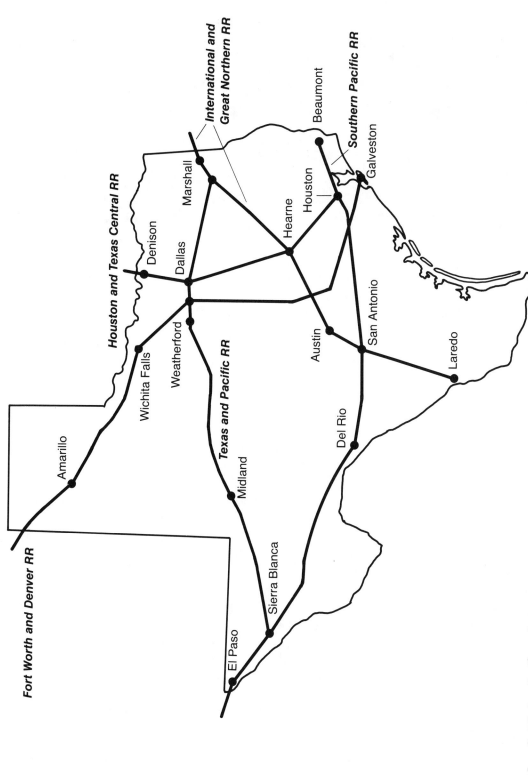

Map 3. Major Railroads in Texas

Judge Roy Bean's saloon and court, Langtry, Texas, about 1900. Judge Bean is shown holding court. Photo by the Lippe Studio, Del Rio. Barker Texas History Center, The University of Texas at Austin.

the treeless plains of West Texas. From 1875 to 1900 lumber products provided the leading tonnage on the railroads.

Large organizations included the Kirby Lumber Company, the first multimillion-dollar industrial firm in the state, which produced 400 million board feet per year. Its president, John Henry Kirby, born in Tyler County, was a lawyer who had worked in the lumbering trade. He bought lands during the depression years of the 1890s and built his first sawmill in 1896. In 1901 he formed Kirby Lumber Company, which at its peak of activity, 1910–1920, employed 16,500 people. It was said that the sun did not rise in East Texas until tall, robust John Henry Kirby rolled over in bed, stretched, and opened his eyes. During the 1920s, however, the industry and Kirby along with it declined sharply due to the exhaustion of the forests. It did not recover until the establishment of a second growth of trees a generation later.

What Kirby accomplished and what various cotton factors such as Anderson, Clayton and Company did was to carry a raw material to a semifinished level—cut lumber or compressed cotton. In the process of industrialization an economy has to mature from this colonial situation of exporting raw materials and importing finished goods to a reversed condition of using raw materials to produce finished products that are sold elsewhere. In 1900 only 1.6 percent of the workers were involved in industry. Texas, like the South, got stuck in the intermediate stage of semifinished production. So it was with cotton, lumber, beef, and later petroleum.

There were some unsuccessful attempts at industrialization. The Galveston Cotton Mill, for example, began producing cloth in 1889. It employed 550 people, mainly women and children, and consumed thirty to thirty-five bales of cotton per day. The women labored sixty-six hours per week and earned ninety cents per day. The mill, however, was unable to compete with larger textile makers and closed before the turn of the century.

As might be expected with such a slight manufacturing effort and the bulk of the population living in the countryside, there was comparatively little union activity. There existed a few interesting and successful unions, however, such as the Screwmen's Benevolent Association, from 1866 to 1924, in Galveston. Screwmen worked with two-hundred-pound jackscrews in five-man gangs to compress cotton bales against a ship's bulkhead. It took extra days to screw a transport, but the vessel could then carry 15 percent more cotton and return a 4 percent greater profit.

Because of their skill, strength, and usefulness, the screwmen became the elite laborers of the docks. Their union formed a closed shop for whites and demanded the highest wages. Rival blacks formed their own group, the Cotton Jammer's Association, in the 1880s, but the advent of faster, larger steel ships and high-density compresses made screwmen obsolete. Both unions declined after 1910.

Although only 17 percent of the Texans of 1900 lived in the cities, urbanization was going on at a rate faster than the growth in total population. All over the United States there was a massive shift from the countryside into the urban areas, and even though Texas and the more recently settled West lagged in this movement, the state followed the same pathway. The future was to be found in the cities.

In 1870 the top six towns were Galveston (14,000 people), San Antonio (12,000), Houston (9,000), Brownsville (5,000), Austin (4,000), and Jefferson (4,000). Galveston, on the island, was the state's main port, and Houston served as its transshipment point into the interior. The Bayou City was the place where water-borne transport changed to land-borne transport—steamboat to oxcart or railroad. San Antonio served the cattle industry of the Southwest, and Brownsville, which had begun as a fort in the War with Mexico, had profited as a shipping point for contraband cotton during the Civil War. When the rail-

Judge Roy Bean

At the turn of the century at Langtry, a small oasis on the Southern Pacific route between San Antonio and El Paso, Judge Roy Bean administered the "Law West of the Pecos." He had been appointed justice of the peace in 1882 to help the Texas Rangers clean up the railroad towns, and he ran his court in tyrannical fashion. When confronted with a corpse possessing forty dollars and a pistol, Bean fined the dead man forty dollars for carrying a concealed weapon and put the money in his own pocket.

Between sessions Bean sold beer from a one-room shack, sported a sombrero, and greeted the passing trains. He was ignorant, opinionated, crude, and untidy with a large gut overhanging his belt. Yet he sustained an enduring platonic love for Lily Langtry, a beautiful actress of the day. He longed to meet her, but died in 1903, ten months before she was able to visit her namesake town to meet the old man.

Lily Langtry, popular stage performer for whom Judge Roy Bean had an unrequited love. Western History Collections, University of Oklahoma Library.

ways built westward, Brownsville became a gateway into Mexico. Austin had an assured future as the state capital, but Jefferson was destined for failure.

Named for Thomas Jefferson, the East Texas town started in 1836 on the banks of Big Cypress Creek, which fed into Caddo Lake and the Red River. The merchants enjoyed deep water, and the large steamboats from St. Louis and New Orleans brought success to their wharves. During the Civil War Jeffersonians manufactured boots and canned meat. The town established the first brewery in the state, but it all came to nothing. In 1873 U.S. engineers used nitroglycerine to blast the Red River raft, a longtime damming log obstruction. The raft fell apart, the land drained, Caddo Lake dropped, and Jefferson was left high and dry. The town's business also evaporated, and Jefferson, thus dehydrated, remained a small town into the present time.

In 1900 the top five cities in Texas were San Antonio (53,000), Houston (45,000), Dallas (43,000), Galveston (38,000), and Fort Worth (27,000). San Antonio continued to supply the Southwest, added railroads, and developed a modern military establishment. The U.S. Army completed the first segment of Fort Sam Houston in 1879, and by 1900 the post was the largest in the nation. Teddy Roosevelt rounded up his Rough Riders at San Antonio in preparation for his charge up San Juan Hill during the Spanish-American War at the end of the century.

Houston grew because of its railroads, its small-scale manufacturing, and its use of barges to bypass the Port of Galveston. The merchants transferred cotton and other items directly to blue-water ships anchored outside Galveston Harbor in Bolivar Roads and thus avoided the wharfage fees. Railways provided the inspiration for the growth of Dallas and Fort Worth. Dallas citizens provided $200,000 in bonds, 142 acres, and $5,000 in cash to entice the rail magnates. It worked. In 1872 the Houston & Texas Central arrived from the Bayou City on its way to Denison, and the next year the Texas & Pacific stoked its first locomotive to within six blocks of the courthouse.

In those few years the population of Dallas leaped from 1,200 to 7,000, and in 1873 the town erected 725 buildings. Dallas was an "instant city." In 1875 the *Dallas Herald* commented, "With the exception of a few old residents, the great body of our people are strangers to one another." This was particularly remarkable since it was a depression time when even the Texas & Pacific went bankrupt.

A cotton compress, nonetheless, arrived in 1874, and in that year Dallas sent 5,700 bales to the east and north, and only 350 to Galveston. The railroad shifted the business direction. As the Kansas City *Journal of Commerce* explained, "While the back door, so to speak, was closed, the trade was all forced to the Gulf to reach the markets of the world, and the interior was supplied from the same ports—cotton went to market that way, and bacon, flour and goods came in that way, for all the state." The Texas & Pacific opened the back door, and North Texas found it cheaper to deal with St. Louis and Kansas City. This explains also why Dallas, even today, has a tendency to look northeastward for orientation.

After reorganization the Texas & Pacific moved on to Fort Worth, where the eager citizens volunteered to help lay track. The same jump in activity occurred, and the population increased from 500 to over 6,000. Fort Worth had begun as a village and army post in 1849, named for Brigadier General William J. Worth, a soldier of the War with Mexico. It had become a county seat in 1856 while still quite small, but with the arrival of the railroad the town built stockyards to attract the passing herds of cattle. Fort Worth became the first Texas cow town, and for that reason, in contrast to its North Texas neighbor, Fort Worth has a tendency to look westward.

Galveston, meanwhile, had slipped. The port lay at the terminus of the south-north rail development, which had lost to the east-west thrust of the transcontinental lines.

Military Plaza, San Antonio. Barker Texas History Center, The University of Texas at Austin.

Damage from the Galveston storm, 1900. Rosenberg Library, Galveston.

Still, it held a ranking in 1900 as the leading cotton port of the nation. This was accomplished by persuading the U.S. Congress to appropriate funds for harbor improvement. So much for vaunted self-reliance. Army engineers dredged the harbor and built two stone jetties to direct the current to scour the channel. In 1896 Galveston possessed a deep-water port that could handle the largest cargo ships in the world.

In early September 1900, however, the Island City suffered the worst loss of life due to a natural disaster in the history of the United States. A West Indian hurricane swept over the island and killed six thousand people. This helped to blunt the city's future development. For survival its citizens had to devote their energy to building defenses against the ravages of the sea. They thus missed the benefits of the oil bonanza that swept the state in the first part of the twentieth century.

In spite of the myth that cities were evil, corrupting, and dangerous, in Texas they became the focal points for information, business, entertainment, and inspiration. As

Texas farmers and ranchers moved into commercial production, they became dependent upon city facilities for transportation and service. Financing, for example, came from the credit offered by city banks and merchants. Citizens had long held an aversion for banks—a characteristic of westerners since the time of Andrew Jackson—and state banks had been regularly prohibited with a few exceptions until 1869. Briefly, until the rewriting of the Constitution in 1876, they were allowed. Then, new institutions were not permitted until the establishment of the state banking system in 1904. Private banks, factors, national banks, and those banks in existence, therefore, had to carry the financial load into the next century. It was a crippling situation for a necessary business function and a hindrance for efforts at manufacturing and commercial farming.

There is a theory that for a society to thrive it must have access to ideas and the intelligence to understand them. It has to be "open." The cities and towns in Texas provided this transmission of information and took the major role of explanation so that the ideas could be understood. It was done through transportation and communication facilities, and through the educational and cultural institutions. The Republic of Texas set up a postal system and routes in 1835 before independence—it cost twenty-five cents to send a letter two hundred miles. From the beginning, newspapers flourished like weeds in Texas drainage ditches. Between 1813 and 1846 eighty-six titles appeared, but few of them lived more than a few seasons. Of lasting significance were those in the larger cities.

The *Galveston Daily News* started in 1842 and became the oldest existing newspaper in the state. Alfred H. Belo,

Galveston Hurricane of 1900

The resident climatologist Isaac M. Cline knew from the reports of the Weather Service and the long swells breaking on the beach that trouble was on the way. On September 8 he warned people living near the Gulf side of Galveston to move to higher ground and sent his brother to telephone for aid from Houston as the dreaded red and black tandem hurricane flags were sent whipping in the wind to the tops of the flagstaffs. The hurricane broke that night over the island, destroyed about one-third of the city, piled up a long line of wreckage, and killed an estimated six-thousand people, including Cline's wife. Another five thousand people died on the mainland. The 1900 hurricane is considered the worst natural disaster in the history of the United States.

The city faced enormous tasks of rebuilding, disposing of the dead, and designing protection for the future. With admirable courage Galvestonians built a seawall, raised the grade level of the city, and constructed an all-weather causeway to the mainland. This was done while pioneering the commission form of municipal government. Their efforts succeeded, but the city spent its patrimony for defenses against the sea while the rest of Texas exploited the oil bonanza.

The Galveston seawall in 1915. Rosenberg Library, Galveston.

Commission Government

During the recovery from the hurricane of 1900, Galveston civic leaders fashioned a new form of city government whereby the governor appointed a mayor and four commissioners. Each commissioner was responsible for a particular function—finance, police and fire, water and sewers, streets, and public improvements. The plan was patently undemocratic, and the Texas Supreme Court forced a modification to require the election of the officers. In Galveston the plan was put into effect one year after the storm and lasted until 1960.

The commission form became widely popular with progressives before World War I, but was found to be inefficient. Commissioners combined executive and legislative authority within their own spheres and often failed to cooperate. In the 1920s and afterward the city-manager plan became popular and by and large replaced the commission form.

who bought a part of the paper after the Civil War and took it over completely in 1875, started an affiliate, the *Dallas Morning News*, in 1885. The *San Antonio Express* began in 1865, the *Austin Statesman* in 1871, the *Houston Post* in 1880, and the *San Antonio Light* in 1881. These early newspapers and dozens of others that proved of shorter lifespan often expressed the personal views of the editor. Yet even with that bias they provided a daily diary of news for the community. Their business was the dissemination and gathering of information, and they worked hard at their task.

The telegraph line which the Texas and Red River Telegraph Company strung through the treetops in 1854 brought instant news items to the editors—much quicker than the deliveries of mail and other newspapers from which they copied stories. A second company, the Texas and New Orleans Telegraph Company, strung wires to Galveston, San Antonio, Austin, and New Orleans. Western Union began in 1866, and by 1870 there were 1,500 miles of live wire in Texas. By 1876 wires interconnected the frontier military posts, and telegraph poles measuring the progress of transcontinental railroads marched across the dry expanse of West Texas. The *Galveston Daily News* was the first paper to capitalize on the technology, leasing a wire to Dallas in 1885 when Belo set up his affiliate paper. Articles headed "By telegraphic intelligence" appeared after the availability of this invention. Texas thus tapped into the thought of the world.

The telephone improved the situation. It could be used without the knowledge of Morse code and specialized personnel. All you had to do was talk, and most Texans were good at that. Colonel Belo visited the Philadelphia Centennial, where Alexander Graham Bell demonstrated his new device, and two years later, in 1878, Belo strung a telephone line between his home in Galveston and his newspaper office. Others liked the novelty, so a Galveston exchange began operating in 1879. Houston established a telephone system in the same year, followed by Dallas and San Antonio in 1881, Lubbock in 1902.

Intercity links began with a double-copper circuit between Houston and Galveston in 1893, and the first conversation involved the weather. To the common question about conditions in Houston, the Galveston reporter received a common answer: "Horrid and warm." By the end of the century long distance lines stretched from Texas towns to St. Louis, Kansas City, and Chicago. Even the sprawling XIT Ranch of West Texas strung phone lines as the top strand of its barbed wire fences. The world, to be sure, had become much smaller.

It is one thing to transmit ideas over a charged wire, on the pages of a letter, or through a newspaper; it is another to be understood on the other end. Communication requires educated people, and this was the main job of libraries and schools. For the most part, before the Civil War schools and libraries were private affairs. An exception was the Texas State Library, which the congress of the republic authorized in 1839. Its early history was one of sporadic appropriations, acquisitions, and care. It was of little matter, however, because the contents burned in the fire that destroyed the capitol in 1881.

Following that, the efforts of the State Library, like those of public libraries in cities, did not become consequential until after the turn of the century. In the first decade, inspired by the work of Andrew Carnegie, the state began an outreach program, the Texas Library Association formed, and most of the major cities started their own public libraries.

Austin, 1876, looking up Congress Avenue to the capitol. Barker Texas History Center, The University of Texas at Austin.

Main Street, Dallas, at the turn of the century. Barker Texas History Center, The University of Texas at Austin.

Of fundamental importance was the founding of public schools. When the Radical Republicans came to power during Reconstruction, they started a centralized secondary and elementary system supported by taxes and compulsory attendance. They continued and encouraged the black schools established by the Freedmen's Bureau, but did not challenge the segregation of races. People objected to the taxes, argued that age six was too young for school, and complained that older children were needed for work around the farms. When the Radicals lost power, consequently, the system was thrown out as part of the Reconstruction bath water.

The Constitution of 1876 left education to the counties, but this did not work and results were uneven. In 1884, therefore, the legislature reinstituted the Radical system with an elected superintendent and supporting revenues. Through the end of the century elementary and secondary education improved. The black schools, although assigned the worst buildings and teachers, managed nonetheless to lower the black illiteracy rate from 75 to under 40 percent.

There existed a longer-standing concern about higher education. The enactment locating the seat of government in 1839 included provision for a university, and a subsequent bill allocated fifty leagues of land to support two colleges. Nothing, however, was done, and in 1858 the legislature gave additional land plus $100,000 in U.S. bonds from the $5 million gained in the Compromise of 1850. The Civil War submerged matters, but the idea of a state university resurfaced in the Constitution of 1866.

To take advantage of the Morrill Act, which provided federal support for agricultural colleges, the legislature at last created Texas Agricultural and Mechanical College in 1871. The purpose was to provide a practical, low-cost education for white males. It opened with forty students in 1876 on a 2,400-acre rural site in Brazos County near Bryan. The school almost lost a student when a pack of wolves attacked the young man in daytime in sight of the main building. A similar institution for blacks under the auspices of Texas A&M and without the wild beasts opened in 1885 at Prairie View.

The Constitution of 1876 required the establishment of a university "of the first class," with a location designated by vote of the people. This time the state was serious, and a small, forbidding man with a prickly temper aided in bringing the thought to reality. Ashbel Smith, born in Connecticut, had studied medicine at Yale and Paris, and he arrived in Texas shortly after the revolution. He served Texas in various capacities, acquired a large plantation on Galveston Bay, and collected a four-thousand-volume library. At the point of decision about the University of Texas, Smith was designated a trustee.

Various towns competed for the site of the school—Austin and Tyler wanted everything, whereas Houston and Galveston wanted the medical branch and threatened to support Tyler unless Austin cooperated. Smith, who was also president of the Texas State Medical Association, argued that Galveston deserved the medical school because it provided a greater diversity of disease. He won. In the plebiscite the people designated Galveston for the medical branch and Austin for the main campus.

The city placed the university on College Hill, a forty-acre tract set aside at the same time as the capitol site. Classes began in 1883. For its financial support the constitution provided one million acres of West Texas land, to which the legislature added another million in 1883. The politicians also set aside a million acres to establish a permanent fund for secondary and elementary schools.

This land was not much better than nothing. It was among the last remnants of the public domain, was considered nearly worthless, and had been rejected by the Texas & Pacific. Ashbel Smith, the president of the Board of Regents, nevertheless pronounced dramatically at the laying of the cornerstone of the first building in 1882, "Smite the rocks with the rod of knowledge and fountains of unstinted wealth will gush forth." In 1923 wildcat prospectors discovered oil on the university lands.

Other, private institutions of higher education, many reflecting a religious bias, could be found around the state—Southwestern (established in 1840), Baylor (1845), Trinity (1869), Texas Christian (1873), and Hardin-Simmons (1891). Altogether, these schools and libraries, private and public, provided the foundation of knowledge necessary for the advancement of society. They made possible minds that were open to fresh ideas, and people who could understand news received "By telegraphic intelligence." They preserved and passed on the heritage of western civilization.

The educational institutions flourished in the towns and cities, and by necessity urban Texas also set the example for improvements in water supply, sewerage, street lighting, pavement, public health, fire and crime control, and local transportation. Population increases, especially at the rate of Dallas or Fort Worth, exacerbated those issues. Most important was water. No city in history has survived without a pure and adequate water supply. It is necessary not only for drinking, but also for fire fighting, cleaning, industry, and sewerage.

In Galveston, surrounded by undrinkable seawater, people caught rain in cisterns for drinking. For fires they built a saltwater system of hydrants in 1884. Nevertheless, an out-of-control nighttime conflagration in 1885 cut a charred swath through the heart of the city and destroyed forty-two blocks of homes and business offices. Sparks swirled overhead on twisting wind currents and landed on wooden shingles while thousands of seabirds soared high above with their wings illuminated by the red glow. Every major city has a history of fires. Underwriters in Galveston, however, raised their rates and forced the city to develop a better system of water supply. This was accomplished by drilling for artesian water on the mainland and pumping the fresh water to the island through a pipe.

In Houston both fire and disease forced a quest for pure water. The city drew its drinking water from Buffalo Bayou and dumped its raw sewage from toilets and slaughter-houses into the same source. In the 1890s, while the "germ theory of disease" was becoming popular, Houstonians complained of "bowel" trouble, offensive odors, and eels in the pipes. This problem was solved by drilling artesian wells, something Dallas did at the same time.

Houston still had a sewage problem, however, and army engineers told the city it would have to clean up before it could receive money for dredging the bayou for shipping purposes. The city responded by building one of the most advanced disposal systems in the world. Alexander Potter, a consulting engineer, designed a method to collect the sewage from around the city, pump it to a station, and then filter it through rough stone, gravel, sand, and coke. The final effluent flowed back into the bayou, and at the opening of the installation in 1902 Potter bragged about its purity. To answer jests about his claim Potter scooped up some effluent, drank it, and pronounced it palatable. No one challenged him, and Houston got its funding for deepening the bayou.

It was in this same period in the latter part of the century that Texas cities eliminated pigs as city scavengers and began to use dumps. It was part of the effort to clean up and pave the streets. In 1882 a writer described Houston as "a huddle of houses arranged on unoccupied lines

Austin, 1888, looking up Congress Avenue to the new capitol. Barker Texas History Center, The University of Texas at Austin.

Capitol dome. Photograph by
David G. McComb.

of black mud." Its streets, like those of Dallas, were notorious as being bottomless mud holes in wet weather
and dust bins in dry times. In the 1880s and into the next
century Houston and Dallas experimented with planks,
bricks, gravel, bois d'arc blocks, macadam, and asphalt. In
Galveston the problem was sand, and there the city tried
pavements of oyster shells and wooden blocks covered
with tar. The blocks were easy on horses' hooves and
quiet compared with brick, but they floated away like
corks during hard rains and floods. Outside the cities, the
roads remained dirt pathways.

City dwellers, particularly in the business section, provided sidewalks of planks or brick at their own expense.
The places were still "walking cities," where traffic moved
on foot, horseback, or animal-drawn wagons. With the ex-

ample of the railroad it was only a short while before en-
trepreneurs provided rail cars pulled by mules along tracks
for urban transportation. Houston had mule cars in 1868,
Fort Worth in 1876, and San Antonio in 1878. They were
no faster than walking, but did provide a certain entertainment. In Houston a mule slipped on a curve, fell, and
ended up on its back underneath the car. The driver
thought it was dead until the mule kicked its way through
the floorboards and stood up. The remainder of the night
was spent trying to figure out how to get the mule out of
the car.

Electric trolleys appeared on city streets during the late
1880s and early 1890s. They spluttered and sparked on
wet days, but they were much faster and permitted an expansion of the urban boundaries into streetcar suburbs.
Electric lighting, too, changed the nature of Texas cities
and placed them even farther from the realm of rural existence. In 1882 the Brush Electric Company demonstrated
a string of arc lights in downtown Galveston, making the
streets "light as day." The same thing happened in Dallas,
and two years later in Houston a crowd cheered as five
lights sputtered to life on Main Street.

In 1894–1895 the Fort Wayne Electric Company from
Indiana built a series of thirty-one towers, 165 feet high,
to provide Austin with artificial "moonlight." Each arc-
light tower provided a three-thousand-foot-diameter circle
of blue-white light strong enough to read a pocket watch
by. The lights, however, needed daily attention. Electric
lighting also began to appear in businesses, and with all of
the wires—lighting, trolley, telephone, telegraph—the
sky over Texas city streets became a geometric silhouette
of crisscrossing black lines intersecting at sharp angles.

Segregation of the races, which was a part of Texas life
before the Civil War, remained afterward despite the
Emancipation Proclamation. Churches, schools, and oc-
cupations continued traditional separations. In addition,
following the war urban ghettos formed as residential segregation became the norm. In 1891 the legislature passed
the most famous of the state's "Jim Crow" laws, which
required separate coaches for all railroads. City ordinances in the last part of the nineteenth century and into
the early twentieth century prevented the mixing of races
on trolley cars and in parks. Galveston even segregated
the beaches.

Crime and vice were a part of Texas urban life from the
first, as rural Puritans warned, but by 1870 the wildness
of the frontier towns had been suppressed by police forces,

Elisabet Ney

Born in 1833 in Westphalia, Germany, Elisabet Ney grew up beautiful, talented, and strong-willed. She left home at nineteen to study art in Munich, secretly married a Scots medical student, Edmund Montgomery, and continued to call herself "Miss Ney." Her charm and skill resulted in the production of busts and statues of George V of Hanover, Garibaldi, Bismarck, William I of Prussia, Schopenhauer, Humboldt, and others. Her relationship with Montgomery, whom she referred to simply as her best friend, even when she was pregnant, was seen as so irregular that she and her husband left Germany, first for Florida and then in 1872 to Texas, where they hoped to find German friends.

While living on a cotton plantation in Waller County, she reared her two sons and tried to uplift the neighboring blacks. She had trouble with both. Her two-year-old son died of diphtheria, and she personally cremated him in her own fireplace. Later she and her other son became estranged. For the Texas exhibit at the Chicago World's Fair in 1893 she carved the statues of Stephen F. Austin and Sam Houston which now stand in the capitols in Austin and Washington, D.C. She built a studio in Austin where she did her best work, a recumbent statue of Albert Sidney Johnston, which now lies in the state cemetery. Ney delighted in shocking people with her peculiar ways. She died in 1907, Texas' greatest sculptor.

city ordinances, and state law. Gambling and dueling were illegal, but saloons still flourished, and drunkenness, then as now, was the most common of urban crimes.

In 1894 the minister of the Shearn Methodist Church in Houston, George C. Rankin, toured the fleshpots and exposed them from the pulpit. Crowds packed the church from "vestibule to amen corner" to hear him describe the open gambling and the "hellish" variety theater where young men swilled beer and went straight to hell. The variety theater was, according to Rankin, a "sodomic institution" that offered lewd music and dances by notorious women. He claimed that five hundred prostitutes worked in the city and that many lived near the church. Despite his fulminations, there was no change.

Fort Worth had its "Hell's Half Acre" for the entertainment of cowboys, and Dallas did not neglect this enterprise. According to one story, a madam in the 1880s borrowed $5,000 from a banker and promised to repay it in October after the state fair. She reappeared in September before the fair, however, and paid the debt in full. The curious banker asked how she and her girls had managed that. "Ah well," she replied, "I forgot all about the preachers' convention in August."

Galveston, since it was a port city with heavy transient traffic, had the worst reputation for vice. Following the Civil War, with all of the federal soldiers in town, Galveston began to develop an infamous red-light district around Postoffice Street. There could be found the bawdy houses, saloons, and variety theaters. At such theaters, according to the police captain, women served beer and danced the cancan, and young men developed a taste for both. In contrast to the rest of Texas, however, Galvestonians adopted an easy tolerance for such activities.

On a higher plane the cities provided sources of inspiration. Christian churches common to the United States could be found in all the municipalities—Baptist, Methodist, Episcopal, Lutheran, Presbyterian, and others. The sermons of the various ministers served not only for moral instruction, but also as a type of exercise requiring thought, a sort of education.

The architecture of churches as well as that of other buildings also inspired people by its symbolic nature. There were models of enterprise—for example, the iron-front business building on the Strand in Galveston, a city nicknamed "the New York of Texas." There was also the castellated Waco suspension bridge, which used the same

innovative technology as the famous Brooklyn Bridge of New York, but at an earlier time.

Most important was the new capitol in Austin, a symbol of civic virtue and power. Fire had destroyed the old building in 1881, but the legislature had already appropriated three million acres of Panhandle land to finance the construction of a new statehouse. Elijah Myers, a Detroit architect, drew plans modeled after the capitol in Washington, D.C., and Mattheas Schnell of Chicago took the land, site unseen, in exchange for the construction. Schnell reassigned the contract to a group of Illinois financiers called the Capitol Syndicate, led by Abner Taylor.

The legislature allowed the use of convict labor and stonecutters from Scotland in order to suppress costs, causing problems with local unions. These difficulties were settled in the courts, and in 1888 the new building, made of Texas red granite with the Goddess of Liberty on top, opened. The syndicate used its land to establish the XIT Ranch, which covered parts of ten counties in the Panhandle. The idea was to use the land for ranching until it could be subdivided for farmers. The owners began disposing of the land in 1901 and sold the last of the cattle in 1912.

For entertainment and perhaps also for inspiration the cities offered theatrical performances even from their earliest days. From 1867 to the end of the century Henry Greenwall ran theaters in Galveston, Fort Worth, Dallas, and Houston. He imported troupes from the East and provided minstrels, operas, wizards, troubadours, and plays.

The Waco suspension bridge. Barker Texas History Center, The University of Texas at Austin.

Texas Leaguer

The baseball term "Texas Leaguer" refers to a ball hit just over the reach of the infielders and too close in for the outfielders to catch. It is usually good enough for the batter to reach first base safely. According to Harry M. Johnston, a longtime baseball fan who wrote to the *Houston Post* in 1904, a young man named Ollie Pickering arrived in Houston on a boxcar in 1888, tried out for the local team, and so impressed the coach that he played the same afternoon. He hit the ball seven times for seven times at bat, each one a quick pop just over the infield that dropped in front of the outfielders. This was the start of the Texas Leaguer, and supposedly Pickering went on to play for the Philadelphia Athletics.

Lily Langtry, Edwin Booth, Buffalo Bill, and Fay Templeton appeared on his stages.

In addition, the cities and towns became the centers for sports. Swimming and boating, bicycle riding and racing, tennis, horseracing, boxing, football, and baseball all flourished. Yankee soldiers playing on a field north of the Ursuline Convent in Galveston introduced baseball to Texas shortly after the Civil War. Men and boys quickly took up the game, and an intercity rivalry arose. After John J. McCloskey barnstormed through Texas with a professional team, the Texas League of Professional Baseball Clubs organized in Austin in 1887 to support regular competition. The Texas League was more of a sporting than a business venture and consequently suffered numerous reorganizations and shifting sponsorships. Yet in one form or another it has endured to the present time.

The essence of urban life in Texas was the same as elsewhere. The city provided a central place for economic, military, political, religious, and cultural activity. Sometimes the balance shifted—Austin was noted for politics and education, San Antonio for military affairs, Houston and Dallas for commerce—but all provided a variety and intensity which, in contrast, made country existence seem boring and sterile. The decisions of state life took place in the municipalities, and increasingly the economic strength of Texas shifted inside the city limits. Still, the countryside had one last surprise to offer the people of the Lone Star State.

Football game, Mitchell County, early twentieth century. Barker Texas History Center, The University of Texas at Austin.

5. Texas in Transit

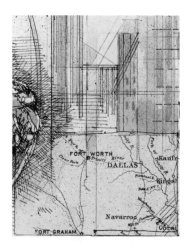

The single most important event in modern Texas history is the discovery of oil and the related global dependence on oil. During bygone geologic eras the sea advanced and retreated over Texas at least nine times. The results were vast sedimentary layers of sand, gravel, and decaying vegetable matter that formed pressurized pockets of petroleum. In Southeast Texas around Houston large plugs of rock salt punched upward through the sedimentary deposits, and into the fractures of stone along the sides of the plug seeped gas and oil. On the surface salt domes usually looked like small hills. These natural resources—salt, gas, oil, and sulphur—combined with the technology and ambition of the twentieth century to establish the economic foundation of the state.

In North America and Europe there was a growing demand for petroleum products to fuel the gasoline engines of the street, grease the machinery of the factory, and light the lanterns of the home. Oil was cheaper than coal. To evaporate 1,000 pounds of water a test in 1913 revealed a cost of thirty cents for coal and half that amount for fuel oil. As a consequence, Texas coal mining declined after that year. The presence of petroleum in the state had long been known. Seepage into the Gulf of Mexico created balls of tar that washed onto the beaches. Indians and early explorers such as de Soto used this natural asphalt for caulking pots and boats. Settlers used oil from springs for medicine, but the first well did not come until 1866.

At Melrose, near Nacogdoches, Lyne T. Barret used an auger clamped to a joint of pipe and rotated by a steam engine to drill 106 feet. He found oil, but this well and another the following year had little impact because of the poor market at the time. Other shallow wells produced oil in Brown and Hicks counties, but the first de-

At about 700 feet or a little over in, why the drilling mud commenced to boil up through the rotary, and it got higher and higher and higher up through the top of the derrick and with such pressure, why, the drill pipe commenced to move up. It moved up and started to going out through the top of the derrick. . . . It didn't last so awful long, but it died down very gradually. Well we three boys then sneaked back down to the well after it quieted down and surveyed the situation. . . . I walked over and looked down the hole there. I heard—sorta heard something kinda bubbling just a little bit and looked down there and here this frothy oil was starting up. But it was just breathing like, you know, coming up and sinking back with the gas pressure. And it kept coming up and over the rotary table and each flow a little higher. Finally it got—came up with such momentum that it just shot up clear through the top of the derrick.

ALLEN W. HAMILL AT THE
SPINDLETOP GUSHER,
JANUARY 10, 1901

The Spindletop oil well coming in as a gusher. Barker Texas History Center, The University of Texas at Austin.

velopment of consequence came in Corsicana in 1894. The city wanted artesian water, and the driller became annoyed when oil seeped into his well at 1,030 feet. He had to go on to 2,470 feet to find the water. A modest oil field of 350 wells developed by 1900 with a production of 836,000 barrels per year.

The early prospectors were individuals who risked drilling at places that looked as if they might produce oil. It was a guessing game, but Anthony F. Lucas was an expert. He was born in Austria, received a military education, immigrated to the United States, married, and worked as a resident engineer in a salt mine in Louisiana. By the turn of the century Lucas probably knew more about salt domes than anyone in the country. He obtained a lease for land in 1899 on a dome near Beaumont known for oil seepages and after initial failure successfully brought in the Spindletop gusher in 1901. When tapped, the pool had so much pressure that it blew out the drilling apparatus and spouted half a million barrels over the countryside in the six days before it was capped.

Spindletop was spectacular. It took the headlines around the nation and changed the course of Texas history. Hereafter, the cotton patch placed second to the oil patch in the state economy. During the Spindletop year the state issued 491 oil company charters, and ambitious drillers perforated the salt domes like pincushions. The fantastic gushers brought more attention and also an overproduction of oil. At one point oil sold for three cents per barrel while drinking water in the field sold for five cents per cup.

Petroleum argonauts tracked back and forth between Houston and Beaumont, paid premium prices for cots in crowded hotel hallways, and traded oil securities in the streets. Local hardware companies began to deal in oil-field supplies, and new companies, prominent later, emerged from this chaos—Gulf, Texaco, and Humble Oil and Refining Company.

There were rapid improvements in drilling techniques. In the mid-nineteenth century well diggers dropped or pounded a steel-tipped iron rod into the ground. In 1881, while searching for water, contractors at Galveston pounded a pipe down 765 feet before it telescoped underground. More useful for deep wells was a technique that revolved a pipe with a serrated rim flushed with water. This led to rotary rigs using specialized drill bits that ground into the rock while piped-in "mud" carried off the tailings and sealed the pipe against leaks.

One night in a bar Howard R. Hughes, a contractor at the Spindletop field, bought an improved drill bit from Granville A. Humason for $150. With partner Walter B. Sharp, Hughes set up a company to make the bit with its revolving cones. It proved ten times faster than other bits and could penetrate hard rock, which others could not. When Hughes died in 1924, his tool company was worth $2 million. It became the foundation for the fortune of his famous son, who died the richest man on earth after a restless life of global flying records, movie stars, and Las Vegas hotels.

There was other technology. Humason produced another bit, which was manufactured by Clarence E. Reed; James Abercrombie invented a device to prevent blowouts due to high gas pressure; and Everett Lee DeGolyer with headquarters in Dallas applied the science of geophysics to the search for oil. Steel derricks and metal storage tanks replaced those made of wood, and wells punched into deeper pools—as much as 4,000 feet in 1930, com-

Port Arthur/Spindletop oil field. Houston Public Library, Houston Metropolitan Research Center.

Modern oil refinery. Houston
Chamber of Commerce.

pared with 20,000 feet today. Refineries followed the oil
discoveries, with J. S. Cullinan from Pennsylvania building the first at Corsicana in 1898. It processed 1,500 barrels per day to produce crude gasoline and illuminating
oil. Using improved techniques to make high-grade gasoline, other refineries appeared in Beaumont and Port Arthur, and by 1925 there were eighty refineries in Texas.

"Oil fever" infected the state, and like conquistadors of
old, the wildcat oil prospectors fanned out over the Southwest with visions of black gold gurgling in their brains. In
the first decade of the century they found oil at Brown-
wood, at Petrolia near Wichita Falls, and in new water
wells at the Waggoner Ranch in North Texas. William T.
Waggoner had made his fortune in the cattle business
with his father. So vast were his holdings that in 1900 he
gave ninety thousand acres and ten thousand head of
cattle to each of his three children. The ranch sprawled
thirty miles east and west and twenty-five miles north
and south. When the petroleum was found, Wagonner
said, "Damn the oil, I wanted water!"

The discoveries continued—Electra in 1911, Burkburnett in 1912, Ranger and Desdemona in 1917, Breckenridge in 1918, Mexia in 1920, Luling in 1922, the Panhandle in 1918–1926, Permian Basin in West Texas in 1921–1929. In 1928 Texas became the leading oil-producing state in the nation, and there was more to come.

In 1930 Columbus Marvin Joiner, an experienced but impoverished independent driller from Oklahoma, brought in a successful well in East Texas where geologists had said there would be no oil. It was a different kind of formation. The field cut across five counties, and others rushed in to complete 5,600 wells in two years around Kilgore and Longview. Joiner, the "father" of the East Texas field, was thus nicknamed "Dad." He needed money and sold out early to H. L. Hunt, who went on to become one of the richest men in the United States. "Dad" Joiner was almost broke when he died seventeen years later.

The oil bonanza produced not only wealthy landowners but also boom towns, a rich university, and laws for conservation. The towns near the oil strikes, like those of the nineteenth-century mining West, quickly fell into chaos due to the overwhelming demand for services. "Bing" Maddox, who experienced the conditions, commented: "Borger was like most all boomtowns. It was made up of corrugated sheet iron buildings, tents, one-by-twelve hunter shacks, people living in their automobiles and trailers . . . and some of them even digging holes back under the caprock and living in caves and half-dugouts."

Streets were unpaved, water supplies and sewerage uncertain, and social life raw. At Hogtown (Desdemona) the prostitutes traveled from rig to rig to sell their services. In a bunkhouse an inhabitant recalled that eighteen of fifty-five men had a venereal disease. In another bunkhouse nine of fourteen suffered. This was a time of poor treatment—mercury and arsenic for syphilis and potash for gonorrhea—and people screamed when they urinated. Whores came into the beauty shops by the back door, and proper women and girls were told by the proprietors to sit on a piece of paper if they used the same chair as a prostitute.

Mrs. Sam W. Webb saw another aspect of this rough existence: "I know there was one young girl. She came in the dance hall down there one night where we were dancing. She wasn't much over sixteen years old. And she saw that crowd of youngsters. She just stood and watched 'em dance for a while. The Holloway girls were there. One of them looked around and seen this girl. Katy Holloway, she started to put on her wraps and leave, and one of the

"The Eyes of Texas"

William L. Prather, president of the University of Texas at the beginning of the twentieth century, often closed his remarks to the student body with the expression "Students of the University of Texas, the eyes of Texas are upon you." He took the expression from Robert E. Lee, who during the Civil War told Hood's Texas Brigade, "The eyes of General Lee are upon you" and later told the alumni of Washington and Lee College, "The eyes of the South are upon you."

As a prank at a benefit for the University of Texas track team in 1903, John L. Sinclair, a student, wrote new words to the tune of "I've Been Working on the Railroad" (the same as "I've Been Working on the Levee").

> The eyes of Texas are upon you,
>   All the livelong day.
> The eyes of Texas are upon you,
>   You cannot get away.
> Do not think you can escape them,
>   At night or early in the morn.
> The eyes of Texas are upon you,
>   Till Gabriel blows his horn.

Prather, who was in the audience, was the first to laugh, and when the audience called for an encore, he joined in the singing. The song became popular and was eventually adopted as the official song of the university. It has also become an unofficial state song voiced in honor of a favorite son or daughter. The official song is "Texas, Our Texas," written by William J. Marsh and adopted in 1929.

boys went and asked the girl to leave. I've always felt sorry for that girl, because she was just left out of life."

In 1926–1927 at Borger in the Panhandle forty-five thousand people arrived in eight months, and a folksong exclaimed:

> Let's sing a song of Borger,
>   Famed for its graft and rot.
> It's just a wide place in the road,
>   This town that God forgot.
> For this village boasts of deeper sin,
>   Than Sodom ever knew,
> Come lend an ear, kind stranger,
>   And I'll whisper them to you.

In 1929 Texas Rangers, operating under martial law, cleaned up the crime of the town. The jail was overloaded, so the Rangers handcuffed prisoners to a chain strung along the main street. Law officers from around the Southwest then came to inspect the "trotline" and to claim their fugitives. Frank Hamer, one of the last famous Rangers, worked to subdue Borger. Hamer, a fearless man who had been wounded seventeen times and left for dead four times in his career, was described as "a giant of a man, moon-faced, always in boots, and as talkative as an oyster." In 1934 Hamer successfully ambushed Bonnie Parker and Clyde Barrow, who had robbed banks and murdered people across North Texas.

The oil discoveries in West Texas, although spawning their share of reckless boom towns, also provided unexpected money for the University of Texas. The near worthless two million acres assigned by the state to support the school returned $40,000 in grazing fees in 1900. As a consequence this "university of the first class" consisted mainly of shacks on College Hill. In 1919, however, Frank T. Pickrell and Haymon Krupp, along with other speculators, began drilling on university land with a rig they called Santa Rita after the saint of the impossible. It was so dry at the site that water had to be hauled from San Angelo. After many delays Santa Rita, using cowboy workers, struck oil at three thousand feet. Other wells shortly followed, and the university began receiving royalty checks in 1923.

Governor Miriam Ferguson signed a bill allowing the use of the money for permanent improvements. "To the average man who sees the miserable-looking buildings at the University," she commented, "it would appear that the state is making an effort to store up hay instead of to store up knowledge." The agricultural college, Texas A&M, which was legally a part of the state system, wanted a share in the largess. U.T. resisted, but when other colleges also began to look greedily at the resource, the administrators compromised. In 1930 Texas A&M got one-third of the royalties. The oil land, nevertheless, allowed the University of Texas to build an endowment that in 1988 was second only to Harvard's. It permitted both Texas universities to compete successfully throughout the United States for scholars and students, equipment, and libraries.

The oil bonanza, however, went too far. At Desdemona the drillers brought up more than could be stored, and at one point an oil stream three feet deep cut through a dirt road to be lost in the ground on the other side. The East Texas field produced 109 million barrels in 1931 and 205 million in 1933; the price of crude oil dropped from $1.10

Oil derrick for offshore drilling on the continental shelf in the Gulf of Mexico. Houston Chamber of Commerce.

Refinery on the Houston Ship
Channel. Shell Oil Company.

per barrel to $.10. Operators who wanted the fast dol-
lar argued with those who wanted to restrict production
in order to force up the price and to conserve the field.
The waste and rapid decline of the fields at Ranger, Desdemona, and Breckenridge demonstrated the need for
conservation.

In East Texas conditions ran amok. During the latter
part of 1931 drillers completed twelve wells per day, while
crude oil prices plummeted downward in a free fall. After
wide discussion Governor Ross S. Sterling, a former president of Humble Oil, ordered operators to shut down and
sent the national guard to enforce the command. Subsequent proration resulted in a price jump and a black market for "hot oil." Forced accounting by refineries, a large
contingent of Texas Rangers, and monitoring by the Texas
Railroad Commission, however, finally brought the field
under control in 1933–1934. This marks the beginning of
serious efforts at oil conservation and also, in consequence, the control of oil production by the Railroad
Commission.

The boom situations ended after this, but Texas oil
production continued to rise to 1,300 million barrels per

year in 1972 and then declined. In 1984 it was 874 million, about where it was in 1950. The story of oil in Texas after the 1930s was one primarily of regulation and the development of already proven fields. Petroleum, however, seeped into the far crevices of the state economy and with a multiplier effect influenced population growth, real estate values, and social attitudes far more than anyone recognized until the oil depression of the 1980s.

Houston blossomed like a native magnolia tree. The city was in the right place for the technological moment and had made the right preparation. Civic leaders had long dreamed of a ship channel like that of Manchester, England, and in 1896 Texas representatives persuaded Congress to authorize a cut through Galveston Bay and up Buffalo Bayou. After delays in appropriations, workers finally dredged to eighteen and one-half feet in 1908 with a turning basin at the old site of Harrisburg.

Houstonians set up a navigation district for special funding, matched federal monies, and deepened the channel to twenty-five feet in 1914. By remote control at the official opening President Woodrow Wilson fired a cannon from Washington, D.C., while the mayor's daughter dropped white rose petals into the water. "I christen thee Port Houston," she pronounced; "hither the boats of all nations may come and receive hearty welcome."

Subsequent improvements took the Houston Ship Channel to a depth of forty feet and a width of three to four hundred feet. Through engineering technology, Houston, fifty miles inland, had turned itself into a blue-water port. It matched Galveston's natural advantage with human effort, something other ports also accomplished. The Port of Houston topped Galveston's tonnage in the 1920s, and in the 1930s Corpus Christi, Beaumont, Texas City, Port Aransas, and Port Arthur also bypassed the old leader. Houston became the major port for the state, and among the top four in the nation, mainly on the strength of oil shipments.

When the fields of South Texas developed, Houston was far enough along with its channel to attract companies that wanted water facilities safe from hurricane damage. Pipelines from the fields snaked into the channel region, and by 1930 there were eight refineries along its banks. Others—Armour, Texas Portland Cement, American Maid Flour, Texas Chemical Company—likewise found the ship channel attractive, and by 1930 there were over fifty companies located there. The Texas Company (Texaco) moved its offices to the Bayou City in 1908; Gulf

Interurbans

Electric railroads catering to passengers flourished in the first forty years of the twentieth century. Steam trains could not compete with the frequent service and convenient stops of the interurbans. The first in Texas connected Denison and Sherman in 1900, and the second linked Dallas and Fort Worth in 1902. In North Texas lines eventually joined Denison, Sherman, Dallas, Denton, Fort Worth, Waxahachie, Waco, Corsicana, and others in between. In South Texas the interurbans served Houston, Galveston, Baytown, Beaumont, and Port Arthur. In West Texas a line connected El Paso, San Benito, and Ysleta. At their height in 1931 there existed 519 miles of interurban track, but eventually highways and automobiles forced their decline.

Oil in 1916; Humble Oil and Refining Company in 1919–1921; and a regional Shell bureau in 1933.

Wealth poured into the city. In 1900 bank deposits per capita in Houston were the same as for the rest of the United States; in 1920 they were one-third higher. This sharp upward climb of bank deposits for the city indicated an economic "takeoff" that coincided with the opening of the ship channel and the development of surrounding oil fields.

In population Houston surged past Dallas and San Antonio in the 1920s to seize first place, a position it has not relinquished. It lost an important plum, however, in the first round of rivalry with its North Texas competitor, Dallas. The Federal Reserve System designated twelve district banks during the Wilson administration to regulate the nation's monetary system. Houston, Dallas, Waco, and Austin competed, but Dallas won the prize for this region. Although the district bank was a "banker's bank," it carried enormous prestige to Dallas and gave it an enduring reputation as a financial center.

On a network of railroad connections, Dallas became the cotton export center for North Texas and then diversified, which was its pattern in the twentieth century. Its possession of the Federal Reserve District Bank allowed it to match Houston in banking assets. Beginning in 1899 with the Praetorians and in 1903 with Southwestern Life Insurance Company, Dallas became the fourth largest insurance city in the nation by 1939. In addition, Dallas revealed a surprising vitality in small manufacturing—furniture, clothing, iron and steel products, leather goods, cosmetics, and printed materials.

Because of its distribution capabilities Dallas evolved into a focal point for the clothing industry. The industry started in San Antonio, however, with Abraham Finesilver, a European who made men's work clothes, uniforms for the army in World War I, and then clothing for J. C. Penney and Company. August Lorch in Dallas, who succeeded first as a wholesale jobber, followed and began making inexpensive housedresses in 1924. They appealed to Texas women because of their coolness and crisp appearance.

Higginbotham-Bailey-Logan began manufacturing Paymaster work clothes for men and Virginia Hart housedresses in 1914 in Dallas. They served as a training ground for other makers. Among their "graduates" were Lester Lief, who with Ernest Wadel made Marcy Lee rayon dresses; Justine McCarty, who fashioned Mary Lou cot-

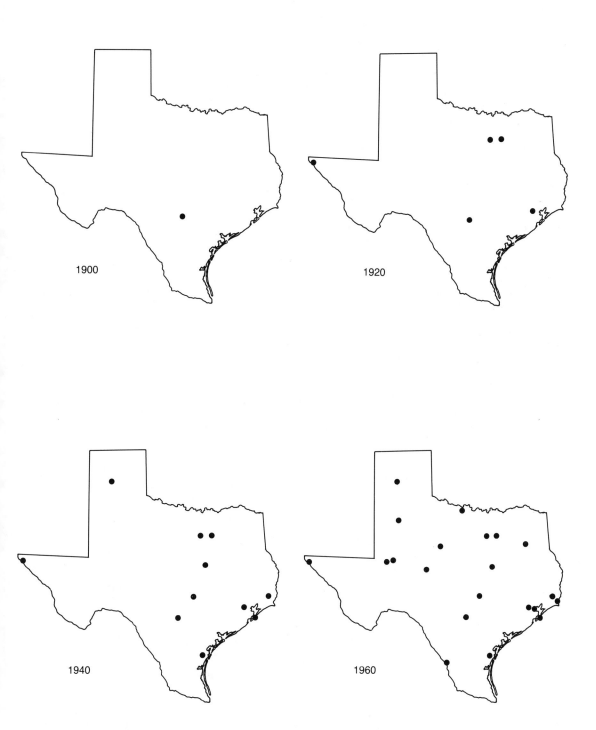

Map 4. Urban Growth, 1900–1960: Cities over 50,000

Post City

C. W. Post invented Postum from knowledge of Texas farm wives who mixed chicory and roasted wheat to make coffee. Postum gave him his start, and he followed it with Grape Nuts and other cereal foods. His company in Battle Creek, Michigan, was making a million dollars in annual profits when he retired in 1902. He then concentrated on building a working-person's community at Post City near the Cap Rock in West Texas in 1906. The community succeeded but has remained a small-sized town.

Post initiated a bizarre set of experiments at the Cap Rock to see if he could make it rain. He had read that there often occurred storms after great battles, and so he thought that explosions might cause rain. From 1910 until his death in 1914 he ordered a series of "rain battles" conducted by setting off dynamite charges on the ground and also from kites. Generally, they were not considered a success. In 1912, however, of the thirteen engagements with the weather, seven resulted in rain.

ton dresses and Justine street dresses; and John B. Donovan, who manufactured Don-a-Tog sports clothes.

One of the more interesting companies was started by Elsie Frankfurt in 1938 when she noted the wretched clothes of her pregnant older sister. Then, expectant women used wraparound styles of little shape, or wore dresses several sizes too large. Frankfurt, a fine seamstress and designer, made her sister a special skirt and jacket which brought so many compliments and inquiries from prospective mothers that Frankfurt went into business. With her sisters she began to produce Page Boy clothing, the name taken from the idea of a trumpeter announcing the birth of a child.

Page Boy sold to upper-income women, and the first store opened in Beverly Hills, California, where it attracted the attention of pregnant movie stars such as Alice Faye, Joan Bennett, and Loretta Young. With the baby boom after World War II the company expanded in Texas and California. Elsie Frankfurt became a national celebrity and the first woman elected to the Young Presidents' Organization.

In yet another Dallas success story, Joseph M. Haggar, born in Lebanon, began to set up factories in small towns where he could find a supply of unemployed housewives. He made "slacks" that men could wear in their slack time. He expanded during the depression years and switched half of his effort into making uniforms during World War II. In Fort Worth Charles N. Williamson and Emmett E. Dickie, makers of heavy-duty work clothes, Dickies, likewise profited from making army uniforms. Another Lebanese, Mansour "Frank" Farah, started a family business in El Paso sewing work shirts in 1920. In the next half-century Farah, with twelve thousand employees, became the largest statewide manufacturer.

For the most part, however, Texas industry along with much else trailed behind the progress made elsewhere in the United States during the first half of the twentieth century. In 1900, for instance, city schools—with the exception of the black facilities—were comparable to those in other states, but the rural schools were far worse. Twenty percent of them were still one-teacher, ungraded schools, and all suffered from lack of tax support. To teach better and conserve resources, a consolidation movement began early in the century and continued into the 1980s—parallel to the rural-to-urban shift.

In 1915 the legislature ordered attendance for children aged eight to fourteen for at least 60 days per year, and

An early Maxwell automobile owned by Dr. Scott, Del Rio. Western History Collections, University of Oklahoma Library.

then revised it to ages six to sixteen for 180 days. A state amendment in 1918 provided free texts, and another amendment in 1920 lifted the limit on tax levies for education. A junior college movement started, supported by Baptist and Methodist churches, and by 1940 there existed thirty-nine junior colleges in the state. The state took over the normal schools at such places as Commerce, Canyon, Kingsville, and Alpine and converted them in 1923 to teachers' colleges. For other constituents in higher education the state established Texas State College for Women (now Texas Woman's University) in Denton in 1901 and Texas Technological College (now Texas Tech University) in Lubbock in 1923.

Although all schools suffered during the Depression, there was a move to add a twelfth grade to the secondary schools to match other states, and by 1941 about half the systems had added the extra year. After the war, with the population on the increase, there was a need for further reform. The Gilmer-Aiken laws of 1949 provided for a broader state board of education, a board-appointed commissioner, teacher accreditation, a minimum nine-month session, and facility standards. The laws quickly showed results with higher school attendance, elimination of weak districts, and teachers returning to college for enhanced education.

In politics, however, Texas failed to benefit from the reforming election ideas of the Progressive era, and regressed. While states like California and Wisconsin expanded popular control and democratized the election process, Texas reduced and restricted voting. A constitutional amendment in 1902 instituted a poll tax of $1.50 to $1.75 as a prerequisite for voting. Residence requirements already amounted to one year in the state, six months in the county, and usually sixty days in the precinct.

Additional legislation passed in 1903 and revised in 1905 required a primary election for any party that drew 100,000 votes in the preceding general election. Leaders of the Democratic Party, the only organization large enough to need a primary, deliberately excluded non-whites from voting. The result was that poor people, blacks, and transients were excluded from the electorate. It took until 1944 for the Supreme Court of the United States to strike down the white primary, and until 1966 for amendments to the Texas Constitution to remove the poll tax and reduce residency to thirty days.

The most liberal of the governors of the early twentieth century was Thomas M. Campbell, who served from 1907 to 1911. His administration was noted for prosecuting monopolies; ending the pernicious convict leasing system; reforming prison policies to eliminate whipping, torture, abuse of women, and the wearing of stripes; requiring insurance companies to invest 75 percent of their reserves in Texas; supporting higher school standards; and encouraging home rule for cities. These reforms were similar to those in other states and generally modest in scope.

Campbell's successor, Oscar B. Colquitt, followed along the same lines, albeit less vigorously. He supported improvement in the state hospitals, factory safety, workmen's compensation laws, and regulations for child and female labor. In the U.S. Senate, meanwhile, Joseph W. Bailey opposed most of the reforms on both state and national levels. He devoted his eloquent oratory, musical voice, and handsome profile to his corporate friends, particularly Standard Oil Company and Kirby Lumber. He was out of step with his state and with his times and finally resigned in 1913 after investigations of corruption and misconduct.

On the national level at the time the most significant

Texas political figure was Edward M. House, an Austin businessman and planter. He was a small, thin, quiet person who preferred to work behind the scenes to shape political events. A master of detail, he helped Jim Hogg in the 1890s, and so influenced the forty Texas delegates to the 1912 Baltimore convention that they stood firm through forty-six ballots to select Woodrow Wilson as the Democratic nominee. House then moved to Washington, D.C., where he served as an informal adviser to the president. He wanted no position for himself, yet he was the first Texan in the modern period to wield power in the nation's capital. He would not be the last.

Neither House nor Wilson, however, could prevent the election of the enigmatic James E. Ferguson as governor in 1914. The son of a poor Methodist minister in Bell County, "Farmer Jim" managed to go through prep school, pass the bar exam, run a farm, and become president of the Temple State Bank before he announced for governor. Although he had no political experience, he spoke of land reform, relief for tenant farmers, and against prohibition. He was part demagogue and appealed to his audience in rural, earthy language which belied his education and intelligence.

Ferguson won the primary against Thomas H. Ball, a Houston attorney and former congressman, with a ferocious campaign in which he accused Ball of being a person who "voted dry, but drank wet." In those days of a one-party state, a victory in the primary meant a victory in the general election. In his first administration Ferguson faced down Joe Bailey, denounced the Ku Klux Klan, obtained a farm tenancy bill that was later declared unconstitutional, and established the Texas Forest Service.

The Forest Service was the beginning of conservation in the state and somewhat a reflection of Theodore Roosevelt's advocacy. Within Texas it was a tribute to W. Goodrich Jones, a businessman and banker who had observed the possibility of reforestation when visiting the Black Forest in Germany. While working in Temple as a young man, he planted hackberry trees along the streets to give shade. For his efforts this small, wiry, bespeckled man became known as a "tree crank" and endured the nickname of Hackberry Jones. He established a forestry association and pushed the state for money to support a state department of forestry. "Why do you need $10,000?" said the incredulous Ferguson, who misunderstood the matter. "Why, for $500 I can get you a good man to cut all the trees you want."

Pancho Villa

Doroteo Arango was born in 1877 in Durango, Mexico. He became a cattle rustler and adopted the name of a local bandit, Francisco Villa. In 1910 he joined Francisco Madero in a revolt against the government of Porfirio Díaz. He was imprisoned under President Victoriano Huerta, but escaped and fought against both Huerta and Venustiano Carranza, another contender for the presidency. When the United States recognized Carranza, Villa turned against the U.S., and his friends in El Paso feared an attack like he had led against Columbus, New Mexico.

President Wilson ordered an expedition to capture Villa, but the Mexican easily eluded the army forces of General John J. Pershing which pursued him across northern Mexico. Pershing did not return entirely empty-handed. Several hundred Chinese who had befriended the troops in Mexico returned with the army to San Antonio, where they settled under Pershing's sponsorship. Mexican Federalists finally bribed Villa into retirement in 1920; he was assassinated in 1923. North of the border Pancho Villa is usually considered a bandit responsible for the death of Americans, including reporter Ambrose Bierce; south of the border he is often viewed as a patriot.

Pancho Villa. Western History Collections, University of Oklahoma Library.

The governor, meanwhile, placed state funds in "pet" banks where he had an interest, and became embroiled in a fight with the University of Texas over budgetary items and faculty. Ferguson vetoed the university appropriation in order to force the administration to fire the teachers who had supported Thomas Ball. Will Hogg, son of the former governor, rallied friends of the school. The Women's Christian Temperance Union and the Equal Suffrage Association also joined in the fight against the governor.

Among other items it was revealed that Ferguson had borrowed $156,000 from an unknown source—later exposed to be a brewery association working to forestall prohibition. The legislature in special session removed Ferguson for the misuse of funds and banned him from ever again holding office. His replacement, William P. Hobby, restored calm by approving the university budget and appointing new regents.

These exciting events obscured the quiet beginning of the Texas Highway Department in 1917. Congress provided matching funds for states in 1916, and to take advantage of this money Texas started the new department. Before this, roads had been left to the poverty of the counties, but now there was an opportunity for a unified system to match the growing interest of motorists. Unfortunately, mismanagement, jurisdictional disputes, irregular funding, and patronage appointments hindered the operation of the department. There were only 7,300 miles of paved roads under its jurisdiction in 1930, but 19,000 in 1940 and 34,000 in 1950.

Lynching near Boonville, Borger County, early twentieth century. Barker Texas History Center, The University of Texas at Austin.

The Ferguson fulminations also distracted Texans from the outbreak of World War I in Europe and the ongoing border irritations resulting from the revolution in Mexico. President Wilson sent punitive and inconclusive attacks against Vera Cruz and Pancho Villa from Texas before settling down to a policy of "watchful waiting." It was not all "waiting" in Texas, however, and border agitation continued, fueled by long-standing prejudice on both sides, Texas Ranger brutality, border raids by Mexican bandits, the movement of Anglo-American farmers into the Rio Grande Valley, and an aborted irredentist movement. In 1915–1917 vigilante groups and authorities lynched some three hundred Mexicans in the county around Brownsville and somewhere between three and five thousand throughout the valley. U.S. troops remained along the Rio Grande until the 1940s.

With America joining "the war to make the world safe for democracy" Texas became a training ground—Camp MacArthur in Waco, Camp Logan in Houston, Camp Bowie in Fort Worth, and Camp Travis in San Antonio. About 200,000 Texans enlisted for duty, and patriotic Texas followed the American flag in conserving food, purchasing war bonds, and forcing conformity. Governor Hobby went so far as to veto the appropriation for the German Department at the University of Texas. This was particularly sad in a state with a long German heritage.

The war, with its movement of people and money, stirred the ethnic pot in other ugly ways. The demons of prejudice were never far away, with or without the encouragement of war. In May 1916, for instance, a frenzied mob in Waco lynched Jesse Washington, an illiterate seventeen-year-old black. He had confessed to the rape and murder of a fifty-three-year old white woman; when convicted, a courtroom mob seized him. Outside, men hoisted him into the air by a chain around his neck and piled dry-goods boxes underneath him.

They doused Jesse and the boxes with coal oil and set them ablaze. As his naked body writhed in the flames, a well-dressed woman clapped her hands in glee. After two hours a horseman lassoed the charred remains and dragged them through the streets until the head pulled off. Boys grabbed the head, jerked out the teeth, and sold them for five dollars each. Finally, the corpse in a sack was pulled behind an automobile and hung from a pole in front of a blacksmith shop. Later, the constable turned the body over to an undertaker for burial.

The racial violence continued. In the wake of a race

riot in East St. Louis and earlier conflict between black
soldiers in Brownsville, San Antonio, and Del Rio, a
bloody protest occurred in Houston in 1917. Northern
black soldiers had been assigned guard duty while workmen built Camp Logan on the west side of town. The soldiers resented the segregation, the arrogance of the police,
and the epithet "nigger" flung their way.

The arrest of a black soldier by local officers and rumors
of his death triggered an explosion in which 75 to 100
black troopers grabbed their rifles to shoot up the town.
Houston authorities struck back with 350 members of
the Coast Guard from Galveston and 602 soldiers from
San Antonio. As a result, 19 people were killed and 11
wounded. Subsequently, after the largest court-martial in
U.S. military history, federal authorities hanged 19 rioters.

World War I also launched Texas and the nation on a
moralistic crusade against alcoholic drinks. Temperance
had been an issue in Texas since the time of Sam Houston, and prohibitionists had been active in the constitutional convention of 1876, elections of 1884 and 1886,
and unsuccessful amendment attempts in 1887, 1908,
and 1911. At the turn of the century the Baptist and Methodist churches especially supported the temperance movement in a recognition of the social implications of their
faith. A Sunday closing law for saloons had been in effect
since 1866.

Even the flamboyant Carrie Nation visited the state
and once broke up a bar in Houston named in her honor.
Instead of her proverbial hatchet she held brickbats in her
apron and hurled them with accuracy through bottles,
windows, and mirrors. In Galveston she lectured loungers
on the Strand: "There you go pouring out some of that
slop. Men, you ought not to drink that stuff, it will ruin
your liver and damn your souls."

The sentiment to protect youthful soldiers before sending them to be killed in the trenches of France and the
national crusade against liquor, however, accomplished
more than the lectures of the Kansas crusader. Texas
passed a law banning saloons within ten miles of military
camps and shortly adopted the federal prohibition amendment in 1918. Despite the good intentions and the efforts
of police officers, prohibition was unenforceable. People
in America continued to drink, and, worse, it became
fashionable to flout the laws.

The Texas coast, particularly Galveston Island, became
a haven for bootleggers. Ships from England filled with liquor anchored outside territorial waters on "rum row."

They were met by the fast speedboats of liquor wholesalers who would smuggle the contraband onto the island and from there by train and truck inland as far as Detroit and Cleveland. Rival gangs in Galveston fought for supremacy. Shootouts occurred on the streets with mobsters ducking behind parked cars and popping their pistols at each other; shotgun blasts in the night came from sleek cars moving without lights; and bullet-riddled bodies were dumped onto the beach by persons unknown.

From this situation emerged the most remarkable gangland family in the history of the state. The Maceo kin had immigrated from Palermo, Italy, at the beginning of the century and settled in the lumber town of Leesville, Louisiana. Rosario (Rose) and his younger brother Sam learned the barber's trade and moved to Galveston shortly before World War I. They opened a shop and at Christmas gave their customers some Dago Red (cheap red wine). Their friends wanted more, and the brothers drifted into bootlegging. They affiliated with one of the gangs, and when fortuitous arrests removed the main characters of the Galveston underworld, the Maceo brothers took charge.

They were interested in gambling and the sale of liquor at the nightclubs they owned and others they controlled. Alcohol again became legal with the repeal of prohibition in 1933, but in Texas gambling remained illegal, as did liquor by the drink until 1971. Taciturn Rose, who remained quietly behind the scenes, and affable Sam, who greeted the customers and wore a white carnation in his lapel, made $3.5 million per year. They owned 80 percent of the slot machines in Galveston County, posted horseracing results by telephone from Louisiana, and owned the Balinese Room, the most famous nightclub in Texas.

Balinese Room

The most famous nightclub in Texas during the time when Galveston was the sin city of the Gulf, the Balinese Room featured dancing to a live band, dinner with mixed drinks, and gambling in a room at the end of a pier extending over the Gulf two hundred feet from the seawall. Rose and Sam Maceo bought the club in 1926 and after several renovations opened it as the Balinese Room in 1942. It was dimly lighted and noisy with the music of Mexican or Cuban rumba bands. As one critic said, "The atmosphere attempts to be extremely El Morocco, but came up extremely rococo."

The brothers operated it as a private club to give some excuse for the illegal drinking and gambling, but there was easy access through the guard at the entrance to the pier. He issued temporary passes and warned of unwanted visitors. According to the legends, when the club was raided by Texas Rangers wearing their ten-gallon western hats, they were readily spotted and the guard pressed a warning buzzer. By the time the Rangers charged down the long pier and into the club, the poker chips and the drinks would be gone into the Gulf and all would be clean and legal. On one occasion as the law officers burst through the door, the band struck up "The Eyes of Texas" as the master of ceremonies announced, "And now, ladies and gentlemen, we give you in person, the Texas Rangers!"

Balinese Room, Galveston. Photograph by David G. McComb.

Destruction of gambling equipment in Galveston. Rosenberg Library, Galveston.

It was located over the Gulf waters at the end of a long pier. Somehow the Maceos always knew when the Texas Rangers would appear and safely hid the illegal gambling tables and the liquor.

The people of Galveston liked the Maceos and tolerated their activities. The brothers brought Hollywood stars to their clubs and contributed heartily to neighborhood churches and civic enterprises. It was difficult not to like them. At the same time, independent of the Maceos, prostitution flourished on Postoffice Street, which became the most notorious red-light district in Texas. Antivice crusades had shut down such "reservations" in most cities—Austin, Dallas, Houston—during the second decade of the century, but Galveston with its easy toleration became a world-class sin city. In 1930 in Shanghai, another front-rank vice capital, the ratio of prostitutes to population was 1 to 130; in Galveston it was 1 to 62.

For thirty years the residents flaunted the "Free State of Galveston," but it fell apart in the early 1950s. Sam Maceo died in 1951 and Rose in 1953. The Internal Revenue Service attacked the estate, the legislature declared it prima facie evidence of gambling to own slot machines, and the federal government made it illegal to transport such machines across state lines. In addition, the Texas attorney general obtained a court injunction to prevent the use of telephone lines for transmitting horse-racing information. At last the Rangers closed down the island and padlocked the doors. Thus ended the "Free State of Galveston," and it has remained a quiet family resort ever since.

Texas governors until the 1950s left Galveston alone; they had other matters to deal with. World War I brought not only prohibition but also women's suffrage. Governor Hobby, who was neither prohibitionist nor feminist, took the lead to allow women the right to vote in primaries. After this move women formed "Hobby Clubs" for the governor's reelection. He won handily, and in 1919 Hobby called a special session that approved the Nineteenth Amendment to the U.S. Constitution. This gave women the right to vote, and on this point Texas led the Southern states.

Less pleasant for Hobby was the labor unrest that disrupted the economy. A longshoremen's strike that began in New York City reached the Galveston docks in March 1920. The basic issue was a raise from sixty to eighty cents per hour in wages and recognition of the International Longshoremen's Association. Galveston businessmen said that there were plenty of workers available, but that they were afraid to challenge the union. The Texas Chamber of Commerce asked the governor to force the port open, and Hobby imposed martial law on the island.

The city commissioners protested this "insult" to their city, but in their agreeable way Galvestonians welcomed the National Guard, which spent $50,000 per month during its stay. The ladies organized dances, the shippers moved their cargo, and the civic leaders presented a loving cup to the commander of the troops when he left. Texas Rangers remained in charge of the police force until 1921, the workers accepted a seven-cent increase, and the union was shattered.

The episode demonstrated the antiunion sentiment found generally in Texas. Hobby's successor, Pat M. Neff, a moderate Waco lawyer, also used the Rangers and martial law to break a railroad strike. Neff, in addition, had to contend with Hiram W. Evans and the Ku Klux Klan. Nationally, the Klan began its rise in 1915 and reached Texas during the 1920s. In 1921 alone there were more than

San Antonio River Walk. Photograph by David G. McComb.

eighty cases of Klan violence against Jews, blacks, aliens, and Roman Catholics. In Galveston the intrepid Rabbi Henry Cohen stood with Father James Kirwin before the city council to block a parade permit for the Klan.

In Dallas, in contrast, a supposed black pimp was whipped and the KKK initials burned into his forehead with acid. A Dallas dentist, Hiram W. Evans, meanwhile, rose through the Klan ranks to the level of Imperial Wizard. Evans concentrated on sympathetic politicians and won enough votes to dominate the Texas legislature in 1922. After that year, however, the 400,000-member Klan declined because of internal dissention, and by 1926 the Dallas and Fort Worth chapters fell into bankruptcy. Seemingly, the weed of prejudice both grows and dies quickly.

The victory of the Fergusons in the 1924 gubernatorial race also hastened the Klan's demise in Texas. Jim Ferguson's motto was "Never say 'die,' say 'damn.'" Barred from political office, he entered his wife, Miriam, and toured with the slogan "Two governors for the price of one." In a furious, gut-level campaign in which "Pa" Ferguson referred to Evans as the "Grand Gizzard," "Ma" beat the Klan candidate. She thus became the first woman governor of Texas and the first elected woman governor in the United States.

With the ever-present Pa next door to her office, Ma

Ferguson attacked the Klan by promoting a law banning
the wearing of masks in public places, vetoed a prison reform bill, and, of course, cut the budget of the University
of Texas. She was most noticed for the large number of
pardons issued—1,161 in two years. Many were former
bootleggers whom she thought could best serve society
by supporting their families. She released so many, however, that people suspected Pa was selling pardons. There
were jokes about this:

> Ma was riding an elevator when another passenger
> accidentally stepped on her foot. "Oh, pardon me,"
> he said.
> Ma replied, "You'll have to see Pa."

> A man went to see Pa at the Ferguson farm to see
> about obtaining a pardon for his son. They toured the
> property and Pa avoided the subject of the pardon. Fi-
> nally, they came to a broken-down mule. Pa said,
> "And this here is a $5,000 mule."
> The exasperated man said, "Now, why would any-
> one pay $5,000 for this broken-down mule that ain't
> worth $25? And what does this have to do with my
> son, anyway?"
> Pa replied with a twinkle in his eye, "Why, if you
> was to buy this mule you could give your son a ride
> home from prison."

The rumors and jokes meant defeat in the next election, and Dan Moody, the new governor, reformed the
prisons, the state audit system, and the highway department. He tried to swing support to Al Smith, the national
Democratic candidate, but Smith was big-city, Irish Catholic, and wet. Although the nominating convention was
held in Houston, the electorate switched and for the first
time since Reconstruction voted for a Republican. Herbert Hoover was a man of integrity, and no imagination. It
was his misfortune to be president when the Great Depression broke over the nation.

The Depression was also the misfortune of Dan Moody
and Ross Sterling, the governor who came next. Neither
knew what to do about failing banks, farm poverty, and
the boxcars of depressed young vagabonds counting the
ties, searching for work, and looking for meaning in their
lives. The number of wage earners dropped from 156,000
to 91,000 between 1929 and 1933. At least Ma Ferguson,
who returned to the Governor's Mansion in 1932, had the

State Fair of Texas

In nineteenth-century Texas many civic promoters held fairs to display agricultural produce, new products, and their community. Dallas made several such starts and then organized a permanent fair in 1886. It first made a profit in 1893 and missed a season only during war years and one in preparation for the Texas Centennial of 1936. The Texas legislature authorized Dallas as the celebration site after a winning bid of $8 million. The money came from various relief agencies. The city erected permanent air-conditioned buildings and welcomed thirteen million visitors over a two-year period. It was an economic boost for Dallas during depressed times and gave the city an identity apart from the rest of the state.

Houstonians, miffed at losing the site, published a booklet of blank pages to illustrate Dallas' role in the Texas Revolution, and the irrepressible Amon Carter of Fort Worth staged his own centennial celebration, which attracted two million tourists. Dallasites argued, however, that their city was best for transportation purposes, and they have continued to hold a state celebration at the fairgrounds ever since. The park stadium took its present name, the Cotton Bowl, from the football classic that started in 1937. In 1941 the Southwest Conference officially took over the sponsorship of the game.

sense to consent to New Deal programs, as did James V. Allred, who followed her. In Washington, D.C., meanwhile, two Texans held prominent positions.

John Nance Garner from Uvalde, who had been Speaker of the House, became Vice President in 1933. Garner had begun his political career in 1903, and his first task as a congressman was to explain why it was economically necessary to keep the cavalry in Brownsville. He said to Secretary of War William Howard Taft: "Mr. Secretary, it's this way. We raise a lot of hay in my district. We've got a lot of stores and we have the prettiest girls in the United States. The cavalry buys the hay for its horses, spends its pay in the stores, marries our girls, gets out of the army and helps us develop the country and then more replacements come and do this same thing. It *is* economics, sir. It *is* economics."

Taft and Teddy Roosevelt had a good laugh and ordered the cavalry to stay in Brownsville. Garner rose through the committees of Congress, became minority leader, and instituted a meeting room called the "Board of Education" where there was liquor in a cabinet and a faucet for "branch water." The Eastern press nicknamed him "Cactus Jack," his homefolks addressed him as "Judge," and his wife called him "Mr. Garner." The election in 1932 revealed a successful bonding between the Southwesterner and the New York aristocrat, but in office Garner had little to do. As he later said to Lyndon Johnson, "I'll tell you, Lyndon, the Vice Presidency isn't worth a pitcher of warm spit."

At the same time Jesse H. Jones, a conservative Houston lumber and real estate man, continued under Franklin D. Roosevelt as the chairman of the Reconstruction Finance Corporation. This was Hoover's most credible effort to ease the crushing losses in the financial community. In 1939 Jones became the Federal Loan Administrator, responsible for funding war industries, and then concurrently served as Secretary of Commerce from 1940 to 1945. He managed enormous amounts of money and at one time was overheard to say in a telephone conversation about a proposal, "I'll not give a nickel more than two billion dollars for it!"

The alphabet agencies of the New Deal came to Texas to provide unemployment relief—W.P.A. (Works Projects Administration), C.C.C. (Civilian Conservation Corps), N.R.A. (National Recovery Administration), and others. Young Lyndon Johnson led the state N.Y.A. (National Youth Administration). Federal money and Texas labor were used to work on roads, bridges, public buildings, parks, and conservation projects.

The San Jacinto Monument at the battlegrounds on the banks of Buffalo Bayou, the tower of the Main Building at the University of Texas, and the internationally famous River Walk of downtown San Antonio resulted from such governmental work. The Federal Writers' Project of the W.P.A. hired unemployed historians to compile *Texas: A Guide to the Lone Star State,* organize archives, and write city histories. Their effort is still of value. So also is the work of artists employed to decorate public buildings; in so doing they developed a style of Southwestern art.

Despite the belated doubts of conservative business leaders, most Texans welcomed the relief programs. Blacks and Hispanics generally benefited, some gaining economically from the programs even while subjected to a degree of discrimination. The experience contributed to the establishment of a permanent relief system in the state. Sharecroppers and tenants, the answer to farm labor since the Civil War, counted for most of the rural need cases. They abandoned the myth of the self-reliant farmer, and over half of them left for the cities. These people, who survived the hard times through governmental help, provided a solid block of votes for the Democratic Party. As one of the many variations of the Twenty-Third Psalm read, this one printed in Weatherford:

> Depression is my shepherd; I am in want.
> He maketh me to lie down on park benches; He leadeth me beside the still factories.
> He restoreth the bread lines; He leadeth me in the paths of destruction for his Party's sake.
> Yea, though I walk through the Valley of Unemployment, I fear every evil; for thou art with me; the Politicians and Profiteers they frighten me.
> Thou preparest a reduction in mine salary before me in the presence of mine creditors; Thou anointest mine income with taxes; my expenses runneth over.
> Surely unemployment and poverty will follow me all the days of the Republican administration; and I shall dwell in a mortgaged house forever.

The total cost of the New Deal in Texas amounted to $1,457 million. In 1933–1935 the Federal Emergency Relief Administration, which often simply handed out money, helped 300,000 Texans; the C.C.C. employed 110,000 between 1933 and 1938. Cold statistics, however,

San Jacinto Monument

Completed in 1939 on the San Jacinto Battlegrounds near Houston, the San Jacinto Monument was part of the 1936 Texas Centennial celebration. Alfred C. Finn, a Houston architect, designed the monument, which was made of reinforced concrete and faced with Texas Cordova shell limestone. It thrusts 570 feet, 4½ inches above ground level, almost 15 feet higher than the Washington Monument. To avoid national criticism, however, Jesse H. Jones, who helped obtain the federal funds for the monument, told people that it was 5 inches shorter than the one in Washington, D.C. This is true if measured from the top of the star to the platform on which the octagonal shaft rests.

San Jacinto Monument. Photograph by David G. McComb.

Audie Murphy

In twenty-eight months during World War II Audie Murphy won every U.S. Army award for valor, two of them twice, while still too young to vote. He was also too young to shave when he entered the Army in 1942 after being rejected by both the Marines and the Paratroopers. He was only five feet five inches tall and weighed 110 pounds. He came from a poor northeast Texas sharecrop farm where he learned to hunt small game. He enjoyed the training in boot camp and relished front-line service, where he rose quickly through the ranks from private to lieutenant.

He won the Congressional Medal of Honor by repulsing a German attack of six tanks and infantry in January 1945. He ordered his men into a defensive position in woods while he remained with the field telephone in a forward position to direct artillery fire. He was asked repeatedly how close the enemy was to him, and he finally said in exasperation, "If you'll just hold the phone, I'll let you talk to one of the bastards!"

He was armed only with a carbine, and as the Germans began to overrun his position, Murphy climbed onto a burning American tank destroyer, rolled the dead commander out into the snow, and began firing its heavy machine guns. He killed or wounded fifty enemy soldiers and after running out of ammunition retreated to the woods. The burning tank destroyer then exploded. Murphy refused treatment for an old wound that had reopened and rallied his men to a counterattack. The Germans retreated.

Murphy returned home in June 1945 as a hero, our most decorated soldier. He went on to two marriages, Hollywood stardom, and a fatal plane crash in 1971.

often fail to convey the depth of need and desperation. Three children starved to death in Lubbock in 1930, and the next year officials converted the useless grass of the city hall square into a turnip patch. A W.P.A. recipient in Houston simply said, "You know, it's been a year since I've taken home a pay check. That's a long time to tell your kids there's no money for ice cream."

In West Texas nature compounded the misery with grasshoppers and dust. The heart of the Dust Bowl was the five-state corner of Colorado, Kansas, Oklahoma, New Mexico, and Texas. Drought, overgrazing, and grasshoppers, which not only ate the crops to the bare earth but also gnawed wooden ax and plow handles, presented dry, loose ground to the ever-present wind. A thirteen-year-old Amarillo girl recalled running for home when she saw her first dust storm approaching. "Just as we reached my front porch everything went completely black. . . . We couldn't see each other's faces. We couldn't see our own hands. I remember gasping, 'I can't breathe!'"

In 1932 John Fischer, a future editor of *Harper's Magazine*, drove a Model T Ford from Oklahoma City to Amarillo during a norther which whipped a fifty-mile-per-hour wind over the barren land. He had to wear a wet handkerchief over his mouth and nose, and when he reached Amarillo the right side of his car had been scoured to bright bare metal. In 1934 West Texas dirt blew all the way to the Potomac River and settled on the desks of Washington politicians.

The hard times added impetus to major shifts already underway. Rural population moved to the urban places. Tractors replaced horses and mules on the farms—the number of tractors on Texas farms increased 934 percent between 1925 and 1940. This shift to power farming offset the loss of labor and also released one-third more land, which earlier had been dedicated to the cultivation of feed for work animals.

The drought in West Texas encouraged irrigation, with the biggest increase in 1934–1949. The farmers "mined" the water with little thought of the future. The spread of irrigation brought an ironic shift: at present most of the state's cotton is grown in West Texas, and most of the state's cattle are raised in East Texas. The irrigated cotton plants of the west avoid the boll weevil, and the cattle of the east feed from nearby grain fields.

With the rest of the nation, Texas recovered from the Depression because of the massive spending on World War II. The state's good weather made it a prime location

Panhandle dust storm, 1930's.
Barker Texas History Center, The
University of Texas at Austin.

for training bases. The federal government placed fifteen bases and several prison camps in Texas. Approximately 750,000 Texans served in uniform, and 30 of them won the Congressional Medal of Honor. The home front participated in war-bond drives, air-raid drills, rationing, memorial services, and production of war materials. Farm prices jumped, and the unemployed found ready work in the new factories. The war was the great catalyst for the growth of Dallas, Fort Worth, San Antonio, and Houston.

Houston was the center of vast amounts of oil, natural gas, salt, and sulphur, the basic materials for a petrochemical industry. When the war clouds began to rumble on the American horizon in 1940, the War Department gave Humble Oil a $12 million contract to produce toluene, an ingredient in high explosives. Shell Oil at the same time worked around the clock to build a plant in four months to manufacture the same material. In 1943 the federal government built an installation at nearby Baytown to use butadiene from Humble and styrene from Monsanto at Texas City to make Buna-S rubber. Sinclair Oil and Goodyear joined in the production. Half of the synthetic rubber used in the war came from Texas, but it was finished into tires, lifeboats, and blimps at Akron, Ohio.

During the conflict government and business invested $600 million in petrochemical plants in the Houston area and added another $300 million immediately thereafter. From the nearby raw materials came sulphuric acid, methane, ethane, propane, butane, toluol, and xylol; through

The Main Building tower at the University of Texas at Austin. Built during the Depression, the tower was the site of the Charles Whitman shootings in 1966. Photograph by David G. McComb.

interconnecting pipelines flowed butylene, hydrogen, hydrogen chloride, ethylene, butadiene, sodium chloride, acetylene, acetone, chlorine, and ammonia. The output of one place was the input of another, and it made economic sense to place installations in close proximity.

What emerged in a "golden triangle" of Houston to Freeport to Port Arthur–Orange was one of the two major petrochemical complexes of the nation. The list of involved companies reads like a roll call of the chemical industry, and the Houston Chamber of Commerce magazine observed in 1957: "If an air to ground X-ray were made of Harris County, these interlaced pipelines would show up like a nerve system around the backbone—the Houston Ship Channel—of an industrial giant."

Natural gas became useful. Before the 1940s the gas was little more than a dangerous nuisance. The City of Amarillo spent $60,000 in the 1930s to advertise five years of free gas to any business that would move to the West Texas town. They got no takers. Operators habitually burned off the gas in giant flares in the fields, and in 1934 in the Panhandle one billion cubic feet of gas per day was thus consumed. Even without a demand the spooky glow of red-orange flares dancing in the night indicated a fearful waste. Starting in 1938 the state forced producers to recycle their gas wells—take out the hydrocarbons from the wet gas and put the dry gas back into the ground. The Railroad Commission, which was in charge of conservation, did not stop the flaring of gas from all wells, however, until 1947–1949.

By this time a market had developed for natural gas as a heating source, particularly in the eastern United States. The federal government built the "Big Inch" and "Little Inch" pipelines during the war, and the Tennessee Gas Transmission Company (Tenneco) formed in 1944 to operate a 1,300-mile line to West Virginia. Texas Eastern Transmission Company took over the government projects in 1947.

One of the more dramatic coastal war industries was shipbuilding. The U.S. Maritime Commission contracted with Todd Shipyards to build Liberty Ships, mid-sized transport vessels, on the Houston Ship Channel. In four months in 1942 Todd expanded from six thousand to twenty thousand employees with only 3 percent possessing a knowledge of ship construction. Yet, by using assembly-line techniques, Todd cut the time of building from 254 days to 53 and turned out 222 ships during the war. Utilizing the same techniques, Brown Shipbuilding

Company produced 300 subchasers, destroyer escorts, and landing craft on nearby Green's Bayou. They launched their vessels broadside with a tremendous splash into the water.

Less successful were the concrete barges constructed by San Jacinto Shipbuilding Corporation. Oddly enough, concrete ships will float and actually become stronger as time passes. Some had been built for World War I, and one of them from Mobile had been deliberately run aground near the Galveston Channel after it had been damaged. Through mismanagement the San Jacinto company failed, but firms elsewhere built concrete ships that saw combat service during the war.

By the middle of the war forty-five Houston companies held prime government contracts. In the decade of the 1940s the population of the city more than doubled, and in 1945–1948 Harris County led the nation in the value of industrial construction. In 1948 Houston was the fastest-growing city in the country, which prompted Oveta Culp Hobby, the wartime leader of the Women's Army Corps and director of the *Houston Post,* to comment, "I think I'll like Houston if they ever get it finished."

Other Texas cities experienced similar leaps in population—Austin, 50 percent; Dallas, 47 percent; Fort Worth, 57 percent; and San Antonio, with its military influx, 60 percent. In North Texas the war brought North American Aviation to Dallas and Convair to Fort Worth to build B-24 bombers. The two companies employed sixty thousand people. Afterward Convair began to assemble B-36 bombers, but North American abruptly halted and sold out to Texas Engineering and Manufacturing Company (Temco) and Chance Vought, which between them employed twenty-five thousand persons.

These companies enhanced the manufacturing base of Dallas and Fort Worth, which already had clothing, meat packing by Armour and Swift, and a Ford automobile assembly plant from earlier in the century. Following the war, when the new shiny Fords became available to the public, they sported a back windshield sticker: "Made in Texas by Texans."

This bit of chauvinism reflected the Texas mystique, a strong myth that Texans were tough, independent, direct, proud, heroic, successful, and different. The myth also included the idea that minorities and women "knew their place," which was subordinate to the white male. The mystique had roots in the glories of the Texas republic, a Southern heritage, and the conquest of a difficult frontier.

But it emerged at a time of rapid transformation when the Texas of old was becoming a fading memory, and people needed an ethos to know who they were.

In 1950 60 percent of the people lived in the cities, the state had grown by 20 percent, and for the first time the actual number of people, not just the percentage, living in the countryside declined—by 400,000. Soldiers had gone to war, been pressed into a G.I. mold, and returned with a new sobriety. Every fifth person was a newcomer. Texas had changed, and the mystique gave migrants and natives alike a common ground on which to stand.

In 1938 W. Lee O'Daniel, a flour salesman from Fort Worth who had acquired popularity with a radio show and a hillbilly band, ran for governor and won. He was well liked but inept, and when he moved to the U.S. Senate in 1941 his critics said that Texas possessed only one senator. His successors in the Governor's Mansion, Coke Stevenson and Beauford H. Jester, although competent, did little to adjust the state to the postwar world. Texas remained loyal to the Democratic Party, supported Harry S. Truman in 1948, and then began to question his liberal policies. The difficulty was that the nation and the world were uneasy, and Texas also revealed an undefined restlessness. Things did not fit right; there was an imbalance; the ethos did not serve contemporary life.

A. C. Greene, a critic and writer, told of a rancher in Scurry County who had allowed oil drillers to invade his land to make him rich. He hated the change, the noise, the disturbance, and spent his nights shooting at the light bulbs of the rigs from his front porch with a .22 rifle. He sipped bourbon from a bottle while he took his pot shots and muttered to himself, "Sons of bitches . . . sons of bitches."

6. The Texas Mystique

The Texas mystique—paternalistic, chauvinistic, wealthy, aggressive, friendly, exploitative, prejudiced, independent, optimistic, enterprising, boisterous. All of these adjectives belong more or less in modern Texas history. They are the descriptive words of a myth—widely believed, casually followed, occasionally helpful, and painfully misleading. The mystique led a rancher in Scurry County to shoot out the lights of a drilling rig and a Vice President of the United States to profane the Taj Mahal, a burial chamber, with a Texas yell.

The image of the Texan was broadcast to the nation with the opening of the Shamrock Hotel on St. Patrick's Day, 1949. Glenn McCarthy, wildcat oil millionaire and land speculator, built this prosaic, eighteen-story hotel in Houston and decorated the interior with sixty-three shades of green. Architect Frank Lloyd Wright, when he witnessed it, said, "I always wondered what the inside of a jukebox looked like." But it opened with 175 movie stars, 50,000 people, and the Dorothy Lamour radio show.

The crowd was so dense that it took thirty minutes to move through the lobby. Jesse Jones got stuck in the entrance, and Mayor Oscar Holcombe had to wait outside for two hours. The radio actors had to shout their lines over the noise, unidentified people cut into the broadcast, and members of the audience grabbed the microphone to hoot into it. NBC cut off the broadcast, and the star of the show went to her room to weep. This scene provided a model for Edna Ferber's epic of modern Texas, *Giant*.

The state's literary tradition has supported and, to an extent, created the mystique. At the center of the tradition were three writers from the University of Texas—J. Frank Dobie, a folklorist; Walter Prescott Webb, a historian; and Roy Bedichek, a naturalist. They lived and

Texans, we are Americans. Americans, we are human beings. That is the real transition, and should be. But this is hard, I think, for us to accept and much harder to enjoy, because the essence of our idea of self, of Texas as a culture, is independence. For this key self-idea of ours, the meaning of interdependence is penetration. Or, to be exact, our being penetrated: penetrated by national commerce, penetrated by news we don't want to be, much less read about. Penetrated by foreign people's problems, penetrated by fear of enemy missiles that can penetrate us and explode us.

RONNIE DUGGER, TEXAS IN TRANSITION CONFERENCE, AUSTIN, 1986

Shamrock Hotel, Houston. Photograph by David G. McComb.

Walter Prescott Webb, a builder of the Texas mystique and the foremost historian of Texas. Barker Texas History Center, The University of Texas at Austin.

worked together in Austin for thirty years after World War I and were close friends. Once a month they met at Dobie's Hill Country ranch, Paisano, sometimes with invited guests, to sit around a campfire, sip whiskey, swap stories, and talk of intellectual matters. They stimulated each other. Dobie wrote about lost gold mines, buried treasure, longhorns, mustangs, and cowboys. He once said, "They call me a folklorist, but I am not a scientific folklorist. After I have heard a story, I do all I can to improve it." This was warning to those who sought unvarnished truth in Dobie's work.

Webb, after failing graduate work at the University of Chicago, returned to Texas to complete revolutionary studies of frontiers and a history of the Texas Rangers. He was responsible for the view of the Ranger as "a man standing alone between a society and its enemies." He wrote in 1935, "The real Ranger has been a very quiet, deliberate, gentle person who could gaze calmly into the eye of a murderer, divine his thoughts, and anticipate his action, a man who could ride straight up to death." He thus added to the Texas mystique.

Bedichek for most of his life worked as the director of the University Interscholastic League of Texas and did his publishing after retirement. In his sensitive way he wrote about Indians and the natural history of his homeland. Dobie encouraged him, and the respect between the two was touching. "You are as good as grass," Dobie said to his friend. Bedichek answered, "Don Quixote once told Sancho Panza, 'You are as good as bread. Nothing but the sexton and his spade will ever part us.'"

Bedichek died of heart failure in 1959, Webb died in a single-car accident in 1963, and Dobie succumbed to old age in 1964. The generation thus passed, but together they turned the minds of writers to the rural countryside. As Dobie said, "Great literature transcends its native land, but none that I know of ignores its own soil." They were western, not southern, however, and the Texas mystique at this point began to wear a Stetson.

A group of younger transitional writers led by Larry McMurtry challenged their dominance in the late 1960s. McMurtry accused the "Big Three" of making a fetish of nature and ignoring urban themes. "The world outside never heard of Bedichek, hasn't read Webb, and isn't particularly interested in Dobie," he wrote. "The world inside doesn't read much and doesn't read well, but the three men were loved and honored there. Their merits as men were long ago confused with their merits as writers . . ." McMurtry, who followed his own advice for a while, became an expatriate like many Texas writers and finally gave in to the lure of the Old West with the 1985 Pulitzer Prize novel *Lonesome Dove.*

This novel may well represent the highest literary point of the Texas mystique, but there were other thrusts into the outside world to support it. Since 1978 the television show *Dallas* has portrayed the saga of the oil-rich Ewing family. The Southfork Ranch, which used to be the Duncan Ranch, became the number one tourist site in Dallas, and when Miss Ellie, the matriarch on the show, announced a Jock Ewing Memorial Scholarship, fifteen Southern Methodist University students applied. It was a mixup of illusion with reality, and to avoid embarrassment Lorimar Productions provided a scholarship to the school.

The Best Little Whorehouse in Texas, written and produced by Larry King, Peter Masterson, and Carol Hall, gave Broadway and moviegoers another glimpse of the mystique, and the "outlaw" country music of Willie Nelson, Waylon Jennings, and Kris Kristofferson carried it on the radio waves. Their music built upon the residual western swing that was a combination of cowboy and cotton-farmer songs that went back to the 1920s. Bob Wills had popularized western swing regionally while playing for politician W. Lee O'Daniel. His later group, the Texas Playboys, performed into the 1950s. In 1970, however, various alienated musicians began to drift into Austin, a liberal haven that also tolerated Janis Joplin, to play a combination of western, rock, blues, and gospel music at Armadillo World Headquarters. Willie Nelson, Jerry Jeff Walker, and Michael Murphy were among them. Nelson's "Red-Headed Stranger" (1975), an allegory of love and

The Chicken Ranch

It was just "a lil' ole bitty pissant country place," according to a song in Broadway's *The Best Little Whorehouse in Texas.* And so it was. It began in 1844, moved a half dozen times around LaGrange, and persevered as the oldest operating house of prostitution in the United States. The citizens of Fayette County were tolerant. Their motto was, "Work hard, play hard, and mind your own business."

Jessie Williams from Waco took over the house in 1905 in order to pull herself out of poverty. She did well during World War I and had trouble during the Depression like everyone else. The cost for sin was $1.50 in 1932, but in this rural area near Houston a chicken could be traded for the service. Hence the name, the Chicken Ranch. Williams died in 1961 at age eighty, but thirty-two-year-old Edna Milton bought the business the same year. Operating with twelve to fourteen women at a rate of $15 per visit, Milton made $500,000 annually. Unfortunately for her, Marvin Zindler, a consumer affairs reporter for Houston's KTRK-TV, began an exposé in 1973. Under such pressure the local sheriff had to close the ranch permanently.

Willie Nelson

With a twangy voice that sounded like the distillation of a hundred smoky honkytonks, Willie Nelson cut through the slick sound of Nashville to establish outlaw country music at his Fourth of July picnic at Dripping Springs in 1972. He was born in Fort Worth in 1933 and reared in the small town of Abbott, worked for a while as a disc jockey, and went to Nashville in 1960 to seek his fortune as a songwriter. He wrote "Crazy," "Night Life," and "Funny How Time Slips Away," which became classics, but the Nashville sound led in another direction.

Seeking honesty in music and life, Nelson left Nashville for Austin in 1972 and began performing at the Armadillo World Headquarters. Other rebels followed, and "honky soul" music "flowed like good wine" at the Fourth of July picnics. From that point Nelson's records, performances, and movie acting gained recognition. He disliked, however, the categorization of his work. "I look at it all as just being American music, sound or whatever, and if you like it, you like it," he commented in the late 1970s. "It don't need a name to be enjoyable."

murder, was among the best products of the time. Nelson sang about the myth, a reality that had never existed.

Until 1982, when plummeting oil prices reined in the Texas economy, few voices were heard to question the mystique. In fact, so much was accomplished from 1945 to 1982 that the period might well be considered a Texas renaissance. With their rich endowment the two major state university systems climbed into the front ranks of public institutions of higher education. The University of Texas retained its main campus and law school in Austin and its medical school in Galveston. It added, however, health science centers in Dallas, San Antonio, Houston, and Tyler in addition to branch campuses in Arlington, El Paso, Dallas, San Antonio, the Permian Basin, and Tyler. Texas A&M obtained a medical school in 1971 to enhance its College Station campus and veterinary medicine school. It opened a maritime branch in Galveston in 1962. Other schools—Texas Tech, the University of Houston—likewise expanded.

In public higher education Texas developed twenty-four four-year universities, five upper-level universities, forty-nine community colleges, seven medical schools, two dental schools, and an institute for the deaf. In the private sector the state possessed thirty-seven senior colleges and universities, four junior colleges, one medical school, and one dental school. Altogether these accounted for 762,000 students in 1986. In the public secondary and primary schools there were 2,933,000 students in 1,100 school districts. Youth, hopefully, would be well educated.

State expenditures for education have varied from a low of 36 percent of the total state budget in 1960 to a high of 45 percent in 1980 and 1984. About one-quarter goes to higher education. In 1985 students in the colleges and universities were paying only 3 percent of their actual costs, which made Texas one of the great bargains in education across the nation. Due to a pinched budget, however, the legislature ordered a rising tuition rate for the following ten years. Even with that, the rates were expected to remain among the lowest in the nation. Despite its financial troubles, therefore, Texas continued its generous support of education.

Schools and other institutions have also benefited from the philanthropic efforts of individuals and foundations. Millionaire Hugh Roy Cullen, for example, gave away 93 percent of his wealth, much of it to the University of Houston. The Sealy and Smith Foundation practically built the University of Texas Medical Branch in Galveston. The Moody Foundation, which started in 1960 as one of the top fifteen largest in the nation, gave money to hundreds of programs throughout the state. One of the more interesting efforts, however, has been that of the M. D. Anderson Foundation in Houston.

At his death in 1939 Monroe D. Anderson, a prosperous cotton factor, gave the bulk of his estate, about $20 million, to the foundation in order to advance medical knowledge and relieve human suffering. The major effort of the organization was to establish the Texas Medical Center south of downtown Houston near the Shamrock Hotel. There was already a nearby Veteran's Administration Hospital, and in time the center—fifty buildings on 546 acres—included Baylor Medical School, Texas Dental School, Arabia Temple Crippled Children's Clinic, Texas Children's Hospital, University of Texas M. D. Anderson Hospital and Tumor Institute, University of Houston School of Nursing, and a half-dozen major hospitals. Here, Drs. Michael DeBakey and Denton Cooley began their revolutionary heart transplants, and M. D. Anderson Hospital (now M. D. Anderson Cancer Center) became one of the top two cancer institutes in the country. Dr. Russell W. Cumley recorded the spirit of the hospital, noted for its research, in a widely copied poem:

> I am a cancer cell.
> Study me, know me,
> And you will hold the world in fief.
> Neglect me, man,
> And as surely as the fingers of the dawn,
> Grasp first the temples of the East,
> I will strike you dead.

Honkytonk Dance Halls

Scattered in the towns and cities across Texas are dance halls that continue the working-class tradition of drinking beer and dancing to guitars and fiddles. The custom goes back to early Texas when pioneers danced the splinters off puncheon floors during all-night parties. It was a lot of trouble to gather enough people, and so, once together, everyone took advantage of the situation.

One cowboy of the nineteenth century, for example, rode 12 miles from his ranch to ask for a date, and then home again. He traveled 16 miles to town to hire a buggy, drove to the girl's house, then to the dance, attended the party, took the girl back home, returned the buggy, and rode his horse to his bunkhouse—a 128-mile jaunt.

The dance hall tradition lives on in places like Gilley's of Pasadena (Houston), Billy Bob's in Fort Worth, Longbranch in Kerrville, and Gruene Hall in Comal County, where people dance polkas, waltzes, spoke dances like the Cotton-eyed Joe, and two-step shuffles. The famous Texas two-step, danced with the feet close to the floor and the lady moving backward, uses six counts with several shifting steps to complete the sequence. Jeans, boots, and cowboy hats are customary, and the entire floor of dancers moves counterclockwise.

Billy Bob's at the Fort Worth Stockyards. Photograph by David G. McComb.

M. D. Anderson Hospital in the
Houston Medical Center, 1954.
Barker Texas History Center, The
University of Texas at Austin.

Beyond the medical research there were other triumphs
for Texas. Aided by state funding through the Texas Commission on the Arts, which started in 1965, the larger cities sponsored and improved symphony orchestras, opera
companies, ballet troupes, and stage theatres. During the
interwar period the Houston Symphony Orchestra pro-
gressed from ten to forty concerts per season, and Maestro
Ernst Hoffmann learned to deal with a cigar-smoking
timpanist and a bassoonist who performed with his shoes
off. Under a string of internationally known conductors,
including André Previn, who went native and pranced
around the city with girlfriend Mia Farrow wearing jeans
and sandals, the orchestra rose to first-class competence.

The symphony, along with a top-rated opera company
that developed in the early 1980s, found a splendid home
in Jones Hall for the Performing Arts, donated to the city
in 1966 by the Houston Endowment Foundation. There is
always a question in such construction about the acous-
tics, a phenomenon little understood by engineers. Proper
sound is easy to miss, as at Lincoln Center in New York
City. But Houston was lucky, and on opening night, as a
music critic put it, "Music burst forth like a sparkling
bubble of champagne." In 1987 the $72 million Wortham
Center opened as a home for the Houston opera and ballet companies. Here the Houston Grand Opera presented
the world premiere of *Nixon in China* and the Houston
Ballet offered the world premiere of *The Hunchback of
Notre Dame.*

Across the street from Jones Hall in downtown Houston contributors built the new Alley Theatre in 1968. Theatrical groups have been a part of the cultural life of almost every city in Texas, but they have suffered high mortality rates. The Alley, however, which was started by Nina Vance in 1947, developed into an enduring repertory theatre. It was able to attract large donations from the Ford Foundation and Houston Endowment, and presented the debut of Paul Zindel's Pulitzer Prize play, *Effect of Gamma Rays on Man in the Moon Marigolds*.

Similarly, in Dallas Margo Jones followed a dream of community theater and with the help of the Rockefeller Foundation developed theater-in-the-round. In 1954 her production of *Inherit the Wind* traveled from Dallas to Broadway. Jones died suddenly in 1955, however, apparently after inhaling the fumes of a carpet cleaner by mistake. Dallas recently built an orchestra hall, but according to A. C. Greene, who has analyzed the city, Dallas has only a pseudo-culture. Patrons looked to New York City for approval and were generally ignorant of art. Dallas does have, however, a new art museum in its downtown cultural district.

Fort Worth patrons, on the other hand, assembled one of the nation's best collections of western art and photographs at the Amon Carter Museum, a building designed by Philip Johnson and made of Texas shellstone. The city also possesses the Kimbell Art Museum of European and British art. It opened in 1972 in a structure of multiple vaults and gardens designed by Louis I. Kahn and was hailed as the best small art museum facility in the United States. Fort Worth competed with Houston's Museum of Fine Arts, but the Bayou City developed a reputation as an art market which before the oil recession was the second best in the United States. Through the promotion of enthusiasts, moreover, a "Houston School" of avant garde artists emerged which contrasted with the more conservative artists in Dallas, Austin, and Fort Worth.

Important for the reputation of Houston as an art center has been the interest of John and Dominique de Menil. In 1971 they built the Rothko Chapel on the campus of the University of St. Thomas in the quiet Montrose section of the city. The small brick building contained no symbolic imagery—only fourteen huge black abstract paintings by Mark Rothko. Outside in a small reflection pool they placed Barnett Newman's sculpture dedicated to Martin Luther King, *The Broken Obelisk*—a twenty-six-foot truncated steel shaft, naturally rusted and balanced on a pyramidal point. From around the world came pilgrims seeking the chapel as a sacred place of meditation.

The de Menils gave more. John de Menil had been chairman of the board of Schlumberger, a manufacturer of oil tools. When he died, his wife, with the Schlumberger fortune, continued their concern for the welfare of their adopted city. They were both from France and had been patrons of the arts since 1931. In 1987, one block away from the chapel, Dominique de Menil opened a long gray and white gallery designed by Renzo Piano of Italy to display her 10,000-piece collection of modern art. Other cities—Paris, Los Angeles, New York—had tried to obtain the collection, but she found the informality she wanted in Houston. At the opening celebration residents in the neighborhood gathered outside in shorts and raised their Lone Star beer cans in salute. This was what she wanted, and at the dedication she said, "Artists are economically useless—yet they are indispensable. A political regime where artists are persecuted is stifling, unbearable. Man cannot live by bread alone. We need painters, poets, musicians, filmmakers, philosophers, dancers, and saints."

In the art of architecture both Houston and Dallas built stunning skylines, showcases of modern and postmodern buildings. With ruthless disregard for the past, Houston and Dallas cleared and excavated, assembled and soared. Gerald D. Hines, a Houston contractor with a national reputation, put up the startling twin black trapezoid towers of Pennzoil Place, designed by Philip Johnson of New York. He also constructed the 998-foot-high, five-sided shaft of pale gray granite of the Texas Commerce Plaza, designed by I. M. Pei of New York City.

Pei, in turn, drew the plans for the cantilevered, reverse-tiered city hall of Dallas. A large bronze statue, "Dallas Piece" by Henry Moore, presided in front. Trammell Crow of Dallas, who started as a bank teller, became the largest commercial builder in the country. He opened the World Trade Center in 1974 and in 1984 the Dallas Market Center, which combined a cluster of buildings covering 160 acres designed especially for wholesale marketing.

For its 250th anniversary San Antonio hosted a HemisFair in 1968. Officials razed ninety-two slum acres near the Alamo for the construction of permanent display buildings, including the dramatic Tower of the Americas. They rejected a plan to integrate the older structures of the site with the new ones; as a result, the city possesses a huge, nearly lifeless white scar in the heart of the down-

Rothko Chapel, Houston. Photograph by David G. McComb.

town. The fair, like most modern world fairs, lost money.

Despite their glittering, attractive downtown buildings, Dallas, Houston, San Antonio, and Fort Worth sprawled into the countryside with a scattering of ten- to twenty-story office buildings, thrown as if by centrifugal force onto the hinterland. In 1988 three-quarters of Houston's office space was outside the central business district. Bankers, lawyers, government agents, and oil people remained downtown, but engineers, architects, doctors, insurance agents, and retail merchants moved to the suburbs. Shopping centers such as Houston's exclusive Galleria with an indoor ice-skating rink sought the distant rich neighborhoods where people lived and where there was room to park cars.

The Bayou City's first mall opened in 1956; its first superhighway, the Gulf Freeway, in 1952. This marked the emergence of an automotive city, which added cost to the urban services because of the distance covered. Citizens and politicians repeatedly rejected the idea of zoning to channel growth, with the result that Houston became the largest unzoned city in the United States. There existed, moreover, no natural barriers to impede the spread and force concentration.

To some people this signaled a dynamic spirit; to others it meant chaos. A visiting French journalist commented in 1962, the time of the last zoning defeat, "There is no plan. I am horrified. Everyone is doing just as he pleases, building here and building there . . . Houston is spreading like a spilled bucket of water." Architect Philip Johnson said in contrast, "I like Houston, you know. It's the last great nineteenth-century city . . . what I mean is that Houston has a spirit about it that is truly American. An optimism, if you will. People there aren't afraid to try something new."

One of the most daring examples of this spirit was the Astrodome. Judge Roy Hofheinz, a millionaire and former mayor, took the idea from the ancient Romans, who covered their coliseum with an awning in bad weather and cooled it with the spray of fountains. Houston had beastly

Menil Collection, Houston. Photograph by David G. McComb.

weather and was well on its way to becoming the most air-conditioned city in the nation in the 1960s. Hofheinz and R. E. "Bob" Smith, moreover, had acquired a National League franchise and needed a baseball stadium.

The judge consulted engineers and then presented a plan for an air-conditioned domed stadium to the people of Houston and Harris County. Although such an arena had never been built before, the people voted county bonds for financing, and in 1965 the Astrodome opened. President Lyndon Johnson slipped in with a special pass from Hofheinz; the four-story-high billboard flashed "Tilt" when Mickey Mantle lofted his home run; the crowd of forty-eight thousand roared; and sportswriter Mickey Herskowitz wrote, "Fantasy met reality, and the New York Yankees lost. It was, in short, Domesday." The Astrodome became a national sports sensation. Since then other cities have constructed covered stadiums, larger and at greater expense, but the Astrodome was the first. Houstonians were not afraid to try something new.

Even with zoning ordinances, other major Texas cities sprawled into their surroundings in much the same manner. Dallas worked out a comprehensive growth plan, Goals for Dallas, in 1966, reworked it in 1977, and then partially ignored it. Fort Worth did much the same with its revolutionary Gruen Plan of 1956. Leaders in both of these cities feared that urban renewal with the use of necessary federal dollars would lead to control by Washington bureaucrats.

Texans, meanwhile, took to automobiles as Comanches had taken to horses. Motor vehicle registration lagged only slightly behind the population—in 1986 there were 16.7 million citizens and 14.3 million vehicles. In Dallas the mayor's wife dramatized the love affair in 1949 by christening the new Central Expressway with a bottle of cologne. After a 1946 amendment passed to protect the highway fund from the periodic raids of the legislature, the Texas Highway Department built a superb network of roads, which doubled the miles of state roads to 72,000. The federal interstate program started in 1956, and the result was superhighways encircling and cutting through the major cities, bypassing the towns, and encouraging automobile travel.

Automobile registrations jumped at a rate of 14 percent per year from 1946 to 1950 and then leveled off to a 5 percent growth rate. This meant that in the 1980s San Antonio gained 75 vehicles per day, Dallas 85, Fort Worth 77, and Houston 120.

Astrodome

Completed in 1965, the Harris County Domed Stadium, or Astrodome, was the first enclosed, air-conditioned sports arena large enough for baseball and football games. It was funded at a cost of $45,350,000 by the taxpayers of Harris County and the Houston Sports Association, which owned the Astros. The rigid dome was 710 feet in diameter, 218 feet high, and offered a 642-foot clear span. It was designed to withstand winds of 130 miles per hour and gusts of 165. It could seat forty-five thousand baseball fans and fifty-two thousand football spectators, shielded in comfort from the heavy heat of summer and the blue northers of winter.

When it opened, New York's Mickey Mantle belted a home run to right center field, but the Astros won 2 to 1. Although the players could not hit the ceiling, there was an initial problem of lighting. The sun shining through the translucent plastic panels made the ball impossible to track across the network of girders. Painting the outside solved that problem, but then the grass died on the field from lack of light. Roy Hofheinz, the entrepreneur who put it all together, contacted Chemstrand, which was then experimenting with an outdoor carpet of artificial grass. This was placed on the floor of the stadium and renamed Astroturf. The impact of this bold venture was the construction of other enclosed stadiums and the widespread use of artificial playing surfaces across the nation.

To repair the leaky roof and catch up on maintenance, the county spent $49 million in 1986, which matched the original construction cost, and then voted another $50 million in 1988 to expand the seating and replace the Astroturf. This was necessary in order to keep the Houston Oilers football team in the city.

There were consequences. The last passenger train left Dallas in 1969; Houston had only one left in 1974, the year private passenger train service ceased in Texas. Amtrak in the 1980s continued to run two passenger trains to serve eighteen cities. Trolleys stopped in the 1940s and 1950s. Bus service, particularly within the metropolises, suffered, and traffic jams became a part of the daily routine.

In Houston a journalist stuck behind a white Lincoln Continental containing men with big cowboy hats observed a helicopter dropping to the grass beside it. One of the men left the car, boarded the helicopter, and whirled away. It was a way to beat a traffic jam—if you were in a hurry, if you had the money, and if you had a telephone in your car. Still, the time of the daily commute averaged fifteen to twenty minutes in the early 1980s. The improved technology—roadways, automobiles, rationalization of traffic patterns—allowed people to travel from greater distances in the same amount of time as earlier. It was generally thought that thirty minutes, whether by walking, bicycle, horseback, streetcar, subway, bus, train, or car, was the common limit of human tolerance.

The shortages of gasoline in 1973–1974 and 1979 provided an unlearned lesson about dependency on automobile transportation. About 40 percent of the filling stations in the big cities ran out of fuel at some point. They closed on the weekends and served customers on a basis of odd- or even-numbered license plates. Traffic jams on the freeways almost disappeared because people were waiting, sometimes as long as an hour, to obtain gasoline. In Houston, an auto-dependent city where 87 percent of the people use a car to get to work, it was rumored that half the population had become neurotic.

Between the cities the airlines took over much of the passenger traffic—it sometimes took less time to cover the distance between the towns than it took to travel by car or taxi to and from the airports. In the late 1930s Braniff and Eastern began to fly regular schedules in Texas, and after the war Southern, Mid-Continent, Pan American, and Trans-Texas joined in the competition. Houston opened Hobby Airport in 1954 and Intercontinental in 1969, but much of its air traffic, like the railroads of old, went north and south. Dallas, with Love Field, an expanded World War I training base, and Dallas/Fort Worth International, which opened in 1974, dominated the heavy east-west flow of air traffic.

In 1987 Dallas/Fort Worth, the "Air Harbor of the World," scheduled 1,750 flights, more than twice as many

as Houston, and travelers polled by *USA Today* in 1987 considered it second only to Atlanta as the best airport in the nation. The traffic amounted to about half of the total for the state; Houston had 28 percent, and other places shared the remainder. The new Dallas/Fort Worth airport also represented a truce in the rivalry of the two Trinity River cities and has been a major factor in the development of the "metroplex," the combined metropolitan units. The detente had to wait for the death of Amon Carter in 1955.

The Fort Worth promoter and newspaperman had bashed Dallas with enduring passion. He referred to his neighbor as "Big d" and printed cards that read, "Please flush twice when you use the washroom. Dallas needs the water." After World War II he promoted a joint airport, Greater Southwest International, but both the airlines and Dallas refused to cooperate. It was a bitter defeat for Carter, but in the 1970s federal officials forced cooperation between the two rivals with the new airfield located a few miles farther to the north.

Arlington, a sleepy town between Dallas and Fort Worth, awakened in the 1950s with the jet noise, a General Motors plant, interstate highways, and amusement parks to become the host for a branch of the University of Texas and the Texas Rangers baseball club. Nearby Irving welcomed the Dallas Cowboys football team.

Astrodome, Houston. Photograph by David G. McComb.

Dallas City Hall. Photograph by
David G. McComb.

Major league professional sports teams began to arrive
in the early 1960s to add to an already rich sports tradition. The state had contributed Jack Johnson to boxing;
Tris Speaker to baseball; Ben Hogan and Babe Didrikson
to golf; Sammy Baugh, Doak Walker, and Bobby Layne to
football; Bobby Morrow to track; and Skippy Browning to
diving. Major league baseball, beginning with the Colt
45s in Houston in 1962 (they became the Astros in 1964)
and the Rangers in Arlington in 1972 damaged but did not
kill minor league ball. The Texas League survived. Professional basketball started with the San Antonio Spurs in
1967 and continued with the Houston Rockets in 1971
and the Dallas Mavericks in 1980.

If Texas embraced a "national sport," however, it was
football. Hulking linemen, smart quarterbacks, lean
runners, prancing bands, buxom cheerleaders, frazzled
coaches, crazed fans—those were the ingredients of a fall
Texas weekend. Small towns painted the schedule of their
high school team on city-limit billboards and bragged
about past triumphs on their water towers. Big towns followed the Southwest Conference and reveled in the annual "shoot-outs." The games dominated life and thought.
At the Plano versus Odessa game in 1978, for example, a
local minister giving the invocation said wistfully: "Bless
each of us as fans: teach us to want the Kingdom of Heaven
with all the fullness of spirit with which we want a touch-

down for our team on this glorious evening. In Jesus' name we pray. Amen."

At times things got out of hand. In 1926 during a riot after the Baylor–Texas A&M game a cadet died. The Aggies were so angry that they decided to march to Waco with a cannon and level the Baylor campus. The administrators dissuaded them. In 1981, to illustrate that a sanguine spirit endures, an Aggie cadet drew a sword and threatened an S.M.U. cheerleader who had stepped on the sacred football turf of Kyle Field.

During the 1980s the National Collegiate Athletic Association managed to condemn most of the Southwest Conference schools for infractions. The worst, however, fell on SMU in 1987 when the NCAA gave it a "death penalty" (a two-year ban on football) for repeated violations. The scandal involved payment to athletes, and implicated Governor William Clements, who had been the chairman of SMU's board. The school vowed to return to the football wars, however, and meantime advertised its soccer season on a sign at the edge of the campus.

Sports historians argue that the games people play reflect their character, and if that is true, then Texans like a disciplined, male-dominated, competitive, violent game of strategy and strength in which the women sit on the sidelines and cheer. For the most part, football satisfied the Texas mystique. There was to be no nonsense, either. In 1948 the high school coach at Stinnett noticed a girl named Frankie Groves at a school picnic. She was sixteen, 105 pounds, and a ruthless tackler. The coach recruited her and let her play in the homecoming game. Said Frankie, "They weren't so tough. Heck, I didn't even get my lipstick smeared." The Interscholastic League, however, ruled females ineligible, and the school fired the coach. Football was a game reserved for males.

The sports image has been changed somewhat, however, in recent years by the winning women's basketball team at the University of Texas, where fan attendance has outpaced that of the less successful men's team. The fans slowly embraced the professional teams, too, entranced initially by the stellar play of Doak Walker and Bobby Layne with the Detroit Lions on flickering black and white television sets.

Unable to obtain franchises, K. S. "Bud" Adams in Houston and Lamar Hunt in Dallas founded the American Football League in 1959–1960. With the help of television revenue they succeeded and forced a merger with the National Football League in 1970. The Houston Oilers

Sammy Baugh

Sammy Baugh was nicknamed "Slinging Sammy" after he turned Southwest Conference football into an aerial circus during his years at Texas Christian University in the mid-1930s. During one game between TCU and the University of Texas, the TCU center openly announced to the Texas players, "Gentlemen, Mr. Baugh is going to pass again. I don't know just where it'll go, but it'll be good. Ready?" The completed pass gained twenty-five yards.

Baugh was a six-foot two-inch, 175-pound all-around athlete born in Temple who played both quarterback and defensive back. He was a master of the quick kick; he threw the ball with a sidearm, slinging motion and took his sport with deadly seriousness. His only "vice" was playing pinball machines for fun. His professional career with the Washington Redskins, 1937–1952, did much to change the game to a passing offense. He led the National Football League six times in passing and four times in punting. In 1945, one of his best seasons, he completed 70.3 percent of his passes. Following his professional playing, Baugh coached for Hardin-Simmons University from 1955 to 1959, the New York Titans in 1960 and 1961, and the Houston Oilers in 1964.

"Babe" Didrikson Zaharias

Born in Port Arthur in 1914, Mildred Didrikson grew up in Beaumont with a love of sports. She practiced hurdles by jumping the hedges between her house and the corner grocery, and earned the nickname "Babe" after Babe Ruth from the homeruns she hit while playing sandlot baseball. She competed in basketball for an insurance company in Dallas in 1930 and by herself won the team championship at the national A.A.U. track championships in 1932. She went on that summer to set two world records and take two gold medals and one silver at the Los Angeles Olympics.

In 1935 she started a golf career and between 1940 and 1950 won every major golf title. In 1938 she married George Zaharias, a professional wrestler from Colorado. In 1953 she began to suffer from cancer, but continued her career, which included playing benefits for cancer research. She died of the disease in Galveston in 1956. The Associated Press voted her the greatest woman athlete of the first half of the twentieth century. Slat thin in her younger days—5 feet 7 inches and 105 pounds—she spoke with a Texas twang and sometimes irritated others with her self-confidence and practical jokes. She was not a feminist, but an athlete who loved competition. To a reporter she once poignantly commented, "I know that I am not pretty, but I do try to be graceful."

won the first few years, lost, and then revived in the 1970s under Coach "Bum" Phillips. He wore western-style hats and boots, kept his hair brush-cut short, spoke with the humor of a West Texas cowboy, and had problems with the Steelers:

> Ever been to a circus when the bears got loose? The people scatter. That was us out there the second half. (Houston v. Pittsburgh, 1976)

> When we play them, it's not a game—it's a collision. The team with the most band-aids wins. (Comment about Pittsburgh)

> The behinder we got, the worser it got. (Division championship against Pittsburgh, 1979)

> An all-Texas Super Bowl? The world isn't ready for that. If you think we're obnoxious now . . .

The Dallas Cowboys, an NFL franchise, began play in 1960 at the Cotton Bowl under Coach Tom Landry. The team gradually gained in support, particularly with quarterbacks Don Meredith and Roger Staubach, who popularized the shotgun formation. They lost twice in championship games to Vince Lombardi's Green Bay Packers in 1966 and 1967; and in the Super Bowl they lost in 1971, won in 1972, lost in 1976, won in 1978, and lost in 1979.

The Cowboys began playing in Texas Stadium, a half-enclosed doughnut arena in Irving near Dallas in 1971. Cowboy souvenirs outsold those of other clubs, and the team along with its sexy cheerleaders developed a following in Mexico and across the United States. In 1979 a scriptwriter with NFL films used the nickname "America's Team," and the name stuck even though it embarrassed the members. There was a certain truth in it at the time, but the byname did imply a responsibility the team was unwilling to carry.

There was a problem, too, with the Texas mystique. The myth masked the changes, hid the problems, and clouded the truth. And what was not seen by Texans did hurt. Oil, the most dynamic element in the state economy, injured Texas the most. In the 1930s, with the outpouring of East Texas crude, the Lone Star State became the leading producer of the world. In time, with the development of the Middle Eastern fields, Texas became less important but remained the number one producer in the United States. Offshore exploration aided in this ranking. Through litigation and politics Texas was able to retain state possession of its tidelands, which extended three leagues (10.3 miles) from shore. By the mid-1960s sixteen fields had been uncovered beneath the shallow Gulf waters of the continental shelf.

Peak production for Texas came in 1972 and then dropped to about two-thirds that amount. Proven reserves of gas and oil likewise declined, and there appeared no new discoveries of major consequence. From the late 1950s the imports of crude petroleum into Texas ports have steadily increased to feed the coastal refineries. The outlook, therefore, was one of declining resources of petroleum to a point of depletion, along with an established petrochemical industry increasingly dependent upon foreign supplies.

Houston, old and new. Photograph by David G. McComb.

Houston freeways. Houston Chamber of Commerce.

In the early 1980s 59 of the 100 largest Texas companies were oil-related; half of Texas' industrial production was oil-related; 25 percent of the gross income from goods and services was oil-related. The income from oil was almost three times that from agriculture. In 1983 the petroleum business employed 350,000 people (6 percent of the work force). It was estimated that by spending and respending, wages multiplied some ten times in the economy. Compared with the rest of the United States, the oil and gas industry was two and a half times more economically significant for Texas. The state, therefore, was partially dependent upon the fortunes of a global petroleum industry. An upswing or downswing in oil prices would have a strong effect on the Texas economy.

Beginning in late 1981 with the breakdown of the OPEC cartel which had manipulated world production since the early 1970s, petroleum began to glut the market and prices dropped. Texas suffered a boom and bust. In 1970 the average price of crude oil per barrel was $3.18; in 1980 it was $21.59; in 1981, $31.77; in 1985, $24.08; and in 1988, $18.00. The high was $39 in 1981 and the low was $10 in 1986. It takes roughly $15 per barrel for a company to break even. The welfare of the state, therefore, depended upon the monopoly control of oil by nations halfway around the globe. So much for economic self-sufficiency. This was a blow to the independence and wealth of the Lone Star State and the Texas mystique.

Texas, along with other oil-dependent states, slid into a depression. Companies stored their rusting drilling rigs in open fields; oil stock-market values dribbled downward; unemployment rose as high as 17 percent in the Rio Grande Valley, 12 percent in Houston; real estate prices dropped; banks became shaky and anxiously looked for out-of-state mergers. The 50 bank failures of 1987 almost doubled the previous record for other states. During 1988 Texas lost 113 banks.

Early in 1988 federal officials tried to work out a "Southwest Plan" to merge 109 (39 percent) insolvent Texas savings and loan companies. In August the Federal Deposit Insurance Corporation had to save the prestigious RepublicBank of Dallas with $4 billion, the largest bank rescue in U.S. history, and *The Economist* reported, "Almost every major bank in Texas has had a recent change of ownership. Texans no longer own Texas banks."

Celebrities such as heart surgeon Denton Cooley and former governor John Connally went bankrupt. The King Ranch retired or laid off more than half its seven hundred employees, and Eddie Chiles, whose shrinking fortune suffered with the oil industry, began to look for a purchaser of his professional baseball team, the Texas Rangers. In announcing a $1 billion state deficit in 1987, state comptroller Bob Bullock commented, "The last time you invited me to speak, you asked me to talk about money. I said at the time that I could make the shortest talk in legislative history: You didn't have any. Today, I would say you have even less."

It was not as bad as the Great Depression of the 1930s, but it was sobering. There was no end in sight. Life was no longer so easy. There were lean economic wolves stalking the plush suburbs of Highland Park in Dallas and River Oaks in Houston. "How do you get a Texas oilman out of a tree?" went the joke. "Cut the rope" was the answer.

Other industries remained reasonably healthy within the strong U.S. economy. High-technology industries involving communications, aircraft, and electronics aided the crippled economy. In Texas, they had located mainly in Dallas, Houston, and Austin, and they involved only 4 percent of the work force. Among the more famous was Texas Instruments of Dallas, which emerged from a geophysical firm in 1951. TI was one of the first to purchase a license to manufacture transistors, and consequently entered the electronics field at an early date. Jack St. Clair Kilby of TI invented the integrated circuit, which made possible the critical breakthrough to miniaturization in 1958. He also presented the world with the pocket calculator in 1971.

General Dynamics, Rockwell, LTV, Lockheed, E-Systems, and Bell Helicopter located in the Dallas–Fort Worth area in the 1940s and 1950s, providing Texas with a pool of first-generation electronic industries. Others spun off from these, such as Datapoint and Tandy Corporation, and by 1984 the industry employed 226,000 people, over half of them in the Dallas–Fort Worth area. This, in addition to its hold on the clothing business, gave Dallas a certain insulation from the oil depression.

Houston attracted its share of high-tech workers with the founding of the Manned Spacecraft Center in 1961–1962. Through a series of intricate moves Humble Oil Company gave Rice University 1,000 acres of land southeast of Houston. Rice gave it to the National Aeronautics and Space Administration. NASA financed a $60 million facility, and Brown and Root Construction Company built it. George R. Brown of Brown and Root was also chairman of the Board of Trustees at Rice, and Rice received a grant to establish a department of space science. It was a happy circumstance, and Houston assumed the sobriquet "Space City, U.S.A." The space center with the affiliated firms of the enterprise generated about 5 percent of Houston's income at the end of the 1970s.

In the countryside, the supposed bastion of independence, farmers and ranchers, with the aid of outside research, education, and government programs, turned to agribusiness. This meant larger, highly capitalized, dependent places, which were expensive to operate but more productive. Agribusiness called for the use of irrigation, pesticides, herbicides, feedlots, artificial insemination, nutrition analysis, and cooperative marketing. Average farm investment changed from $6,000 in 1940 to $481,000 in 1984; the number of people working changed from 1,475,000 in 1940, to 205,000 in 1983, to 160,000 in 1987.

A severe drought from 1950 to 1957, which blew dust from the Panhandle to Dallas, impelled the broader use of sprinkler irrigation on the high plains. The unnatural green spots dotting the light brown earth seen by air travelers were the result of center-pivot sprinklers that drew water from the Great Plains aquifers. Cotton remained the leading crop, followed by wheat, sorghum, corn, hay, rice, soybeans, and peanuts. Livestock production, particularly cattle, was five times in value ahead of cotton cultivation. Cattle feedlots boomed in the 1960s and

Manned Spacecraft Center (NASA)

The National Aeronautics and Space Administration constructed the Lyndon B. Johnson Manned Spacecraft Center twenty-five miles southeast of Houston on 1,620 acres donated mainly by Rice University. It opened in 1961–1962 and by mid-decade employed almost five thousand people and had attracted 125 space-related companies to the Houston area. Its purpose was to control the communications of space flights, and in 1969, when the astronauts landed for the first time on the moon, Neil Armstrong triumphantly announced, "Houston . . . Tranquility Base here. The *Eagle* has landed!"

Saturn rocket, NASA Manned Spacecraft Center. Photograph by David G. McComb.

Tower of the Americas, San Antonio. Photograph by David G. McComb.

1970s, overproduced, and then declined. Nonetheless, there still exists about one cow per person in the state.

Between 1940 and 1980 over one hundred reservoirs were built, increasing water in storage by ten times. There emerged, nonetheless, a vague worry on the plains about the continuing decline and pollution of the aquifers. Like the eventual exhaustion of the oil, the depletion of water was predictable. Without water and without oil West Texas would face a bleak future. What then of the Texas mystique?

The urbanization and population growth of Texas, of course, continued in the postwar years. Between 1950 and 1980, Texas population doubled from seven to fourteen million, with an estimated seventeen million in 1987, and the state moved from sixth to third largest in the nation. One-third of the population had been born elsewhere, and two-thirds of the migrants came from places outside the Old South. Texas passed the average national figure for percentage of people in cities by several points. Eighty percent were urban Texans. Houston gained a million people to become officially the fifth largest city in the United States; estimates now place it in fourth place, ahead of Philadelphia and behind New York, Chicago, and Los Angeles. Dallas attracted a half-million and moved into seventh place; San Antonio became tenth with a gain of one-third million.

Only a little over 1 percent of the population were actual working farmers and ranchers; others simply lived outside a defined urban area. It made little difference. With television sets, radios, big-city newspaper delivery, magazines, books, mail, paved roads, and an easy means of travel, the people living in rural Texas became as ur-

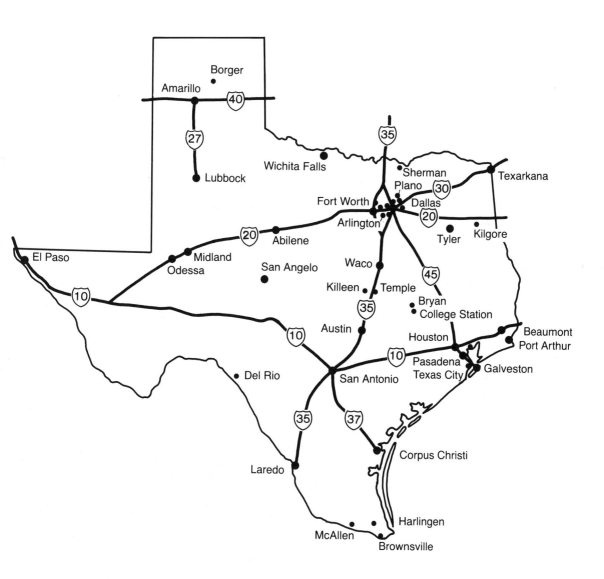

Map 5. Major Cities and the Interstate Highways

banized as the rest of the population. For all its open spaces, Stetsons, and high-heeled boots, modern Texas was an urban state within a nation of cities held together by a national network of connecting economic, political, military, and cultural strands. Ronnie Dugger was right when he spoke about penetration. Texas citizens were tied to a larger fate.

As might be expected, Texas suffered indigestion from big-city problems like the rest of the country. Air pollution was one difficulty. In 1958 commercial airline pilots could find their way to Houston by following a mile-wide plume of industrial haze streaking inland to Austin and Dallas. Before then, as early as the 1940s people complained of industrial odor, and in 1953 Harris County created a pollution control section in its health department.

The main difficulty came when a rare east wind blustered up the ship channel, concentrated the bad air, and blew the pollutants into the city. The sulphur compounds

Houston Ship Channel/Port of Houston. Houston Chamber of Commerce.

were occasionally high enough to blacken lead-based paint and damage foliage. Efforts to improve air quality helped, but Houston was second in the nation to Los Angeles for ozone levels. Dallas and others also suffered, particularly from auto emissions, but the open, flat terrain of most Texas cities and the prevailing winds mitigated the problem. It was generally not as bad as in Denver or Los Angeles.

Conditions were not so pleasant, either, in some of the waterways. After a good start early in the century, Houstonians allowed sewage control to slip, and Buffalo Bayou became increasingly polluted. By the end of the 1940s the bayou was the receptacle of industrial wastes, blood from slaughterhouses, grease, chemicals of all sorts, and raw sewage from overloaded treatment stations. The water was 80 percent sewage. As much as four feet of disease-laden sludge silted the bottom of the ship channel every year. There was no oxygen in the bayou between the San Jacinto Monument and the turning basin, and when heavy rains flushed the watercourse, there were massive fish kills in Galveston Bay.

Students from San Jacinto College went so far as to hold a funeral service for the bayou, and in 1967 a commissioner of the Federal Water Control Administration said, "The Houston Ship Channel, in all frankness, is one of the worst polluted bodies of water in the nation. In fact, on almost any day this channel may be the most badly polluted body of water in the entire world. Most days it would top the list."

At this point the local attitude was one of indifference—the natural environment was for exploitation. That had long been a western premise. In this case, however, a change occurred. Federal officials, the Texas Water Quality Board, and the Houston Chamber of Commerce insisted upon improvement. In the 1970s the city upgraded its sewage plants, industrial developers placed deed restrictions on pollution in their real estate contracts, offending companies were taken to federal court, and county vigilance increased through the efforts of Walter A. Quebedeaux, Jr., the pollution control officer. This intrepid investigator once had garbage dumped on his head from the stern of an Italian tanker while he was out in the channel in a rowboat searching for an oil leak.

Eighteen species of biological life returned to the waterway in 1972, thirty-four by 1975, and in 1980 fish were seen in the turning basin. Noting seagulls hovering around an outfall, Armco officials, who had been forced to clean up after their factory discharges were found to kill fish within minutes, triumphantly dipped healthy shrimp from the water and served them in the cafeteria. The watercourse was not perfect, yet it was a clear improvement.

Quebedeaux also developed instruments to identify an air polluter from as far as ten miles away. One of the major improvements for air quality, however, came when the state banned the burning of garbage in 1968. Many places burned refuse until then. Galveston, for example, greeted the tourists traveling over its causeway with a smoky exclamation point that continually undulated over its smoldering dump.

After 1968 Galveston and most other places resorted to sanitary landfills. This simple burying of garbage proved to be the cheapest solution, but there was always a problem of the location of the dump. As Mayor Louie Welch of Houston once lamented, "You know, when it comes to garbage, people want us to pick it up, but they don't want us to put it down again, especially if it is near their house."

Crime in the modern era, as folk wisdom indicated, was a big-city problem, and in Texas crime statistics generally Houston was followed in rank order by Dallas, San Antonio, and Fort Worth. The long Texas border on sea and land, furthermore, made it hard to stop the marijuana, heroin, and cocaine smuggled across by modern gangsters. As Assistant U.S. Attorney Terry Clark in Houston stated, "I don't care what anyone says; this is a war. Whoever has the most assets wins—and I am not at all sure we will."

The customers for the drug dealers were the city populations of the nation, and the desire for drugs added to the crime potential. In Texas Houston had long maintained a murderous reputation, but the most common of urban crimes, there and elsewhere, was still drunkenness. The breadth of the cities, the scattering of bars, the low police budgets, and perhaps an enduring frontier attitude contributed to high Texas crime rates.

A story told about Amon Carter, who liked to play the role of the mythic Texan, demonstrates the recklessness. At the 1928 Democratic Convention in Houston, Carter and a Fort Worth sheriff had to wait in the crowded Rice Hotel while the elevator passed by them four times. Finally, Carter could stand it no more. He snatched the sheriff's .45-caliber pistol and shot six times through the glass doors of the elevator into the shaft. No one was hurt, but the next time the elevator stopped.

This sort of attitude continued. Wesley West in the late 1940s regularly parked his bright green Cadillac in a bus zone outside his downtown Houston office. He just as regularly paid his $5 fine. He was an oil millionaire who lived in River Oaks, and no one seemed to mind the inconvenience. His brother, Jim, cruised the streets with police officers while he acted out a role of amateur cop. This stopped after he shot at a burglar and reportedly hit his police companion in the foot.

Texans have always liked their guns, and a gun rack in the back windshield of a pickup truck was a symbol of the macho mystique. Citizens wore handguns into the 1930s, and the number of guns still carried around can be surprising. In August 1966, for example, Charles Whitman, a Marine sharpshooter and sometime student at the University of Texas, went insane. He killed his mother and wife; filled a footlocker with food, water, ammunition, and six guns; and headed for the library tower on the campus. At the observation deck he clubbed the receptionist, killed two people, wounded two more, and opened fire on students 231 feet below.

With deadly accuracy the cross in his rifle scope found victims—walking on the bypaths, riding bicycles in nearby streets, and peering with curiosity through windows. He shot them all in one of the country's worst mass murders, a slaughter of seventeen killed and thirty wounded before a courageous policeman and a volunteer stopped him. During the hour-and-a-half fusillade private citizens from all around the campus pulled rifles from their cars and shot back. Afterward the chief of police noted that these people had acted responsibly and had helped to keep the sniper pinned down.

The most notorious crime in modern Texas history, however, was the assassination of President John F. Kennedy during a motorcade in downtown Dallas on November 22, 1963. Lee Harvey Oswald had grown up in Texas and Louisiana, trained with the Marine Corps, and spent some time in the Soviet Union. When Kennedy traveled to Texas on a political fence-mending trip, Oswald, apparently acting alone, shot the president with a high-powered rifle from the sixth floor of the Texas School Book Depository. Kennedy, struck in the head, was killed, while Governor John Connally, riding in the same car, was hit in the back, wrist, and leg. Connally survived. Oswald killed a policeman while making an escape but was caught in a movie theater. In turn, Jack Ruby, owner of a Dallas lounge, killed the assassin in the basement of the city jail while the police were transferring Oswald to new quarters. Ruby was convicted of murder and imprisoned.

Since Oswald died so abruptly and without trial, there was lingering speculation about the event, despite an official multivolume report issued by a presidential commission. This bloody episode brought nationwide questioning about the unbridled conservatism of Dallas, the lax gun laws, and the cowboy ethic. It did not help the situation that Lyndon Johnson, in many ways an embodiment of the Texas mystique, then became President of the United States.

Until the 1960s there was a certain callousness in Texas toward crime because the majority of victims were minorities. Kennedy's assassination and the ongoing drive toward civil rights served to change that insensitivity. Under the weight of federal law, court decisions, NAACP pressure, and good sense, segregation in Texas began to break down in the 1950s.

The National Association for the Advancement of Colored People, after being subdued by the Ku Klux Klan in the 1920s, had reorganized in the late 1930s. In 1944 the NAACP successfully struck down the white primary, and from 1945 to 1956 the association backed a series of cases to end segregated education. They attacked, for example, the situation at Moshier Valley near Fort Worth, where the black school had no lights, no heat, no water, as well as one at LaGrange, where three classes were held in the same room and the teachers also served as janitors.

Most important, the NAACP backed Heman Marion Sweatt's application to the University of Texas law school in 1945. The university resisted, and while the case climbed to the Supreme Court, the state created Texas Southern University in Houston with a law school. Blacks refused to apply there for legal training, and in 1950 the high court ruled in favor of Sweatt. Integration of undergraduate classes began in 1952 at Del Mar College in Corpus Christi, followed by Southern Methodist University of Texas in 1955. Other major Texas universities integrated in the 1960s, including Rice, which had to go to court to break the will of the founder. In 1965–1968 the All-American talents of Jerry LeVias, who played football for SMU, broke the color line in the Southwest Conference.

The famous case of *Brown v. Board of Education of Topeka*, meanwhile, started integration in the grade schools. The NAACP pushed hard on cases across the state and met resistance. Black teachers who protested lost their jobs in LaGrange and Rusk. In Sulphur Springs a black teacher was told by a city official to move away. "We don't like nine men in Washington telling us what to do," he said. Pistol shots and shotgun blasts through the teacher's house punctuated the warning.

In 1954 Allen Shivers won reelection as governor in opposition to integration, Texas Rangers were used to impede the efforts of black students to go to school in Mansfield and Texarkana, and the state district attorney harassed the NAACP to a point of ineffectiveness. After this, however, the state government remained passive, and enforcement came from the federal government.

Sixty-six school districts, including those in Austin, San Antonio, San Angelo, El Paso, and Corpus Christi, began to integrate in 1955–1956. In 1957–1958 over 120 districts were integrating, and court orders in Dallas and Houston in 1960–1961 forced those large districts to begin the effort. There were contrived delays, and the big-city systems did not complete the task until the 1970s.

Fort Worth Water Park. Photograph by David G. McComb.

One long-term result was a white flight of students in these large cities. In 1968 the Houston Independent School District was 29 percent black and 71 percent white (Hispanics were counted as white at the time). In 1974 the system was 42 percent black, 39 percent white, and 19 percent Hispanic. In 1980 it was 45 percent black, 27.5 percent white, and 27.5 percent Hispanic. Concurrently, total numbers declined, and the average skill levels of students dropped below state norms.

The same pattern also occurred in the Dallas Independent School District, where the white representation shifted from 80 percent to 20 percent over three decades. Ironically, in Dallas this shift in school population eventually resulted in black minority students being bused into schools where the minority was the majority. No responsible person argued, however, that the struggle was not worthwhile.

Integration, meanwhile, occurred in other areas. In 1950 five blacks filed suit in Houston to use the municipal golf course for which they had paid taxes. In Galveston, after being given the runaround for five years, a group of blacks simply went out, put their balls on a tee, and began to play. The greens keeper came out and collected a fee, and that was it. Through protests, blacks also integrated the beaches, lunch counters, restaurants, and theaters.

Housing, however, remained largely segregated, in part

by choice and in part by the actions of homeowners, real estate agents, and others. Public housing projects had never gained much support because of the fear of federal interference. It took courage to protest social convention as an individual, but blacks all over Texas, nevertheless, took up the fight for their civil rights.

In 1950 the Baptist General Convention set up a commission led by Thomas B. Matson of Fort Worth to explore the problems of race in theological terms. The Southern Baptists had become the largest denomination in Texas—2,660,000 members in 1980—and Matson's writings reached them through hundreds of pamphlets, articles, and columns. Archbishop Robert E. Lucey of San Antonio exhorted Roman Catholics—the second largest denomination with 2,340,000 members in 1980—to support racial integration, unionization, and aid for migrant farm workers.

Under this weight the segregation laws crumbled in the 1960s. A greater humanity emerged, not only because of the courage of the protestors, but also because of a prevailing sense of decency on both sides. John Graves, an expatriate Texas writer, for instance, recalled from his youth a job he had moving cotton bales on a two-wheeled hand truck. It was a mixed racial crew, and he got into an argument with a "crazy mean" black man with red eyes and razor scars on his stomach. Everyone was afraid of this man, and so was Graves.

As the red-eyed man came at him, a larger black with whom Graves had never spoken stepped between them and said, "You old Mist' Graves' grandbaby?" Graves said, "Yes," and the big man shoved the troublemaker away with the comment, "Go on, trouble pot. Go 'round the other way. This here's my folks." There sometimes existed a kinship, a fairness, that reached across racial lines.

In a scene repeated a hundred times over across Texas people met to make a decision on the question of integration. In Galveston at a gathering of retail people caught in the turmoil of lunch-counter sit-ins, George Clampett, a local druggist, stood up and related a conversation with his partner. "You know, Grady and I got together and discussed this business about losing business, causing trouble, and we finally got around to the ultimate question—what is right? What is right?" They concluded that if blacks could buy Kleenex and toothpaste, they could also buy hamburgers and Cokes. That was right. The druggists led the way to integration in Galveston, and they lost only one indignant white customer—who returned in a week's time.

Hispanics in Texas followed the lead of the blacks. The state's population of Mexican-Americans had declined in the nineteenth century to a low of 4 percent in 1887. With a high birth rate in Mexico and the possibility of jobs in Texas, Mexicans moved northward after 1890. There were no border restrictions until the Immigration Act of 1917, which required a literacy test and a head tax. After that, the migrants waded the Rio Grande, and the term "wetback" became common.

The boundary was like a sieve with a daily flow of people back and forth, a characteristic still common in the 1980s. Crossings slowed during the Great Depression but increased with the World War II bracero agreements on farm labor. These ended in 1945, and illegal entry resumed. The distribution of races in 1980 for Texas was 66 percent white, 21 percent Hispanic, 12 percent black, and 1 percent other.

As might be expected, the highest concentrations of Mexican-Americans were found in South and West Texas, where they provided the bulk of the cheap labor. Curiously, the intensity of prejudice against Hispanics varied—the worst in farming areas, the least in ranching country, in between in the cities. There had been some earlier stirrings of difficulty.

During the Depression, for example, Hispanic pecan shellers in San Antonio struck after a reduction in wages. The mayor said the strike was communist-inspired, and the police used tear gas and clubs on the pickets. Over a thousand were arrested and jammed into city jails, where the police turned fire hoses on them to keep them quiet. Governor Allred obtained an agreement to arbitrate, and the matter was settled. The union obtained a contract, but when the managers discovered they had to pay the minimum wage of twenty-five cents per hour under the Fair Labor Standards Act, they opted to mechanize the business. They laid off workers, and the union died.

Hispanics gained more success in 1972–1974 with a statewide strike of the Amalgamated Clothing Workers against Farah, the El Paso–based manufacturer. They won a three-year contract. Texas' "right-to-work" law, which prevented closed shops, the turnover of population, decentralization of the industry, and the often desperate need of employees, however, prevented other such union achievements in the apparel business. In general,

Texans remained unfriendly to union activity—people were supposed to stand on their own feet, not lean on each other. Unionization violated the mystique.

In part, for the same reason Texas cities resisted public housing efforts. Father Carelo Tranchese, a Jesuit priest, however, agitated successfully in the late 1930s for public housing in the San Antonio barrios, where half the families depended upon government relief. He invited Eleanor Roosevelt for a visit and argued, "The city and state regulate stables for horses and cows; why not regulate human habitations also?" The Alazan-Apache Courts opened in 1941–1942, and applicants exceeded space two times over.

Somewhat like blacks, Hispanics lived a segregated life with larger contact mainly in the economic sphere. There were separate schools, churches, shops, living quarters, and folk customs. One of their heroes was Gregorio Cortez Lira, who early in the century had been falsely accused of stealing a horse. Cortez—lithe, handsome, and adored by women—killed the sheriff who had shot his unarmed uncle. With a price on his head he eluded posses and bloodhounds in a desperate race to reach the Mexican border. In the ten-day chase he killed a second sheriff before being captured at a sheepherder's camp. At his trial in 1904 the court acquitted Cortez of killing the first man but gave him life in prison for the death of the second. He became a hero to Mexicans on both sides of the border, received a pardon in 1913, and passed into the folksongs of his people.

Gregorio Cortez, seated between two officers at the Bexar County jail. Western History Collections, University of Oklahoma Library.

Then said Gregorio Cortez
With his pistol in his hand,
"Ah, how many cowardly rangers,
Against one lone Mexican!"

Various organizations tried to unite and lead the Mexican-Americans—the League of United Latin American Citizens (LULAC), founded in 1929; the American GI Forum, 1948; the Political Association of Spanish-Speaking Organizations (PASO), 1961; the Mexican-American Youth Organization (MAYO), 1967; and La Raza Unida, 1970. The groups differed in style and tactics, and although they often wanted the same goals, they had trouble cooperating. There were too many internal factions. As a Houston priest put it in 1965, "The Negro's problem is the white man. But the Latin's problem is the Latin."

A glimpse of the political potential, however, came at Crystal City in 1963. This town of ten thousand inhabitants was one hundred miles southwest of San Antonio and forty miles from the border. It boasted a six-foot-high statue of Popeye to proclaim its status as the center of spinach cultivation, a fact recognized by Del Monte, which had established a packing plant there after World War II. The trouble started in a small way.

Andrew Dickens, a retired oil-field worker who owned a doughnut shop, lost his property to the entrenched Anglo officials who wanted a right-of-way. Dickens swore vengeance and talked to the Teamsters' Union at Del Monte about organizing the Mexican-American vote to oust the city council. The Teamsters and PASO worked to activate the population, which was 80 percent Hispanic. In a sweep the Anglo elites lost for the first time since the founding of the town in 1907. With continuing efforts by MAYO and La Raza Unida, there was compromise, division, and accommodation on both sides.

Elsewhere, particularly in San Antonio, some capable Hispanic politicians came forward. Henry González, who had served on the San Antonio City Council and in the Texas legislature, became a U.S. congressman in 1961. He was noted for his fights against segregation, which included a thirty-six-hour filibuster in the Texas Senate in 1957. Henry Cisneros became a successful mayor of San Antonio in the 1980s and was touted as a possible presidential candidate for the election of 1988. Cisneros was one of the few Hispanic mayors of that traditionally Hispanic city. In 1980, however, there were over a thousand

Mexican-Americans in various political positions around the state.

With this sort of activism and the work already accomplished by the blacks, the barriers blocking civil rights were knocked flat. Most people recognized the greater humanity of the issue and adjusted to accept it. The continued migration northward across the leaky border, however, created pressure on the cities. Business owners liked the cheap labor, but the heavy presence of illegal aliens created problems for society. Was a public school system, for example, obligated to educate the children of such people? The legislature said "no" in 1975, and the Houston school system tried to charge the illegals $162 monthly for tuition.

Judge Woodrow Seals of the U.S. District Court, however, overturned this effort and ruled for the free education of all children. The tax injustice and the economic burden could not be denied, but the judge wisely observed that the lack of education would only create a dependent subclass of people roaming the city streets. "Children," he said, "are the basic resource of our society." It was a humane triumph.

Another group, women—a majority rather than a minority—also sought recognition and changes. Although the paternalistic Texas mystique placed women on a pedestal, the question of "women's place" was national. It was described by Betty Friedan in 1963, defined further by Gloria Steinem, and politicized by the National Organization of Women. Until 1970 female leaders in Texas were rare and exceptional—Oveta Culp Hobby, Ma Ferguson, Nina Vance, Babe Didrikson, Ima Hogg. In Houston Poppy Northcutt, a political leader, described the situation: "Resembling a parfait, white males float like whipped cream at the top. Underneath are minority males. They are followed by white females, and at the very bottom are minority females."

J. B. Priestly wrote in 1955:

Here was a society dominated entirely by the masculine principle. Why were so many of these women at once so arch and so anxious? There was nothing wrong with them as women. Superficially, everything seemed blazingly right with them. But even here in these circles, where millionaires apparently indulged and spoilt them, giving them without question or stint what women elsewhere were for ever wistfully hoping for, they were haunted by a feeling of inferiority, resented, but never properly examined and challenged. They lived in a world so contemptuous and destructive of real feminine values that they had to be heavily bribed to remain in it. All those shops, like the famous Neiman-Marcus store (a remarkable creation) here in Dallas, were a part of the bribe.

The current conditions have remained the same to an extent. For example, women constituted only 9 percent of the legislature in 1986, the bicentennial year. But there have been changes, too. President John F. Kennedy appointed the feisty Sarah T. Hughes to the U.S. District Court in Dallas in 1961; the Texas legislature ratified the Equal Rights Amendment in 1972; Barbara Jordan, a black congresswoman, became famous during the Watergate hearings; Frances Farenthold ran for governor in 1972; Anne Armstrong served as ambassador to England; Sarah Weddington of Austin won *Roe v. Wade*, the Supreme Court case granting women the right to abortion; Lorene Rogers was president of the University of Texas in the latter part of the 1970s; Lila Cockrell was mayor of San Antonio in the 1970s; Kathy Whitmire won the mayor's job of Houston in 1981 and gained a national reputation for competence; Ann Richards won the position of State Treasurer in 1982, the first woman in fifty years elected to state office; Lady Bird Johnson promoted beauty in the landscape; Mary Kay Ash built a successful cosmetics company; Myra McDaniel as Texas Secretary of State in 1984 became the first black to hold an appointive cabinet position; Annette Strauss became mayor of Dallas in 1987. These women were exceptional, too, but in contemporary Texas it was no longer a surprise to find women in responsible positions. That was a change.

The Texas mystique, which dictated a subordinate place for women and minorities, was no longer operative in the 1980s. The destruction of the myth can also be seen in the arena of politics, particularly in the breakdown of the single-party system. In 1952, in part because of the tidelands struggle, Texas voted Republican for the second time since Reconstruction. Governor Allen Shivers strongly endorsed Dwight Eisenhower, and the conservative-liberal split in the Democratic Party became apparent. The liberals, supporting Adlai Stevenson, formed a separate organization, the Democrats of Texas, and Eisenhower made Republicans respectable in the state.

Although reared in Kansas, "Ike" had been born in Texas, and the success of his administration depended

Neiman-Marcus

The store began in Dallas in 1907 as the first specialty store in Texas. The owners, Herbert Marcus, his sister Carrie Marcus Neiman, and her husband Al Neiman, bought high-quality merchandise that they priced for profit, but not exploitation. Stanley Marcus, a man of "subdued elegance" who was brought up in the store, went on to build the company's reputation and influence during his tenure at the head of the store from 1952 to 1979. When his son, Richard Marcus, retired from the firm in 1988, General Cinema Corporation owned 60 percent.

"Publicity and beautiful stores are fine," Stanley Marcus said, "but they are not sufficient to build an enduring reputation in the field of merchandising. The goods must represent honest value, the best available at the various price ranges carried, and the customer service must be superior. Neither of these objectives is accomplished by broad executive directives, but rather by painstaking attention to the thousands of details involving both."

Stanley Marcus became one of the few liberal influences in his conservative hometown and a legend in the history of merchandising. On one Christmas occasion, for example, he observed a man rather desperately searching the store for a present for his wife. The man said that he did not know what he was looking for, but would recognize it when he saw it. Marcus asked about the woman and her sizes and told the man to wait ten minutes. The merchant then took a giant brandy snifter that had been used for a display. He filled it with colored layers of cashmere sweaters like a pousse-café, placed a white angora sweater on top to suggest whipped cream, and topped it with a ten-karat ruby ring to act as a cherry. The price was $25,350. The customer exclaimed, "That's exactly what I was looking for! I'll take it!"

Lyndon B. Johnson

Lyndon Baines Johnson was born in the Hill Country west of Austin in 1908, went to college at Southwest Texas State in San Marcos, taught briefly in Houston, and became a secretary to Congressman Richard Kleberg in 1931–1935. He married Claudia (Lady Bird) Taylor from East Texas in 1934 and worked as National Youth Administration director in Texas for two years before winning a congressional seat in 1937. Johnson was reelected to the House until he won a position in the Senate in 1948. There he became minority leader and then majority leader during the Eisenhower administration. In the Senate he was noted for his hard work and detailed knowledge of people and issues. "I seldom think of politics more than eighteen hours a day," he said.

In 1961 he agreed to run for Vice President with John F. Kennedy, and at Kennedy's death in 1963 Johnson became the thirty-sixth President of the United States. He was elected in his own right in 1964, but because of the difficulties over Vietnam and civil protests, he chose not to run in 1968. Johnson returned home to his ranch on the Pedernales River and died in 1973.

He had a notable sense of humor, and once explained why the United States had to fund missiles with the following story:

> In 1861 a Texan left to join the rebels. He told his neighbor he'd return soon, that the fight would be easy "because we can lick those damyankees with broomsticks."
>
> He returned two years later, minus a leg. His neighbor asked the tragic, bedraggled, wounded man what happened. "You said it'd be so easy that you could lick the damyankees with broomsticks."
>
> "We could," replied the rebel, "but the trouble was the damyankees wouldn't fight with broomsticks."

upon the two Texas Democrats who ruled the Senate and House of Representatives. Sam Rayburn from Bonham had been elected to the house in 1912 and then reelected twenty-three more times until his death in 1961. His mentor was Cactus Jack Garner; his hero was Franklin D. Roosevelt. In his congenial way Rayburn served variously as minority leader, majority leader, and Speaker of the House after 1937.

Rayburn continued the tradition of Garner's "board of education" and tutored young congressmen in the ways of politics. His best pupil was Lyndon Baines Johnson from the Hill Country near Austin. Johnson, a New Deal liberal, won election first to the House in 1937, and then to the Senate in 1948. A masterful and hard-driving politician, he moved quickly through the ranks to become majority leader in 1952. Much of the Eisenhower program depended upon the cooperation received from Johnson and Rayburn, and for the most part, the three men worked cordially together for the benefit of the nation.

By 1960 Johnson had developed presidential ambitions, but the young senator from Massachusetts, John F. Kennedy, won the primaries while Johnson labored in Washington. Kennedy swept the convention on the first ballot, and Johnson, contrary to Rayburn's advice, accepted the vice-presidency. For their party it was a fortunate combination because Texas, a swing state in the election, narrowly voted for the Democratic ticket.

With delicious irony, Johnson as Vice President had to swear in John Tower, the Republican who had won his empty Senate seat. Tower, a short, combative political science professor from Wichita Falls, beat seventy-one others for the position. He was able to hold his place through three more elections, in part because of liberal Democrats. This was another delicious irony. The liberals tried to force the conservative Democrats to declare themselves Republicans. These "kamikaze" politics worked. The Republicans found support in the white, urban, middle, and upper classes; worked hard on organization; and elected William Clements, a Dallas millionaire, governor in 1978 and 1986.

The Republicans did not have a majority, but it was clear by 1960 that Texas was no longer a one-party state. The party of Lincoln, moreover, had penetrated and undermined part of the foundation of the Texas mystique, that resting on the Southern heritage and symbolized by the Democratic Party, the party of the solid South.

John Connally, a Johnson protégé who had been Kennedy's Secretary of the Navy, meanwhile, won the position of governor. The liberal-conservative fire within the Democratic structure smoldered, and Kennedy traveled to the Lone Star State to keep it under control in case the conservative Barry Goldwater decided to run in 1964. Even though the assassination cast Dallas and Texas in bad light, it made Connally a national celebrity. He held the Texas conservatives in check for a while, but then joined the Nixon Republicans and tried unsuccessfully for the presidential nomination in 1980.

The assassination also made Lyndon B. Johnson President of the United States. In many ways Johnson's exaggerated personality was the Texas mystique personified. He was paternalistic, chauvinistic, energetic, successful, crude, dominating, and gallant. To the surprise of Eastern detractors, "Uncle Cornpone" grasped the failing Kennedy legislative program, added a mountain of ideas of his own, and crammed through Congress the laws necessary for a "Great Society."

Johnson meant the program to complete the New Deal and end poverty, discrimination, slums, and poor education. The growing involvement in Vietnam, however, drained the lifeblood of the Great Society. The "shootout" in Southeast Asia could not be won. In the end Johnson refused to run again and returned to his beloved Hill Country a broken man.

Hubert Humphrey was able to carry Texas for the Democrats in 1968, but Richard Nixon won for the Republicans in 1972. Jimmy Carter carried the state in 1976 in the wake of Republican scandals, but Ronald Reagan dominated the next decade. He won in 1980, and after the Republican convention held in Dallas in 1984 Reagan was able to carry Texas Republicans with him to a second victory. In the legislature Reagan's followers were able to capture 51 of the 150 house seats, up from 37 in 1983, and 6 of 31 senate seats, a gain of 1 since 1983. George Bush, a sometime Houstonian, served as Reagan's Vice President, and then was elected to the presidency in 1988. Yet another Texan, Democrat Jim Wright of Fort Worth, served as Speaker of the House of Representatives from 1986 to 1989.

The year 1986 was also the year of the Texas sesquicentennial. It was celebrated throughout the state with a great deal of emphasis upon past glories. The fete was generally good-hearted, but the heavy hand of the oil depression could not be entirely lifted. Texas was still the third-largest state in population, the second in square miles,

Johnson, in addition, was a complicated man with exaggerated faults and virtues. Wilbur Cohen, a cabinet secretary, after meeting with the president at the LBJ ranch, talking about politics, looking at the cattle, and watching the sun set over the low Texas hills, recalled about Johnson:

Now, there within one hour was a man being three different things. First, he dealt with our business problems, the president of the United States dealing with matters of momentous national policy on an executive planning basis. Then he was a small-time cattle breeder in the way any two-bit farmer is who wants to get better cows or calves. And then, a half hour later, the same man was talking in the most emotional terms about the earth and the world and the incomprehensibilities of life. He was like a combination of Boccaccio and Machiavelli and John Keats. When I went away I said to myself, "This man is larger than life." He simply does not fit into any pattern.

Photograph courtesy of the Lyndon Baines Johnson Library.

the first in roads and railroads, the second in air traffic, the first in oil and gas reserves. It had a Gutenberg Bible at the University of Texas, Frederic Remington paintings at the Amon Carter Museum, the Rothko Chapel in Houston. "America's Team" still played in Irving. Yet the old bumper stickers from the 1960s and 1970s telling drivers to let Yankees freeze and encouraging secession were now faded.

Too much had happened—the oil depression, civil rights, feminism, JFK in Dallas, Vietnam, television, Republican Party victories, national sports—Texas, the United States, the world were no longer the same. The old myth that inculcated white male dominance, unbridled wealth, and unrestrained individualism could not be sustained or trusted. The ethos, the social compass, no longer gave the correct directions. It did not work any more. So now, after two hundred years, Texans have to look for a new mystique, a new reason for being. Hopefully, the new ethos will retain the openness, optimism, and pride of the past without the paternalism, prejudice, and arrogance. It will include, perhaps, such a sensitivity to the environment and intelligent compassion that people will write proudly on their change-of-address card at the post office, "Gone to Texas," to join in the new adventure.

7. Afterword: Books and Themes

All writers have an ax to grind or, to put it more politely, a point of view. I am no different. I think that history is shaped by inspired people working with the tools and resources at hand. That is more complicated than it sounds, because inspiration can come from various directions—greed, necessity, patriotism, curiosity, kindness, anger, God—and is frequently mixed in unique proportions. Tools can be tangible, like shovels and automobiles, or intangible, like statutes and forms of government, which are the tools for ruling people. Resources are often a gift of nature, but without the inspiration and the technology the gift remains unused. Altogether, people, technology, and resources make up the stuff of history. To weave them into a tapestry of the past is a craft and an art.

This narration about Texas was written with such thoughts in mind, but it could not have been accomplished without the prior work of scholars and others who have been interested in the land and its inhabitants. It is impossible to mention all of the books that have been helpful and all the events of Texas history, but for a reader who wants more, here are some suggestions. For elusive facts nothing can beat *The Handbook of Texas* (Austin: Texas State Historical Association; vols. 1 and 2, ed. Walter Prescott Webb, 1952; vol. 3, ed. Eldon Stephen Branda, 1976) and the *Texas Almanac* (the 1986–1987 version [ed. Mike Kingston; Dallas: Dallas Morning News, 1985] is particularly worthwhile). The *Handbook* is undergoing revision at the Texas State Historical Association, and a new version should be ready in the mid-1990s. For bibliography there are John H. Jenkins, *Basic Texas Books* (Austin: Jenkins Publishing Co., 1983), and Light Townsend Cummins and Alvin R. Bailey, Jr., eds., *A Guide to the History of Texas* (New York: Greenwood Press, 1988). For current ideas, articles, and book reviews

To read a writer is for me not merely to get an idea of what he says, but to go off with him, and travel in his company.
ANDRÉ GIDE, "THIRD IMAGINARY INTERVIEW," 1903

I recommend the *Southwestern Historical Quarterly*, published by the Texas State Historical Association.

To my good fortune the Sesquicentennial inspired some useful anthologies: Donald W. Whisenhunt, ed., *Texas: A Sesquicentennial Celebration* (Austin: Eakin Press, 1984); Ralph A. Wooster and Robert A. Calvert, eds., *Texas Vistas* (Austin: Texas State Historical Association, 1987); and Archie P. McDonald, comp., *The Texas Experience* (College Station: Texas A&M University Press, 1986). These anthologies work well with the general histories available: Archie P. McDonald, *Texas: All Hail the Mighty State* (Austin: Eakin, 1983); Ben Proctor and Archie P. McDonald, eds., *The Texas Heritage* (St. Louis: Forum Press, 1980); Walter L. Buenger, ed., *Texas History* (Boston: American Press, 1983); Joe B. Frantz, *Texas: A Bicentennial History* (New York: W. W. Norton, 1976); Rupert N. Richardson et al., *Texas: The Lone Star State* (Englewood Cliffs, N.J.: Prentice Hall, 1988); and T. R. Fehrenbach, *Lone Star: A History of Texas and the Texans* (New York: Macmillan, 1968). Most of these also have bibliographies.

Although narrower, I would also recommend the following books for someone in pursuit of Texas: W. W. Newcomb, Jr., *The Indians of Texas* (Austin: University of Texas Press, 1961); Elizabeth A. H. John, *Storms Brewed in Other Men's Worlds* (College Station: Texas A&M University Press, 1975); D. W. Meinig, *Imperial Texas: An Interpretive Essay in Cultural Geography* (Austin: University of Texas Press, 1969); Ann Fears Crawford and Crystal Sasse Ragsdale, *Women in Texas* (Austin: Eakin, 1982); Terry G. Jordan with John L. Bean, Jr., and William M. Holmes, *Texas: A Geography* (Boulder: Westview Press, 1984); Leo J. Klosterman, Loyd S. Swenson, Jr., and Sylvia Rose, *100 Years of Science and Technology in Texas* (Houston: Rice University Press, 1986); A. C. Greene, *Dallas, USA* (Austin: Texas Monthly Press, 1984); David G. McComb, *Houston: A History* (Austin: University of Texas Press, 1981) and *Galveston: A History* (Austin: University of Texas Press, 1986); Craig Edward Clifford, *In the Deep Heart's Core* (College Station: Texas A&M University Press, 1985), a discussion of the Texas literary tradition; Robert F. O'Connor, ed., *Texas Myths* (College Station: Texas A&M University Press, 1986); and Michael Gillette, ed., *Texas in Transition* (Austin: LBJ Library and LBJ School of Public Affairs, 1986), transcripts from a forum on the Texas past, present, and future.

These books will lead the traveler in Texas history to provocative vistas and new roads of inquiry. They all have their branch paths to entice the intellect.

References

Chapter 1. Land and Nature

Amos Andrew Parker, *Trip to the West and Texas* (Concord, N.H.: White and Fisher, 1835), p. 183.

G.T.T. story from Frederick Law Olmsted, *A Journey through Texas* (1857; reprint, Austin: University of Texas Press, 1978), p. 124.

Thomas Jefferson, Philip Sheridan, Berta Hart Nance, and John Steinbeck quotes from Peter Yapp, ed., *The Travellers' Dictionary of Quotation* (London: Routledge & Kegan Paul, 1983), pp. 962–963.

Randolph Barnes Marcy quote from Marilyn McAdams Sibley, *Travelers in Texas, 1761–1860* (Austin: University of Texas Press, 1967), p. 53.

Georgia O'Keeffe quotes from John F. Matthews, "The Influence of the Texas Panhandle on Georgia O'Keeffe," *Panhandle Plains Historical Review* 57 (1984): 107–136, and Elaine Partnow, ed., *The Quotable Woman, 1800–1981* (New York: Facts on File, 1982), p. 209.

On Benno Matthes, see Terry G. Jordan et al., *Texas: A Geography* (Boulder: Westview Press, 1984), p. 27.

Norther description from David G. McComb, *Galveston: A History* (Austin: University of Texas Press, 1986), pp. 23–24.

Pecos Bill stories from Harold W. Felton, *Pecos Bill, Texas Cowpuncher* (New York: Knopf, 1949), pp. 125, 139.

William A. McClintock quoted by Terry G. Jordan in Walter L. Buenger, ed., *Texas History* (Boston: American Press, 1983), p. 156.

Cabeza de Vaca observations from Cyclone Covey, *Cabeza de Vaca's Adventures in the Unknown Interior of America* (New York: Collier, 1961), p. 81.

George W. Kendall, *Narratives of the Texas Santa Fe Expedition* (Austin: Steck, 1935), p. 78.

George C. Frison quoted from *Fort Collins Coloradoan*, December 26, 1987.

Athanase de Mézières quote from W. W. Newcomb, Jr., *The Indians of Texas* (Austin: University of Texas Press, 1961), p. 257; Ferdinand Roemer quote, ibid., p. 165.

Olmsted, *Journey through Texas*, p. 293.

Observations on Lipans from Newcomb, *Indians of Texas*, p. 112.

John Holland Jenkins, *Recollections of Early Texas*, ed. John Holmes Jenkins III (Austin: University of Texas Press, 1958), pp. 77–78.

Roy Bedichek, *Karánkaway Country* (Austin: University of Texas Press, 1950), p. 16.

Rattlesnake sidebar: George W. Kendall, *Narrative of the Texas Santa Fe Expedition*, pp. 91–92; Teddy Blue (E. C. Abbott), *We Pointed Them North* (Norman: University of Oklahoma Press, 1939, 1954), p. 46; John Salmon "Rip" Ford, *Rip Ford's Texas*, ed. Stephen B. Oates (Austin: University of Texas Press, 1963, 1987), p. 116; Arthur and Bobbie Coleman, *The Texas Cookbook* (New York: Wyn, 1949), p. 51.

Armadillo sidebar: Hondo Crouch quote from Larry L. Smith and Robin W. Doughty, *The Amazing Armadillo* (Austin: University of Texas Press, 1984), p. 70.

Chapter 2. The Spanish Legacy

Mary Rabb quote from Fane Downs, "'Tryels and Trubbles': Women in Early Nineteenth-Century Texas," *Southwestern Historical Quarterly (SHQ)* 90 (July 1986): 51.

Sam Houston and Peggy McCormick conversation from Arnoldo De León, *They Called Them Greasers* (Austin: University of Texas Press, 1983), p. 67.

Chapter 3. Texas and the United States

Sam Houston quote from Noah Smithwick, *The Evolution of a State*, comp. Nanna Smithwick Donaldson (1900; new ed., Austin: University of Texas Press, 1983), p. 138.

Ford, *Rip Ford's Texas*, p. 118.

Rabb quote from Downs, "'Tryels and Trubbles,'" p. 51.

Smithwick, *Evolution of a State*, p. 134.

Zachary Taylor quote from Mark E. Nackman, "Citizen Soldier," *SHQ* 78 (January 1975): 239.

Olmsted, *Journey through Texas*, p. 257.

Augustine Haidusek quote from Buenger, ed., *Texas History*, p. 217.

For Jesse A. Ziegler, see McComb, *Galveston*, p. 105.

Lydia Spencer Lane quote from Sibley, *Travelers in Texas*, p. 40.

Shapley P. Ross story from Ford, *Rip Ford's Texas*, p. 442.

For John B. Billingsley and early Dallas, see John William Rogers, *The Lusty Texans of Dallas* (Nashville: Parthenon Press, 1965), pp. 42–43.

Sam Houston quotes from McComb, *Galveston*, p. 73, and M. K. Wiseheart, *Sam Houston: American Giant* (Washington, D.C.: Robert B. Luce, 1962), p. 626.

Jefferson Davis quote from Harold B. Simpson, *Hood's Texas Brigade* (Waco: Texian Press, 1970), p. 59.

Magruder-Lea story from McComb, *Galveston*, p. 77.

Walker Colt sidebar: quote from Walter Prescott Webb, *The Great Plains* (New York: Grosset and Dunlap, 1931), pp. 174–175.

Hood's Texas Brigade sidebar: quotes from Ralph A. Wooster and Robert Wooster "'Rarin' for a Fight': Texans in the Confederate Army," *SHQ* 84 (April 1981): 407, and Francis Edward Abernethy, *Singin' Texas* (Dallas: E-Heart, 1983).

Chapter 4. Settlement

Blue, *We Pointed Them North*, p. 67.

Mollie Goodnight's remedies from Ann Fears Crawford and Crystal Sasse Ragsdale, *Women in Texas* (Austin: Eakin, 1982), p. 115.

Ranchers' resolution from Tkhadis W. Box, "Range Deterioration in West Texas," *SHQ* 71 (July 1967): 45.

Blue, *We Pointed Them North*, pp. 28–29.

Cowboy sayings from Ramon F. Adams, *The Cowboy Says It Salty* (Tucson: University of Arizona Press, 1971).

William H. Haupt quote from Douglas E. Barnett, "Angora Goats in Texas: Agricultural Innovation on the Edwards Plateau, 1858–1900," *SHQ* 90 (April 1987): 368–369.

Lubbock visitor quoted in Lawrence L. Graves et al., *History of Lubbock* (Lubbock: West Texas Museum Association, 1962), p. 239; housewife quoted in John Fischer, *From the High Plains* (New York: Harper and Row, 1979).

Charles Goodnight story from Francis Edward Abernethy, ed., *Built in Texas* (Dallas: E-Heart, 1980).

W. W. Lang quote from Donald W. Whisenhunt, ed., *Texas: A Sesquicentennial Celebration* (Austin: Eakin, 1984), p. 161.

Cotton picking description from J. B. Coltharp, "Reminiscences of Cotton Pickin' Days," *SHQ* 73 (April 1970): 539.

Dallas Herald, January 29, 1875, as cited in *Handbook of Texas* 1:456.

Kansas City *Journal of Commerce* quote from reprint in *Galveston Daily News*, November 12, 1874.

Cowboy sidebar: Blue, *We Pointed Them North*, p. 8.

Chapter 5. Texas in Transit

Allen W. Hamill, "Spindletop, the Lucas Gusher," Oral History of the Texas Oil Industry," Tape No. 84, September 2, 1952, typescript pp. 18–19, Barker Texas History Center, University of Texas at Austin.

"Bing" Maddox quote from Roger M. and Diana Davids Olien, *Life in the Oil Fields* (Austin: Texas Monthly Press, 1986), p. 35; Mrs. Sam Webb quote, ibid., p. 224.

Borger folksong from H. Gordon Frost and John H. Jenkins, *I'm Frank Hamer: The Life of a Texas Peace Officer* (Austin: Jenkins, 1968), p. 114.

Ma Ferguson quote from David F. Prindle, "Oil and the Permanent University Fund: The Early Years," *SHQ* 86 (October 1982): 287.

Pa Ferguson on trees from Robert S. Maxwell, "One Man's Legacy: W. Goodrich Jones and Texas Conservation," *SHQ* 77 (January 1974): 376.

Ferguson jokes from Norman D. Brown, *Hood, Bonnet, and Little Brown Jug: Texas Politics, 1921–1928* (College Station: Texas A&M University Press, 1984), p. 273, and Francis Edward Abernethy, ed., *Legendary Ladies of Texas* (Dallas: E-Heart, 1981).

John Nance Garner quote from Bascom Timmons, *Garner of Texas* (New York: Harper, 1948), p. 37.

Depression psalm from *Weatherford Democrat*, June 10, 1932, as cited in Donald W. Whisenhunt, *The Depression in Texas: The Hoover Years* (New York: Garland, 1983), p. 221.

WPA recipient quote from McComb, *Houston: A History* (Austin: University of Texas Press, 1981), p. 117.

For Amarillo dust storm, see Larry Willoughby, *Texas, Our Texas* (Austin: Learned & Tested, 1987), p. 497.

Ship Channel quote from "Plastics: Will They Boost the Boom?" *Houston* 28 (April 1958): 17.

Oveta Culp Hobby quote from *Life*, October 21, 1946, p. 108.

A. C. Greene, *A Personal Country* (New York: Knopf, 1969), pp. 23–24.

Balinese Room sidebar quotes: see McComb, *Galveston*, pp. 176–177.

Audie Murphy sidebar: quote from Harold B. Simpson, *Audie Murphy, American Soldier* (Hillsboro, Tex.: Hillsboro Junior College Press, 1975), p. 158.

Chicken Ranch sidebar: quote from *The Best Little Whorehouse in Texas* used by permission of Larry L. King.

Chapter 6. The Texas Mystique

Ronnie Dugger, in *Texas in Transition* (Austin: LBJ Library and LBJ School of Public Affairs, 1986), p. 122. The conference took place April 18, 1986, in Austin.

Frank Lloyd Wright quote from McComb, *Houston*, p. 136.

J. Frank Dobie quote from H. Bailey Carroll et al., *Heroes of Texas* (Waco: Texian Press, 1964), p. viii.

Walter Prescott Webb, *The Texas Rangers* (1935; 2d ed., Austin: University of Texas Press, 1965), p. xv.

J. Frank Dobie and Roy Bedichek exchange from Ronnie Dugger, ed., *Three Men in Texas* (Austin: University of Texas Press, 1967), p. 12; Dobie on great literature, ibid., p. 179.

Larry McMurtry, *In a Narrow Grave* (Austin: Encino, 1968), p. 31.

Russell W. Cumley, "I Am a Cancer Cell," reprinted from *The First Twenty Years of the University of Texas M. D. Anderson Hospital and Tumor Institute* (1964) by permission of M. D. Anderson Cancer Center.

Dominique de Menil quote from Greg Smith, "Art for Houston's Sake," *Images*, July 17, 1987, p. 4.

French journalist Pierre Voisin quote from McComb, *Houston*, pp. 138–139; Philip Johnson, ibid., pp. 191–192; Mickey Herskowitz, ibid., p. 188.

Minister's invocation from Geoff Winningham and Al Reinert, *Rites of Fall: High School Football in Texas* (Austin: University of Texas Press, 1979), p. 28; Frankie Groves quote, ibid., p. 78.

"Bum" Phillips quotes from David Kaplan and Daniel Griffin, eds., *The Best of Bum* (Austin: Texas Monthly Press, 1980).

The Economist, August 6, 1988, p. 10.

Bob Bullock quote from *USA Today*, June 23, 1987.

Water commissioner James M. Quigley quote from McComb, *Houston*, p. 148; Mayor Welch, ibid., p. 152.

Terry Clark quote from "The Southwest Drug Connection," *Newsweek*, November 23, 1987, p. 29.

John Graves quote from Bertha McKee Dobie et al., *Growing Up in Texas* (Austin: Encino, 1972), p. 74.

Father Carelo Tranchese quote from Donald L. Zelman, "Alazan-Apache Courts: A New Deal Response to Mexican American Housing Conditions in San Antonio," *SHQ* 87 (October 1983): 135.

Gregorio Cortez lyrics from Américo Paredes, *With His Pistol in His Hand* (Austin: University of Texas Press, 1958), p. 169.

Woodrow Seals quote from McComb, *Houston*, p. 169; Poppy Northcutt, ibid., p. 173.

J. B. Priestly quote from Yapp, ed., *Travellers' Dictionary of Quotation.*

Willie Nelson sidebar: quotes from Irwin Stambler and Grelun Landon, *The Encyclopedia of Folk, Country & Western Music*, 2d ed. (New York: St. Martin's Press, 1983), p. 504.

"Babe" Didrikson Zaharias sidebar: quote from William O. Johnson and Nancy P. Williamson, *Whatta-gal! The Babe Didrikson Story* (Boston: Little, Brown, 1977), p. 74.

Sammy Baugh sidebar: quote from Texas Sports Hall of Fame.

Neiman-Marcus sidebar: quotes from Stanley Marcus, *Quest for the Best* (New York: Viking, 1979), pp. 151–152, and Francis Edward Abernethy, ed., *What's Going On? (In Modern Texas Folklore)* (Austin: Encino, 1976), p. 18.

Lyndon B. Johnson sidebar: joke from Bill Adler, *The Johnson Humor* (New York: Simon and Shuster, 1965), p. 13; Wilbur Cohen quote from David G. McComb's interview with Cohen in the Lyndon B. Johnson Oral History Project, LBJ Library, University of Texas at Austin.

Index

By the same author

GALVESTON
A History

"Maybe it's the mention of familiar places, the old names or maybe it's remembering oral history recited in countless family car trips across the causeway. Whatever the reason, there seems to be a slight aroma of salt air coming from these pages."
—*Dallas Morning News*

Galveston: A History is at the forefront of a trend in writing urban biographies emphasizing technology as the dynamic force in urban development. David McComb explores the often contradictory relationship between technology and the city and provides a guide to both Galveston history and the dynamics of urban development.

ISBN 0-292-72049-1
ISBN 0-292-72053-X, paperback